The History of Menshevism

Leopold H. Haimson, *General Editor*

HOOVER INSTITUTION PUBLICATIONS

The Making of a Workers' Revolution

The Making of a

THE HOOVER INSTITUTION
on War, Revolution,
and Peace

Allan K. Wildman

Workers' Revolution

RUSSIAN SOCIAL DEMOCRACY, 1891–1903

THE UNIVERSITY OF CHICAGO PRESS

CHICAGO AND LONDON

This volume is one of a series arising from the
work of the INTER-UNIVERSITY PROJECT ON THE
HISTORY OF THE MENSHEVIK MOVEMENT

Library of Congress Catalog Card Number: 67-25086

THE UNIVERSITY OF CHICAGO PRESS, CHICAGO & LONDON
The University of Toronto Press, Toronto 5, Canada

Editor's Preface

ALTHOUGH not the first to appear, Allan Wildman's *The Making of a Workers' Revolution* should be regarded as the introductory volume in the series on the history of Menshevism which the University of Chicago Press is publishing under the sponsorship of the Hoover Institution.

The years that Mr. Wildman's study cover in the development of Russian Social Democracy (from 1891 to 1903) antedate, to be sure, the conflicts at the Second Congress of the RS–DRP from which the Bolshevik and Menshevik factions originally emerged, not to speak of the slow and halting process through which the two factions gradually assumed their separate identities. But as Wildman rightly suggests, many of the ideological and social tensions that underlay the split at the Second Party Congress and the subsequent process of self-definition of Bolshevism and Menshevism had beset Social Democracy from its first steps on Russian soil.

The contradictory themes in the outlook and attitudes of the revolutionary intelligentsia which the ideological constructs drawn by the founders of Russian Marxism reflected, even as they sought to reconcile them, have been the object of considerable attention by historians of Russian Social Democracy.

On the one hand, the leaders of Osvobozhdenie truda consistently affirmed that the future of socialism rested, in the last analysis, not on the "subjective" aspirations and will of the individual revolutionaries who espoused its cause, but on the development of a mass movement—the growth, through the unfolding of the "objective" laws of capitalist development, of the numbers, the class consciousness, and the class organization of the industrial proletariat. On the other hand, one can find in the earliest writings of Plekhanov and Akselrod the view that it is the mission of the socialist intelligentsia to guide the industrial workers to the discovery and affirmation of their "real" class interests and needs, to the successful fulfillment of the role assigned to them by history and by the Social Democrats.

The psychological contradictions and potential sources of conflict implicit in this modulated view of the relations between intelligentsia and workers were greatly accentuated by the Russian Marxists' conception of the "bourgeois" revolution and "bourgeois" stage of development that Russia would have to traverse before the establishment of socialism: by the view that, even while struggling against capitalist exploitation and drawing from the experience of this struggle the consciousness of the conflict between their interests and those of their bourgeois exploiters, the workers also had to assume a leading role in the conquest of the political freedom of which their class antagonists would temporarily emerge as the chief, if not the sole, beneficiaries.

An impressive number of scholarly studies have examined in recent years these contradictory elements in the ideology of the Russian Marxists and the debates and factional conflicts to which they gave rise even before the emergence of Bolshevism and Menshevism. The novelty and chief interest of Wildman's analysis are that it seeks to examine systematically how these contradictions were reflected in the early development of Russian Marxism as a social movement: in the changing structure, the changing social and psychological configuration of Social Democratic groups and organizations in different regions of European Russia, the changing pattern of the relations between leaders and led—above all, in the crucial interaction, in different social and cultural settings, of various strata of the Social Democratic intelligentsia and the industrial working class.

Readers may draw a sense of the difficulties that Wildman has had to surmount in this historical reconstruction from the fact that most of the problems that he touches, indeed some of the most basic questions of fact concerning the interaction during the 1890's between Social Democratic intelligentsia and workers, were almost from the outset an object of bitter controversy. By the Second Party Congress of 1903, which saw the partisans of *Iskra* rout their Economist opponents only to discover the divisions in their own ranks, two highly stylized—and conflicting—images of the experience of the labor movement of the 1890's had already emerged in Russian Social Democracy.

The first, the image of the victors, which thereafter remained the dominant view in Russian historiography, was largely drawn from the bill of indictment that Plekhanov and Akselrod had drawn against their opponents in the Union of Social Democrats Abroad at the turn of the century and especially from Lenin's contemporary descriptions of Economism and the labor movement. According to these representations of the Marxist "politiki," their opponents in the Social Democratic emigration and many of the "praktiki" of the Russian labor movement had become exclusively absorbed with the parochial concerns of the workers' day-to-day struggle against their employers, to the neglect of the broader class interests of the Russian proletariat—above all, of its interest in the conquest of the political and civic rights required for the further development of its class consciousness and organization. The sole concern of the Marxist politiki was to rescue the Russian proletariat from this morass, for the sake of the successful prosecution of its struggle for political freedom.

The image of the eventual losers, of *Iskra*'s opposition among the emigrés and on Russian soil, took somewhat longer to crystallize, partly because this opposition included heterogeneous elements whose various arguments and underlying attitudes shifted as they sought unsuccessfully to counter the charges against them and to discover for themselves, as the battle progressed, what its real issues were. By the time of the Second Party Congress, however, the main thrust of their defense had turned to a blanket denial of the charges leveled against them by the Marxist politiki. The partisans of *Iskra*, they vehemently insisted, had largely fought a straw man constructed for their political convenience.

Although at some time or other, a few isolated individuals might have been seduced by the sirens of Revisionism and Economism, the overwhelming majority of Social Democrats and, above all, of the praktiki of the labor movement in Russia were already fully persuaded of the urgency of the struggle for political freedom—indeed were energetically waging it—when Iskra had unleashed its campaign against them. Given this fact, Iskra's efforts to conquer the Russian labor movement, just as the tactics used earlier by the leaders of Osvobozhdenie truda against their opponents in the Union of Social Democrats Abroad, could only be attributed to personal animosities, and especially to an unscrupulous drive for control of existing Social Democratic organizations.

This emphasis is to be found even in the most valuable retrospective accounts of the labor movement of the period, recorded shortly after the Second Party Congress by the Economist Akimov-Makhnovets. But in Akimov's rendition of it, it is translated into the broader conception of an inherent conflict between the outlook, interests, and values of the Social Democratic intelligentsia and of the workers' own "labor intelligentsia"—the more articulate and better educated elements of the working class which, in Akimov's view, the partisans of Iskra had driven away from the labor movement in the course of their struggle for power.*

Wildman's historical reconstruction reaches beyond these two conflicting stereotypes, which by 1905 had already begun to color even the personal recollections of many of the participants in the early development of Russian Social Democracy. He recognizes the legitimacy of many of the threads in Akimov's interpretation; indeed, he emphasizes the degree to which the tensions which exploded at the turn of the century had been present throughout the development of the labor movement. Yet he draws a more balanced picture of this development, emphasizing the elements of both mutual attraction and conflict that consistently appeared in the relations between intelligentsia and workers. Wildman's examination of contemporary sources also shows the validity of

---

* See particularly V. Akimov [Makhnovets], *K voprosu vtorogo s'ezda Rossiiskoi sotsial' demokraticheskoi rabochei partii* (Geneva, 1904); and his *Materialy dlia kharakteristiki razvitiia Rossiiskoi sotsial' demokraticheskoi rabochei partii* (Geneva, 1905).

Akimov's claim that by the turn of the century the praktiki of the Russian labor movement were already emphasizing in their propaganda and agitation the importance and urgency of the conquest of political freedom. But his analysis also clearly shows the conflict between the image of the political struggle to which the leaders of the Russian labor movement were now drawn—in the face of the mutual hostility of workers and employers, and of the seeming political apathy of the Russian bourgeoisie as a whole—and the quite different political conclusions inherent in the conception of "proletarian hegemony in the all-nation struggle against autocracy" which the leaders of Osvobozhdenie truda reached, at the same time, on the basis of much of the same evidence. Most importantly, Wildman's treatment graphically describes how the tactical and organizational implications that the praktiki of the labor movement and the supporters of *Iskra*'s plans drew from their respective conceptions of the political struggle necessarily brought the tensions already present in the relations between the Social Democratic intelligentsia and the workers' "labor intelligentsia" to the breaking point.

One thread of Wildman's analysis of this conflict is worth pursuing, for it sheds considerable light on the subsequent history of Russian Social Democracy, particularly on the travails that the Menshevik fraction (which so many of the praktiki of the labor movement eventually rejoined) would repeatedly experience during critical periods in its history. As Wildman points out, the conception of the political struggle and the character of the political objectives to which the praktiki of the Russian labor movement were drawn at the turn of the century were inextricably tied to the workers' experience of their struggle against "capitalist" exploitation. What this experience immediately suggested to both the leadership and the rank and file of the Russian labor movement was the solidity of the alliance between the autocracy and their "capitalist exploiters," an identity of interests and outlook which appeared to be continually confirmed by the fact that behind the employers stood a police force ever ready to intervene whenever the workers revolted against the oppressive conditions of their existence. This experience necessarily impelled the Russian praktiki to blur the careful distinction which Plekhanov and Akselrod by the late 1880's had drawn between the bourgeois revolution, which was to bring the workers political freedom, and the eventual socialist revolution which would free them from the yoke of capitalist exploitation.

What I am suggesting is that the internal dynamics of the "spontaneous" labor movement were not necessarily calculated to pull it—as its critics charged at the turn of the century—in the direction of Revisionism or trade unionism. They were likely to draw many of the participants in this movement to more, rather than less, radical conceptions of the immediate political tasks ahead, more radical conceptions than even a Lenin was as yet prepared to espouse.

One can, I believe, already discern the traces of this attraction to more radical political goals—of the blurring of the "proper" historical interval which the founders of Russian Marxism had scheduled between the bourgeois and socialist revolutions—in the agitational leaflets that were beginning to appear in Russia at the turn of the century. The equal intensity with which these leaflets urged the workers on to the struggles against capitalism and for the overthrow of autocracy, the equal emphasis with which they presented the slogans summarizing these two objectives—indeed the link that they consistently made between them—provided the first, if as yet purely instinctive, expression of this process of radicalization.

Until 1905, the pull toward a more radical image of political goals and of the political struggle received little explicit formulation, let alone theoretical elaboration. Yet surely the elements for such an explanation are already to be found in the arguments passionately advanced in a number of Social Democratic circles and party organizations after the turn of the century, to the effect that the autocracy could no longer be viewed as the exclusive political spokesman for the traditional forces in Russian society, or even as an impartial arbiter between the "feudal" and "capitalist" elements struggling for supremacy in Russian national life. The autocratic state should already be regarded chiefly as the political expression of the interests of Russia's capitalist class. If this was the case, one might well have asked why Social Democracy should still confine the Russian working class to a struggle for a "bourgeois" revolution.

It was only in 1905 that this question was squarely answered—in the negative—by the advocates of "permanent revolution." The dynamics that we have seen at work in the development of the labor movement in earlier years already suggest why the views expounded at this time by a Dan, a Martynov, indeed a Trotsky, did not constitute—as would be argued in the immediate aftermath of 1905—temporary aberrations in the development of Menshevism. The example of Martynov, who had so vigorously defended Economism against *Iskra's* attacks at the turn of the century, is particularly instructive in this regard. The views and attitudes that Martynov expressed in 1905, and that he would again articulate in 1917 and during the period of War Communism, vividly demonstrate how naturally the cult of the "spontaneous" labor movement, the worship of the workers' capacity for independent initiative, could be combined, especially in periods of revolutionary turmoil, with an attraction to radical political goals and solutions.

To be sure, the defeat of the 1905 revolution temporarily strengthened in the Menshevik faction the counsels of political moderation, the restraining hold of the conception of bourgeois revolution that had been drawn in the 1880's by the leaders of Osvobozhdenie truda. But the emotional drive reflected in the cult of the "spontaneous" labor movement and the intellectual restraint imposed by the conception of a necessary "bourgeois" stage of historical development never enjoyed more than an uneasy coexistence. When a revolutionary storm descended once again on the Russian scene, the conflicting pressures of these two strains in Menshevism tore the movement asunder, and they continued to divide its ranks well after the Bolshevik seizure of power.

Mr. Wildman conducted most of the research for this study, and is now publishing it, under the sponsorship of the Inter-University Project on the History of the Menshevik Movement. This project was launched in the fall of 1959 by an ad hoc committee of specialists in Russian history teaching at various American universities, in collaboration with representatives of the then already fast-dwindling Menshevik community in the United States. The members of this committee assigned themselves two major objectives:

First, to assemble systematically all available data on the history of Menshevism, with particular emphasis on the aspects of its history that were likely to remain largely unrecorded unless a special effort was immediately launched to reconstruct them.

Secondly, to give surviving representatives of the various, often conflicting, tendencies represented in Menshevism the opportunity to articulate and *reconsider* their views—with the benefit of a half-century's perspective—on the course pursued by their movement at crucial turns in its history.

The pursuit of these two major objectives has involved, for a period of over six years, an unusual collaboration between American scholars and survivors of the Menshevik movement in the United States and Western Europe. The fruits of this co-operation have been:

1. The establishment at Columbia University of a permanent archive on the history of Menshevism in which have been deposited a collection of Menshevik documents and publications, records of interviews of survivors of the Menshevik movement, and transcripts of seminar discussions in which conflicting views about the aspects of the history of Menshevism discussed in the Project's various studies were joined.

2. The preparation and distribution in multilith form of recollections by survivors of the Menshevik movement of aspects of its history in which they were directly involved. To date seventeen of these accounts have been deposited by the Project in major American and European libraries.

3. The preparation for publication of a number of longer volumes of reminiscences, as well as of monographic and auxiliary studies, prepared by American scholars as well as Menshevik associates of the Project. Some of these works are being published in English, under the sponsorship of the Hoover Institution, by the University of Chicago Press. Others are scheduled for publication in the Russian-language series of the Hoover Institution.

This summary of the activities of the Menshevik Project cannot be closed without mentioning the broad and generous assistance that they have received since the Project's inception. This assistance has included an initial grant by the Ford Foundation, supporting grants by the Rockefeller and Atran Foundations and by the American Council of Learned Societies, as well as by the Hoover Institution in the concluding phase of the Project's work. Just as vital has been the aid and counsel so generously rendered by individual faculty members and programs of Russian studies at the Universities of California, Chicago, Indiana, and Washington, as well as Columbia and Harvard Universities, without which the Project would not have been conceived and started on its way.

LEOPOLD H. HAIMSON

Author's Preface

WHEN I first undertook research for the present work some eight years ago with the aid of a Ford Foundation grant, I was reasonably certain of entering upon unexplored territory. The pioneer work on Russian Social Democracy of Leopold Haimson (then my doctoral sponsor) entitled *The Russian Marxists and the Origins of Bolshevism* (Cambridge, Mass., 1955) concentrated primarily on the leading personalities, on their ideas and contributions to the formation of the party. Such an emphasis left open the possibility of a companion study on the social and structural foundations of the movement. A preliminary survey uncovered a wealth of previously unutilized materials—pamphlets, underground journals, memoir fragments, organizational documents, police reports—which witnessed to unsuspected threads and connections scarcely hinted at in the available secondary works. Most of the latter, both Western and Soviet, suffer from their heavy reliance on the polemical literature of the subsequent *Iskra* period, above all, on Lenin's brilliant, but very biased political tract *What's to Be Done?* My intention was to see what historical perspectives and images would emerge from a fresh look at the documentary legacy of the period, before it was refracted through the prism of later party controversies.

In the years which often elapse between a doctoral dissertation and a more finished literary product suitable for publication, a host of studies have appeared which overlap or border on my own investigations (see the works in the Bibliography by Keep, Baron, Geyer, Mendel, Kindersley, and Pipes), and a good many more are in various stages of preparation. Although this scholarly profusion has enormously expanded the horizons of our knowledge about the movement, the emphasis has remained for the most part on the scaffolding of ideas, personalities, and party politics. With the partial exception of Geyer, the studies mentioned do not treat Russian Social Democracy as a genuine social movement, whereas my own findings have led me to view it primarily as a dynamic response to a deep-rooted and many-faceted dilemma of evolving Russian society. It appears that a monograph is still needed which concentrates on the substructures of the movement, one that defines the participating social groups, their attitudes and motivations, their interactions and mutual responses, and the resultant inner tensions and conflicts. If there is any justification for yet another work on Russian Social Democracy, it is to help fill in this gap, so that it may be understood as an integral part of the social history of Russia.

In carrying out this task I have found it convenient to arrange the chapters topically rather than chronologically. With the exception of the last, each chapter develops a specific theme important for understanding the movement and carries it up to what I regard as the major turning point, the street demonstrations of March, 1901. This procedure allows me to handle a particular problem exhaustively enough and over a long enough period of time to warrant meaningful conclusions without awaiting the end of the book, when the reader may easily have lost the thread. The logic in the order of the chapters, though far from perfect, is dictated by the overall framework of the study. The Social Democratic movement received its initial impetus from the severe famine of 1891, which exposed the vulnerabilities of the autocracy and generated a sense of urgency among the educated layers of Russian society for doing away with the antiquated political order. Yet the flurry of political activity stirred up by the famine served only to demonstrate the impotence of the educated classes to effect any change either through persuasion or through revolutionary action. The apathy and inactivity of radical Russia during the previous decade had been the consequence of its inability to descry on the bleak horizon a sufficiently imposing array of social forces to justify a renewal of the struggle against the autocracy. Social Democracy was able to take in tow and exploit the new spirit of political activism, precisely because it was able to point to the availability of a powerful new social force, the industrial workers.

The chief goal of the practitioners of the new faith was to demonstrate that this new class could be effectively mobilized and drawn into the political struggle. The technique they developed to accomplish this was to circulate agitational leaflets which articulated the workers' incipient economic grievances and persuaded them to use the strike as a weapon to secure concessions from their employers. They reckoned that the workers would soon become aware that the autocratic regime blocked their advances and that only by overthrowing the existing order could they hope to achieve their aims. In other words, the inevitable course of the economic struggle would lead them to Social Democratic conclusions and incline them to follow Social Democratic leadership. And indeed, within a few years, the Social Democrats achieved a remarkable success in infusing large masses of Russian workers with a revolutionary spirit, preparing the ground for the revolution of 1905.

This external success, however, masked certain powerful internal strains, bound to arise in any social movement which attempts to bridge two diverse social milieus. From the very start value conflicts and mutual suspicions between participating workers and intelligentsia continued to bedevil the normal conduct of local committee work. Faced with persistent demands by the workers for a larger role in the leadership of the movement, the Social Democratic intelligentsia was divided over how to cope with such pressures; although no hard and fast lines were formed in the period under discussion, the outlines of the future divisions of the party may be discerned in these controversies. Those who were most sympathetic to the workers' demands and felt that the intelligentsia should in no way attempt to impose its ideological precepts or "leadership" on the workers were attracted to the underground journal *Rabochaia Mysl'*. Their most articulate opponents, who felt that the workers' movement found its only justification in its contribution to the revolutionary struggle, gathered around the group and journal of the same name, *Rabochee Znamia*. Although the group remained small for a number of years, it evolved views which strikingly anticipated *Iskra,* and with the mounting revolutionary temperature after the turn of the century it preceded *Iskra* in attracting the more revolutionary elements both in and outside the party. Eventually its adherents were either absorbed into the *Iskra* organization or defected to the newly formed party of S.R.'s. Until 1901, however, the great majority of underground workers avoided the two extremes and happily combined reverence for the masses with revolutionary élan. The convoking of the First Congress and the founding of the Russian Social Democratic Workers Party in 1898 was perhaps the supreme expression of this "mainstream" of Russian Social Democracy.

I selected March, 1901, as the terminal point for the main body of the present investigation, because the demonstrations of that month were the most important milestone in the history of the movement thus far. For the first time the educated elements of Russian society clashed directly with the forces of political order and brought to a close the exclusive "hegemony" of Russian Social Democracy over the oppositional movement. The new tactics of the Social Democrats represented a desperate, but in the end unsuccessful, attempt to maintain leadership of the spirit of protest by mobilizing the workers in support of the demands of "society." The workers were indeed caught up in the general revolutionary atmosphere; but *Iskra's* rigid policy, largely inspired by Lenin, of insisting on transforming the movement into a disciplined conspiratorial party (on the order of the People's Will of the 1870's) exacerbated the issues which had already served to embitter the workers, particularly those with long experience in the Social Democratic movement. The book ends on the ironic note that the very success of *Iskra* in calling the Second Congress under its own banner served to complete the process of alienating the workers.

Such are the basic themes of the present work. The reader must be warned that it does not presume to be a comprehensive history of the movement, but rather an in-depth treatment of certain pivotal but neglected phases. There are still several important questions requiring further investigation, a situation which it is hoped will be remedied in the future. For one thing, I have not begun to do justice to the important bearing of the parallel movements within the Jewish and Polish national minorities, which by the end of the period under consideration should include the Letts, the Lithuanians, the Finns, and the Caucasian peoples. The Russian Social Democratic groups abroad, and particularly the clashes between Plekhanov and the younger generation of Social Democrats, though partially covered by Samuel Baron's biography, deserve further treatment. Although my coverage of the *Iskra* period has even less claim to comprehensiveness, I am painfully aware of having neglected to discuss adequately the Zubatov movement, which skilfully exploited the incipient hostility between workers and revolutionary intellectuals. I comfort myself that a study of precisely this question has been undertaken by Professor Jeremiah Schneiderman of the New York State University College at New Paltz.

My acknowledgments are few but, I hope, more than perfunctory. Whatever merit this work possesses owes a considerable debt to two persons no longer living. During their lifetimes they not only contributed greatly to my knowledge of the Social Democratic movement but were part of the movement itself, the one as a veteran participant from the early years, the other as both participant and its most knowledgeable historian-archivist. I refer to Lydia Osipovna Dan and Boris Ivanovich Nicolaevsky, with whom it was my pleasure to be associated through the Project on the History of the Menshevik Movement. With Lydia Dan, one of the few remaining witnesses of the epoch under discussion, I spent many hours of unconstrained, informal conversation, much of which has been recorded on tape and deposited in the archives of the Menshevik Project. Her vivid memory of personalities and events have corrected and deepened my perception of the milieu that shaped the attitudes of the young Social Democratic revolutionaries. I assume full responsibility for the form in which it is represented here, however, as I realize that Mrs. Dan would have taken sharp issue with a number of my conclusions. Mr. Nicolaevsky was an inexhaustible source of factual details which seem to elude the printed sources and are the despair of the investigator. More than once a seemingly unbridgeable gap in my story received sudden illumination through an interview with Nicolaevsky, and somewhere from the mountains of material lining his apartment he would pull out a sheaf of notes or a rare volume which supplied the information desired. Investigators in this field will sorely miss these two important witnesses to a past era.

I would also like to acknowledge the contributions of other Menshevik acquaintances to whom I turned on innumerable occasions for specific bits of information or their judgment on particular points. In this connection Boris Sapir and Grigory Aronson were especially helpful. Iulia Abramovna Kamermacher, our secretary, has through the years been the very soul of the Project; she rendered me help in innumerable practical ways, not the least of which was to advise me on ticklish problems of translation. My thinking was also stimulated by frequent conversations with my research colleagues, Ladis Kristoff and Walter Sablinsky, as well as other young scholars who occasionally made use of the services of the Project.

To the Director of the Project, Professor Leopold Haimson, I am indebted in so many ways that only the chief ones can be recounted. First, in his capacity as doctoral supervisor he guided my professional training, imparting to a freebooting perennial student a healthy respect for the academic calling and for the realities rather than the fantasies of Russian history. Second, by inviting me to participate in the Project, he made possible two years of uninterrupted research for the present volume, in addition to unlimited use of the unique resources at the Project's disposal. Finally, he has labored over the present manuscript with great care in all its various stages, insisting that it meet standards of both historical accuracy and clarity of presentation. I am sure he has rescued me from many a pitfall of careless scholarship, and if I have nevertheless fallen into others, he certainly is not to be blamed.

I wish to express by gratitude to Professor Thomas Rogers of Stony Brook for his meticulous reading of the manuscript to improve its style. Mark Khinoi of New York generously supplied a number of the photographs used for illustrations. Thanks go also to my colleagues Werner Angress, Karl Demuth, and Gunther Roth for reading individual chapters and making suggestions. My wife Helga deserves special recognition for performing the Sisyphean task of typing the manuscript several times over, including the trying footnotes and bibliography in transliteration. To her I also owe the necessary prodding and encouragement to keep at the task, meet deadlines, and finally bring it to completion.

Contents

Illustrations

(Following page 48)

Moisei and Mikhail Lure, Mark Khinoi, I. V. Babushkin

Some of the Delegates to the First Congress of the Russian Social-Democratic Workers' Party (Minsk, 1898)

A Group of Veteran Worker-Intellectuals from Ekaterinoslav

Founders of the Underground Journal *Iuzhnii Rabochii* (1899–1903)

CHAPTER I

The Rebirth
of Revolutionary Hopes

In 1890, life in Imperial Russia appeared to be supremely serene and peaceful, the autocratic power unassailable. Under the watchful eye of the ubiquitous Ober-Prokurator of the Holy Synod, Konstantin Pobedonostsev, the work of counter-reform had been carried on for nearly a decade without serious challenge from below. Stupefied by the assassination of Tsar Alexander II in 1881 and the rapid collapse of the revolutionary organization (the People's Will), oppositional "society" had settled into a mood of passivity and despair.[1] The remnants of the People's Will, having lost the tacit support of this social milieu, were unable to operate effectively and new plots were uncovered with dismal regularity by the Okhrana. The University Statute of 1884, which required students to wear uniforms, forbade student organizations, and re-established the system of curators and inspectors, was another attempt, like the introduction of the classical gymnasium

---

[1] The term "society" in quotation marks will be used as the equivalent of *obshchestvo* as conventionally employed by the Russians of this period; that is, to designate those cultivated Russians who felt they stood for the highest values of the nation, but were denied the opportunity to work for them by the arbitrary restrictions of the autocracy. It was more inclusive than the term "intelligentsia" though similar in import, that is, a term implying commitment to social and political ideals, but including liberals and a large fringe of well-disposed persons not explicitly adhering to one of the intelligentsia creeds or political strategies.

some years earlier, to immunize the youth against political infection. The "provisional rules" of 1882 setting up a preliminary censorship of manuscripts submitted for publication and making possible the permanent closing of a journal on the joint order of four ministers, proved sufficiently effective to mute the liberal press and to silence forever *Otechestvennye Zapiski* (*Notes of the Fatherland*), the leading organ of Populist public opinion. Pobedonostsev himself daily surveyed the press to ensure that the censorship authorities in the Ministry of Education were performing their duties (the Tsar was notified of lapses and oversights). The other personal causes of the zealous Ober-Prokurator —the missionary efforts of the Orthodox Church, the increase in parish schools at the expense of secular schools, the curbs on Jews and sectarians, and the Russification of border nationalities— made significant strides, albeit not without distasteful chattering in the liberal press and (so the Ober-Prokurator felt) lukewarm support from the throne. New repressive laws dealing with the zemstvos, the municipalities, and the creation of a new species of rural officials, the land captains, were, by 1890, in the final stages of drafting. The self-appointed guardian of Holy Russia could take satisfaction that the sources of insane delusion among the educated and of bewilderment among simple Orthodox were being stopped up one by one and that soon not a ripple would disturb his idyll of a beautiful autocracy—a stern but kindly Tsar wedded in the one true faith with a grateful and obedient people.[2]

In the accounts written by members of the radical intelligentsia, the 1880's are represented as the decade of "quiet," the era of "small deeds," "inner soul-cleansing" (*samosovershentstvovanie*), and "step-by-step" progress.[3] The once ardent partisans of peasant uprisings and political terror now found moral gratification in rendering modest, but concrete service to the "people" (*narod*)

---

[2] A good monograph on the domestic scene under Alexander III is yet to be written. The best available treatment, one accurately conveying the reactionary spirit of the age, is K. Stählin's *Geschichte Russlands* (Koenigsberg, 1939), IV, 431–95.

[3] Two such intelligentsia "histories" are R. V. Ivanov-Razumnik, *Istoriia russkoi obshchestvennoi mysli* (St. Petersburg, 1908), Vol. II, chaps. 4–7, and D. N. Ovsianiko-Kulikovskii, *Istoriia russkoi intelligentsii* (St. Petersburg, 1911), Vol. III. The picture here, however, is the author's own, drawn from a variety of sources, particularly memoirs, which will be cited in due course.

as midwives, teachers, doctors, or zemstvo employees. No longer was "the people" viewed as the chosen agency of social transformation; it was now regarded as the helpless object of disinterested service, moral uplift, and protective measures administered by enlightened zemstvo leaders. The great reconstruction of society was indeed to come, but not through concerted revolutionary action; it would be the cumulative effect of countless individual works of benevolence, together with the eventual reduction of the citadels of power through noble example. It might be said that Tolstoy's precepts of non-resistance to evil and indifference to observable results ("The Kingdom of God is within you") influenced a whole generation of the Russian intelligentsia. Although debates between Tolstoyans and traditional Populists were common enough in the circles of the 1880's, the two viewpoints imperceptibly converged with each other.[4] Tolstoy, who until his conversion remained haughtily aloof from the intelligentsia, wove a number of Populist motifs into his new religious teaching—the evil of property, the purity of the peasant way of life, the "debt" owed to the people, and the consequent rejection of all cultural values (art, science, constitutions) in which the people had no share. Though they might ridicule the literalism of Tolstoy's unimaginative disciples, most radical intellectuals felt only reverence for Tolstoy himself. They warmly admired his literary creations (including the religious ones), praised the sincerity of his ideals, and unconsciously incorporated many of them into their own thinking and attitudes. More than a few such intellectuals made the pilgrimage to Yasna Polyana to come away charmed, if not often converted.

There was a notable absence of other new trends among the intelligentsia. The sacred texts of Belinskii, Chernyshevskii, Lavrov, and Mikhailovskii were still piously read, but facile prescriptions of "what to do" were crowded out by involved discussions of the national economy, the role of personality in history, the definition of progress, literary criticism, and statistics on the life and needs of the people. The age seemed to fit Lavrov's prescription of long, intensive theoretical preparation and the bringing

---

[4] See Ivanov-Razumnik, II, 235–45 and 363 ff. and Ovsianiko-Kulikovskii, III, chap. 7.

of enlightenment and culture to the people (*kul'turnichestvo*) before the undertaking of precipitous revolutionary activity.

Students alone kept the vestal fires of the radical tradition burning. The only serious terrorist plot of the period was organized in 1887 by a group of St. Petersburg students that included Lenin's older brother, Alexander. Although terrorism appealed to only a minority of students, a diffuse sense of identification with the radical tradition and of hostility to the restrictive University Statute of 1884 were very widespread. Protest demonstrations were chronic in the late eighties: the celebration of the twenty-fifth anniversary of Dobroliubov's death in 1886 brought several thousand students into the streets of the capital, and only the quick deployment of Cossack troops prevented the outbreak from assuming larger proportions. In the same year at Moscow University, the harsh regime of the Curator Brizgalov provoked disorders which spread to other institutions and led to the temporary closing of five universities.[5] Nonetheless, the majority of students viewed their protests as aimed at the Statute of 1884 and opposed the attempts of the radical minority to channel it into "politics." By 1890, despite the troublesome currents stirring beneath, the surface of public life was undisturbed.

In the following year, the picture changed abruptly. The government found itself in the midst of a deep crisis as the result of a protracted famine, which its clumsy bureaucratic apparatus proved singularly ill-equipped to handle. As the opposition press began to hint at the mounting catastrophe in the course of the summer of 1891, the government was obliged to release an official version, faithfully echoed in the loyal press, representing the situation as a "poor harvest," severe only in a few localities. The

---

[5] A typical incident illustrating the temper of the students is related by V. A. Maklakov in *Iz vospominanii* (New York, 1954), pp. 110–14. Although he was neither then nor subsequently anything but a moderate liberal, when he and a few fellow students heard of the death of Chernyshevskii in 1889, they decided to use the pretext of holding a mass at a nearby church to stage a student demonstration. When the culprits were brought before the level-headed dean of the University, Kapnist, he asked them which one of them had ever read one of Chernyshevskii's works or were acquainted with his views. To their embarrassment not one of them (including Maklakov) could answer affirmatively. Perhaps only Maklakov appreciated the delicacy of Kapnist in handling the situation. The thoughtless demonstration of student radicalism, Kapnist was suggesting, threatened to bring reprisals on the entire university community, the one island of relative freedom and enlightenment under the autocratic regime.

reactionary *Moskovskie Vedomosti* (*The Moscow News*) ominously cautioned that to raise the specter of "famine" (the word itself smacked of disloyalty) would set in motion a "dangerous hubbub" from which only the revolutionaries could benefit.

The famine crisis was especially unwelcome to the tsarist government at this juncture, since it threatened to upset the carefully laid plans for modernizing the national economy. In a monumental effort to overcome Russia's industrial backwardness, the Finance Minister Vyshnegradskii had inaugurated a policy of higher protective tariffs and of forcing the export of grain. To achieve this increase, dues (chiefly redemption payments for land) were collected from the peasants at harvest time. This forced the peasants to market immediately, forcing prices down, and to purchase grain for their day-to-day needs the rest of the year at higher prices. In 1891, the resulting lack of grain reserves among the peasants proved catastrophic, threatening large numbers with starvation and burdening the government with the double loss of huge arrears in taxes and a marked decline in export income. It was clear that to tide the peasants over until the next season, huge financial outlays were necessary. Such sums could be obtained only from classes ordinarily exempt from taxation—i.e., the nobility and wealthier townsmen. A logical solution to the impasse, which would not violate traditional prerogatives, would have been to appeal to the general public for voluntary contributions, thereby drawing upon the long frustrated philanthropic and civic feelings of cultivated Russian "society." This would have been very strong and bitter medicine, since it would have meant giving encouragement to those very inclinations which the era of counter-reform had so carefully held in check.

Despite its qualms, the government bowed to the inevitable, and an imperial rescript of November 17, 1891 (o.s.), called upon the public to form voluntary organizations and rush aid to the afflicted regions. Thus the policy of a decade was abruptly, if but momentarily, reversed, and the "dangerous hubbub" against which the reactionary press had warned set in. Special committees sprang to life, public meetings resounded with heated debates and impassioned oratory, the pages of the press bristled with reports and appeals in bold print. Passions which had been denied legitimate expression since the period of Great Reforms took a

deep draught of the heady wine of freedom. The magnitude of
the operation and the frenzy of activity which enveloped the
non-official sectors of society exceeded all anticipations.[6] Persons
of the most diverse viewpoints found in this enterprise an outlet
for long-repressed strivings: the excitable youth again "went to
the people"; Tolstoyans devoted their practical talents to the relief of suffering; liberals reveled in the dispensation given to free
expression and public initiative; zemstvo leaders sought to prove
their superior administrative capacities; and the philanthropic
gentry generously contributed their wealth. The normal course
of national life was interrupted and all energies were directed
toward the challenge of the moment.

The famine, therefore, was accompanied by a many-faceted
social awakening with which the government now had to reckon.
Feeling itself strong and the government weak, "society" would
no longer reconcile itself to the old strictures and came to look
upon the cause of aid to the starving as peculiarly its own affair.
Vainly, the government attempted to funnel public activity into
organizations of a semi-official character. Grand Duke Nikolai,
the successor to the throne, headed a so-called "Special Committee," while another "Local Committee" in Moscow enjoyed the
protection of the wife of the reactionary governor, Grand Duke
Sergei. The Red Cross had also long been patronized by personages
near the throne and served as a stepping-stone for careerists seeking high office. Those with positions in the bureaucracy or govern-
ment-connected institutions (universities, hospitals, zemstvos)
were often advised of official "displeasure" if their efforts were not
made through these semi-official committees. Undaunted by such
intimidation, the liberal public quickly set up its own organs of
famine relief, such as the committee initiated by the leading members of Moscow "society" to which Tolstoy lent the prestige of his

---

[6] Maklakov thus characterized the atmosphere: "People of the most varied persua-
sions and temperaments threw themselves into the cause. Many forsook their usual
occupations and went about setting up canteens, and during the epidemics, helping
the doctors. In this work not a few lost forever their positions and their health."
(*Ibid.*, p. 167.) Even the hard-bitten foe of liberalism, Victor Chernov, was heartened by the new activism of "society": "Collections for the starving undertaken
by the Free Economic Society brought stupendous results. Literally everyone was
infected by it. People who stood aside from all 'politics' were caught up in the all-
embracing stream." (*Zapiski sotsialista-revoliutsionera* [Berlin, 1922], p. 94.)

name and his untiring efforts. Tolstoy's own flaming appeals appeared in scores of newspapers. He offered such concrete suggestions as, for example, that landowners forage the peasants' horses in their own barns over the winter and return them in time for spring plowing. His wife, Sofia Andreevna, handled the collection of relief funds in the capitals, while he himself worked tirelessly in the provinces, traveling from village to village to assess local needs and make necessary arrangements.

The restless public, facing obstacles to their *ad hoc* organizations, turned to their purpose two institutions which had long enjoyed special status under autocratic laws, the Free Economic Society and the Moscow Society of Agriculture. These organizations had originally been authorized as purely learned societies to allow interested persons to consult together on economic questions, to gather information, and to print scientific works. In the 1880's both had established affiliates, called "Committees on Literacy," which printed large quantities of useful educational materials for the people and in general furthered the cause of popular education. When the famine struck, those involved in this work as a matter of course made use of its facilities for the purpose of famine relief. I. I. Petrunkevich, one of the Moscow liberals associated with the Moscow "Committee on Literacy," has left the following account in his memoirs.

> This fortuitous intrusion of real life into the stuffy atmosphere of the old committee remarkably enlivened it; it introduced passion, it threw bright rays of light on a task put forward by life itself, making demands which seemed remote from educational aims, but in reality inseparably bound up with them. . . . There were members who did not care for this feverish work, these heated speeches, the not always restrained references to the political authorities, which evoked fears that the displeasure of the government might be aroused.[7]

The committees continued to be a haven for normally proscribed public activities long after the famine was over; not until several years later did the government become sufficiently aware of the danger of these sanctuaries and place them under the direct control of the Ministry of Interior.

The new buoyancy of the Russian liberal and radical public

---

[7] *Iz zapisok obshchestvennago deiatelia* (Berlin, 1934), p. 277.

quickly crystallized into a number of groupings, each with its own particular program and strategy for exploiting the situation. Although the shackles of despondency and quietism had been broken, the main body of journalistic opinion still bore the ideological earmarks of the era of "small deeds." The most typical exponent of the Populism of this era was "V. V." (Vorontsov), whose ponderous treatise on political economy, *The Fate of Capitalism in Russia* (St. Petersburg, 1887), supplied the pseudo-scientific rationale for current dogmas and moral promptings. Although the government might give it artificial encouragement, V. V. argued, capitalism was "impossible" in Russia because the intrinsic superiority of the products of peasant labor precluded a mass market for factory-produced goods. V. V. was quite confident that peasant handicraft (*kustar*) production would flourish, once freed of arbitrary restraints and burdensome taxation and encouraged by measures that would put scientific technology and ordinary mechanical improvements within reach. The Populist intellectuals, too rooted in their social positions to be tempted anew by revolutionary panaceas, yet seeing their perspectives fade with the mounting bureaucratic reaction and Vyshnegradsky's new industrial policies, looked increasingly to enlightened zemstvo leaders, liberal professors and journalists—"progressive society" in general—for useful partners in their cause. In turn, the progressive circles, odd compounds of liberalism, Slavophilism, and Tolstoyanism, had also shown a marked tendency toward accommodation with the new orientation of the Populists. The bureaucratic, "Westernizing" liberalism of the Era of Great Reforms had given way to a new liberalism animated by "love for the people," a liberalism concerned with the plight of peasant agriculture and incensed by the bureaucracy's assaults on the integrity of peasant and zemstvo self-administration. Although the leading liberal organ, *Vestnik Evropy* (*European Messenger*), catered to the democratically-inclined urban professional classes—professors, ex-bureaucrats, lawyers, justices and the like—it took great pains to divest itself of the image of "Manchesterism" foisted on it by the reactionary, and sometimes even the Populist, press. It claimed that Russian liberalism, unlike certain types of European liberalism, championed the interests of the whole people and not simply those of the commercial and industrial bourgeoisie. It strongly opposed protective tariffs, heavy excise taxes on items of peasant consumption (sugar, alcohol, kerosene), and the rapid development of capitalist industry with its unthinkable concomitant, a landless proletariat. Conversely, it supported the institution of a Peasants' Bank, a graduated income tax, and a separate Ministry of Agriculture. Like the Populist journals, *Vestnik Evropy* advanced various projects to ease the peasant's lot and enhance his economic viability and self-reliance. Other organs of the liberal press such as the newspaper *Russkie Vedomosti* (*The Russian News*) and the journal *Russkaia Mysl'* (*Russian Thought*) were even more noticeably tinged with an "agrarian" and Populist orientation. (*Russkaia Mysl'* sometimes even published articles by the well-known Populist Mikhailovskii.) The provincial press often reflected the immediate practical concerns of the liberal gentry entrenched in zemstvo institutions; here the "Westernizing" overtones were apt to be even less in evidence, and the Slavophile and Tolstoyan more pronounced.[8]

By the famine year the crisscrossing trends of "people-loving" liberals and "liberal-flirting" Populists were scarcely distinguishable in any essential respect. In unison, they protested against the government's pampering of industry and neglect of agriculture, and they advanced various projects to protect the villages from the rapacity of the money-lenders and the bureaucratic tutelage of the land captains. The new allies felt themselves fully vindicated by the famine crisis, which, in their view, confirmed their diagnosis of the perils of the new industrial policy and the urgency of their program. In scores of journal articles, brochures, public lectures, and learned treatises, liberals and Populists insistently put their program before the public: the easing of the peasant's financial burdens, the establishment of peasant co-operatives, credit on easy terms for increasing inventory, government purchase of surplus lands and resale to the communes on easy terms,

---

[8] A particularly acute analysis of the interrelationship between Populism and liberalism in this period is that of the Menshevik author A. N. Potresov, "Evoliutsiia obshchestvenno-politicheskoi mysli v predrevoliutsionnuiu epokhu" in *Obshchestvennoe dvizhenie v Rosii v nachale XX-go veka*, ed. L. Martov, A. N. Potresov, *et al.* (St. Petersburg, 1909), I, 538–56. Some of the preceding data were drawn from this article. Like any Marxist treatment, of course, it imposes its theoretical scheme on the material, ignoring trends and ideas not easily categorized (for example, Tolstoyanism and Slavophilism).

the resettlement of the surplus population in Siberia, the extension of zemstvo institutions to the volost (sub-district) level and the widening of their tax powers and sphere of competence. The hitherto colorless journal *Russkoe Bogatstvo* (*Russian Wealth*) was taken over by Populists, most of them former collaborators of *Otechestvennye Zapiski* (Mikhailovskii, Krivenko, Iuzhakov). V. V.'s thesis on the "impossibility of capitalism in Russia" was further elaborated by Nikolai ——on [Danielson] in *Outline of Our Post-Reform Economy* (St. Petersburg, 1894), which purported to make use of Marxian analysis; henceforward, the arguments of these authors became axiomatic for the liberal-Populist bloc. The occasional bickering between the liberal and Populist organs, or among the Populist authors themselves (V. V., for example, accused Nikolai ——on of failing to recognize the intrinsic viability of the commune), served only to demonstrate the large body of ideas they shared in common.[9] The liberal-Populist crusaders believed their arguments to be so obvious and unassailable that the government could not resist their logic, and that even if it should, the united force of public opinion would certainly compel it to adopt the proposed measures.

There were, however, many representatives of "society" who maintained a sense of political realism amidst the general euphoria; they realized that the autocracy had undergone no real change of heart and that the concessions won by "society" during the famine would be taken back at the first convenient opportunity. Convinced that the autocracy was steering a course toward national disaster, they hoped to forge a broad coalition of all oppositional elements to wrest basic civil liberties and a democratic constitution from the Tsar. Although such bold spirits constituted a rather small minority, many of them were strategically placed in the zemstvos, the city dumas, the universities, and the prominent professions. Organized expression of this nascent "revolutionary constitutionalism" would probably not have come

---

[9] For these family quarrels see L. Z. Slonimskii, "Ekonomicheskie reformy i zakonodatel'stva," *Vestnik Evropy*, Nos. 5 and 6, 1893, pp. 735–56 and 316–41; Nikolai ——on, "Nechto ob usloviiakh nashego khoziaistvennogo razvitiia," *Russkoe Bogatstvo*, Nos. 4 and 6, 1894, pp. 1–54 and 86–130; and V. V., *Ocherki teoreticheskoi eknomiki* (St. Petersburg, 1895), chap. 2. Nikolai ——on's economic panaceas were far more drastic than the other Populists', but he shared their critique of capitalism, their peasant socialism, and their optimism concerning "reform from above."

about at this time (1892–94), had not returned political exiles, mainly former members of the People's Will, taken the initiative. Toward the end of 1891, Mark Natanson, the founder in the 1870's of the underground party, Land and Freedom, formed a new revolutionary organization called Party of the People's Rights (*Partiia Narodnogo Prava*). The guiding idea of his strategy was that neither the revolutionaries nor oppositional "society" could bring down the autocracy if they acted separately, but that, united on a common platform of a democratic constitutional order, they could muster the necessary support in the country at large. Operating from Saratov, his enforced residence since his return from Siberia, Natanson sent out agents (mainly seasoned revolutionaries) to sound out disaffected circles and persuade them to coordinate their efforts to abolish absolutism through his organization. There was hardly a "sympathizing" liberal or a radical student who was not aware that something was in the wind. Many highly respected people were compromised by carrying on negotiations with Natanson's representatives or offering them aid. Natanson's conspirators acted so cautiously that they were able to carry on their work for nearly three years (until 1894) without interference by the secret police. The plan provided that, at a given signal, all oppositional groups should take to the streets in protest against the existing regime and thus shatter its moral authority. Faced with such a massive demonstration, the Tsar's police and army would be powerless, and, unless he was willing to embark on a universal bloodbath, the Tsar would be forced to capitulate. The police eventually became aware that something was afoot, and a round-up of old revolutionaries who had served their terms of prison and exile sufficed to demolish the master plan. Protesting "society" was again left helplessly atomized.[10]

The famine also gave considerable impetus to the growth of political radicalism among students, which had remained dormant under the regime of the classical gymnasium and the University Statute of 1884. During the famine students went in droves "to the people" to staff canteens or assist doctors in fighting epidemics. The panorama of misery and chaos implanted in their minds a firm image of the complete irrationality of the prevailing

---

[10] For data on the Party of the People's Rights see *Obshchestvennoe dvizhenie*. I, 372–75 and Chernov, pp. 187–97.

social and political order. The radical ideologies offered ready-
made solutions and outlets for their mounting indignation. Forgotten were the former prejudices of the majority against mixing
"politics" with demonstrations against university authorities. The
once more-or-less innocent student corporations, the *zemliachestva* (supposedly, groups of students from the same parts of Russia), now became hotbeds of revolutionary agitation. Their number
and membership increased rapidly, their activities were co-ordinated through central organizations, and they established contacts
with similar organizations in other universities. In Moscow, Viktor
Chernov and his circle of revolutionary Populists took over the
leadership of the student movement and formally "expelled" the
moderates, among whom was the later well-known liberal V. A.
Maklakov.[11] Under Chernov's leadership the "Union Council"
strengthened its authority over member *zemliachestva* and expanded their number considerably. It sponsored frequent "student
evenings" (*vecherinki*) and inter-*zemliachestva* assemblies which
discussed, not the abuses of university authorities, but the respective revolutionary potential of peasantry and intelligentsia,
the advisability of reviving terror, the structure of the future
republic, and the "usefulness" of "cowardly liberals" in the coming
struggle against the autocracy. A secret student congress took
place in Kiev early in 1892, whose deliberations were summed up
as follows by Chernov:

> The organized student body of the country was recognized as a
> legitimate component of the revolutionary intelligentsia and the nat-
> ural avant garde of the nation-wide movement. The students were
> advised not to remain enclosed in the narrow circle of their aca-
> demic interests. The academic hierarchy was recognized as an or-
> ganic component of the political regime. An isolated struggle to

---

[11] The radicals objected to Maklakov's efforts to gain legal recognition for the
student organizations. Chernov's account elucidates their thinking: "The material
basis of mutual aid funds, the foundation of our organization, reinforced by the
principle of comradeship, guaranteed us broad scope in the student masses. Thus
the students' vanguard was moved into the directing position. To tear this organization to pieces, to make its 'visceral' side autonomous and surrender it to the custody
of autocratic laws . . . did this not mean to undermine the implacable hostility of
the students, to operate in a spirit of 'harmony' and conformity to the existing? . . .
Therefore, we anticipated the attack of our position by the 'legalizers' and took into
our hands the 'militant initiative' and became the offensive party." (*Zapiski*, pp.
114–15.) Reflecting on this incident many years later, Maklakov saw here a hint of
"that new ideology which led to Bolshevism" (*Iz vospominanii*, p. 159).

renovate an individual part of it was therefore rejected. Students were summoned to go to the aid of the starving, to enter units for combating the epidemics, to infiltrate the Sunday Schools in worker quarters with the aim of strengthening ties with the laboring masses, and of making use of these ties later on for the revolution.[12]

Because of the policy of biding its time for a concerted revolutionary outbreak, the student leadership frequently found itself in the curious position of restraining the rank and file, who were inclined to demonstrate at every opportunity and to become restive over the inactivity of their leaders. Although in the years immediately following the famine there were no major student demonstrations, the students were becoming ever more infected with political radicalism.

The intoxicating atmosphere of the famine year inevitably produced a flurry of revolutionary enterprises. It only sufficed for some figure from the epic past to return from exile and come into contact with a group of young people for a conspiracy to be born. Chernov's comrades, though suspicious of "constitutionalism," could not resist the temptation to offer their services to Natanson and fell victim in the arrests which followed. Iulii Martov had not yet completed his first semester at St. Petersburg University when he was drawn into several conspiratorial undertakings (besides those he initiated himself); he was implicated in the breakup of a circle of *narodovoltsy* in 1892 and arrested.[13] The story was similar in the provinces: ex-revolutionaries, ostensibly under police supervision, were often in contact with circles of gymnasium youth or university students home for semester vacations and inspired them with tales of the past and counsels on prospective political activities. These groups instinctively revived the doctrines and strategies of previous decades, their impatience untempered by afterthoughts. The inevitable result was a series of affairs which ended in collapse, arrests, and disillusionment.[14]

---

[12] Chernov, p. 121.

[13] See Iu. O. Martov, *Zapiski sotsial-demokrata* (Berlin, 1923), pp. 99 ff.

[14] Another typical conspiracy of the period was that of the Astyrev circle in Moscow in 1892. Its strategy vacillated between the revival of terror and attempts to foment a peasant uprising through systematic agitation. See *Obshchestvennoe dvizhenie*, I, 373.

The beneficiary of this aftermath of futility and stock-taking was Marxism. In the circles of the late 1880's and early 1890's, individual, self-styled "Marxists" were to be found, but they impressed most radical intellectuals as outsiders to the intelligentsia tradition, who were preoccupied with esoteric and irrelevant abstractions. The few clandestine "Social Democratic" groups which conducted propaganda among the urban workers attracted little notice, and their activities differed little from those of rival Populist groups, which had been plying the same program since the early 1870's. The rapid swing to Marxism occurred only after the famine, and the records of the period indicate that it was precisely the famine which provided the stimulus. Henceforward, it was the Social Democratic movement that was to give form and substance to the new militant mood of the radical Russian intelligentsia. It is worth observing that somewhat before Marxism made its literary debut with Struve's *Critical Notes on the Question of Russia's Economic Development* (St. Petersburg, 1894), it already had a strong appeal for the radical student youth, long since noted for serving as "the barometer of society." Indeed, the majority of those who emerged as the Marxist literary figures of the mid-1890's (except, of course, for the veteran émigré, Plekhanov) had either just graduated from the university or were still serving terms of exile for the sins of their student days. The university careers of Struve, Potresov, Martov, Lenin, Bulgakov, Prokopovich, and Kistiakovskii, soon to be the luminaries of the Marxist literary renaissance, spanned the famine year. Only Tugan-Baranovskii and Vladimir Posse could claim a few years' seniority.

The movement known as Legal Marxism was the creation of precocious radical youths who turned to Marxism under the impact of their experience of the hunger years (1891 and 1892). The cases of E. D. Kuskova and S. N. Prokopovich, who belonged to one of the first Marxist circles in Moscow (that of the young Marxist lawyer Riazanov), were typical. Kuskova was one of the student *buntari* (Populist partisans of peasant uprisings) who volunteered to serve in the campaign to stem the cholera epidemic in Saratov which raged in the wake of the famine. She was the horrified witness of one of the riots of peasants and simple townspeople against the doctors and students who had come to inoculate them.

Student agitators who tried to transform the riot into a "popular uprising" against the landowners and the police succeeded only in drawing the wrath of the mob upon themselves.[15] Prokopovich likewise lost his faith in the revolutionary potential of the peasantry during his tenure as a zemstvo statistician working with peasants being resettled in Siberia. Like their predecessors of the "mad summer" of 1874, the student *buntari* underwent a crisis of spirit and cast about for a new revolutionary formula. Like the older generation, many turned to terror. Others, familiar with the fate of their revolutionary predecessors, saw the futility of repeating the same cycle and were ripe for some "new word." This was a period of searching and uncertainty among the revolutionary youth, and on this well-prepared soil Marxism easily brought forth shoots.

The most vivid and illuminating account of this transitional phase in the outlook of the Russian intelligentsia has been left to us by Martov.[16] As a gymnasium student he was already a political radical; he and his companions pored over the secretly obtained classics of Populist literature and the accounts of the exploits of the People's Will. The greatest thrill of Martov's early years was the opportunity to take part in the funeral procession of the bold publicist Shelgunov (April, 1891) which the radical public (students, for the most part) transformed into a political demonstration. Although chagrined by the fact that the procession submitted to the directives of the police escort and failed to denounce the autocracy openly, Martov felt himself a part of a vast underground which would one day help the enraged people to cast off the shackles of the oppressive regime. Moreover, he was deeply impressed by the fact that genuine workers participated in the demonstration, giving him his first opportunity to see representatives of the "people" face to face.

When Martov entered the university his frame of mind was typical of the radical youth of his generation. He described it as follows:

---

[15] On this incident see Chernov, pp. 94–96 and E. D. Kuskova, "Davno minuvshee," *Novyi Zhurnal*, No. 49 (June, 1957), pp. 160–66. On the Moscow Marxist circle see *ibid.*, No. 50 (September, 1957), pp. 171–91 and Chernov, pp. 158–62 and chap. 4 *passim.*

[16] See his *Zapiski*, chaps. 3 and 4.

Vague feelings stirred within me and upon my conscience I would not be able to define what my soul longed for, what I expected from this holy of the holies, the university. . . . Comradeship in the task of pursuing scientific truth was mysteriously intertwined in my imagination with a militant fraternity of youth, hostile to the "social order," although I was not yet able to envisage concretely the form of my future "rebellious" [*buntovshchicheskii*] activity. A romantic sensation that I had entered on the threshold of exploits and dangers was not foreign to me—I was not yet eighteen.[17]

Although the name of Marx was highly revered among radical students, and the more mature of them read articles on the European socialist movement in the liberal press, Martov encountered very few professed "Marxists" among his new acquaintances. Among the older student leaders, A. N. Potresov was negatively disposed toward Populism and tentatively linked to zemstvo liberal circles, yet a convinced revolutionary seeking a "new word"; Struve offered the ambiguous impression of being "now a German Social Democrat, now a liberal from the *Vestnik Evropy*."[18] Martov's other acquaintances were Populists of various shades and seekers for a new gospel.

Martov did meet one bona fide Marxist, a certain D. V. Stranden, an older student of imposing erudition and easy familiarity in political questions, whose reserved yet authoritative manner suggested important connections in the revolutionary underground.[19] Although Stranden was thoroughly familiar with the

---

[17] *Ibid.*, p. 62.

[18] *Ibid.*, p. 91. See P. B. Struve's own account in "My Contacts and Conflicts with Lenin," *The Slavonic Review*, XII (1933–34), 577. Struve had spent much time abroad as a youth and was certainly familiar with Marxism and German Social Democracy before 1891. His own version of his convictions of the time would seem to confirm the ambiguity observed in Martov. However, both versions are susceptible to the distortion of hindsight. An indication that Struve's convictions were not yet fully developed in 1891 and that he shared a good bit of the prevalent student radicalism is given in an incident recounted by Martov. As chairman of the Student Fund of Mutual Aid, Struve was instrumental in drawing up a petition of protest to the famous philosopher Vladimir Soloviev for his public statement that the famine was a judgment of God upon "those who stirred up violence in Russia." The students felt that such a reflection on honor of the *narodovoltsy* was a betrayal of the intelligentsia tradition; Soloviev explained to the chagrin of the students that he was referring to the perpetrators of pogroms! See *Zapiski*, pp. 78–79. For details on the complexities of Struve's development, see Richard Kindersley, *The First Russian Revisionists* (Oxford, 1962), pp. 28–52.

[19] See Martov, p. 85 and *passim*.

views of Plekhanov's Liberation of Labor Group, he apparently felt it would be premature to initiate his young acquaintances into its program until they outgrew their *buntarstvo*. He suggested instead that they undertake a long period of systematic preparation for revolutionary activity, during which time they should work out a well-rounded, scientifically sound "world-view."

Stranden, Potresov, and Martov were put in charge of a student library initiated by the illegal Student Fund for Mutual Aid, of which Struve was the head. Along with the usual Populist-revolutionary fare, many serious works on history, European socialism, primitive culture and political institutions passed through their hands, as well as Plekhanov's first Marxist works, *Our Differences* and *Socialism and the Political Struggle*. Despite this widening of his horizons, Martov was much too eager to engage in genuine revolutionary work to concern himself with serious study—after all, the famine year promised to be the year of the great uprising of the people against the autocracy! His impetuousness only led to his arrest and the collapse of his conspiratorial group.

Freed pending sentence the following year, the chastened Martov resumed "systematic work" on developing his world-view and in this connection read *Das Kapital*. He immediately wrote his friend Stavskii: "*Das Kapital* has opened my eyes to the basic question 'What to Do?'"[20] His friend replied that he had coincidentally undergone the same experience and was convinced of the futility of Populist dreams. Capitalist development in Russia was inevitable, and therefore it was imperative to organize a workers' movement in Russia on the model of those in advanced Western countries. Potresov, like Struve a few years earlier, undertook a trip to Western Europe to acquaint himself with the experience of European socialist parties. He interviewed their leaders and collected their literature. He also called on Plekhanov in Geneva and received a complete stock of the literature of the Liberation of Labor Group, including Plekhanov's most recent tract, *The Tasks of Socialists in the Struggle with the Famine*. With the help of Martov and a few other comrades, this rich collection of literature was smuggled into Russia and eagerly devoured by the circle. "After a short time," Martov relates, "we

---

[20] *Ibid.*, p. 138.

all agreed among ourselves that we were without reservation Social Democrats and adherents of the Liberation of Labor Group."[21]

Their newly formed convictions were reinforced by news of
large scale strikes at Lodz in May, 1892. Martov had met some of
the leaders of the Polish movement in prison and knew that they
were by conviction Social Democrats and adherents of the Second
International. The idea of becoming a part of a grand European
movement excited the imagination of the fledgling Russian Social
Democrats. The isolation of the intelligentsia would be overcome,
for their comrades in the revolutionary struggle would be the
proletariat, not only of Russia, but of all nationalities. Populist
exclusivism and provincialism would be left far behind. Russia
was destined to march in step with Europe. The thoughts which
gestated in the minds of Martov's comrades were a microcosm of
the stirrings of their student generation—the revolutionary
expectations of the famine year and subsequent disenchantment,
the desire to escape the "enchanted circle" of Populism, the ex-
hilarating discovery of new roots in the masses, the confidence of
a "scientific" foundation for their hopes, and, finally, the satisfaction of participating in the general progressive movement of
European civilization. When Marxism entered the arena of the
legal press two years later, it found a well-prepared audience
among the radical student youth.

Early in 1894, the campaign of the Populist intelligentsia to
rally "society" around its program was still at its peak. Each
number of the Populist and semi-Populist journals carried extensive articles on peasant craft industries and the dangers of the
government's policies in the field of economics. Even liberal professors like Postnikov and Chuprov, when discoursing professionally on such matters as the impact of higher grain prices, sought
to advance the tenets of the Populist-inspired coalition. The
phalanx of these crusaders was solid enough for Mikhailovskii
complacently to chide certain unidentified "Russian Marxists,"
and for Nikolai ——on to issue patronizing advice to a certain
"young scholar," P. von Struve, who in some obscure German
journal had dared to challenge Nikolai ——on's thesis on the "im-

_____

[21] *Ibid.*, p. 140.

possibility of capitalism in Russia."[22] But the identity of these "Russian Marxists" remained a mystery, since their works had not yet appeared in Russian publications. Clearly the liberal-Populist coalition sensed no real challenge to its sway over the educated public.

This sanguine atmosphere was abruptly jarred toward the end of the year by the appearance of two successive literary sensations: Struve's *Critical Notes on the Question of Russia's Economic Development* and Beltov's *On the Question of Developing a Monistic View of History* (the unwary Russian censor did not recognize the latter as belonging to the pen of the dangerous émigré, Plekhanov). These works launched a sustained attack on the precepts of Populism and produced something in the nature of panic among the hitherto self-assured Populist intellectuals. The turmoil extended far beyond the pages of the "thick journals" and polemical works. Here was a clear case of the irreverent revolt of the "sons" against their wiser and more experienced "fathers." The circles or *kruzhki* of intellectual intimates, where such ideas were always thrashed out, hummed with the debate; their members assiduously acquired and pored over the writings of Marx, and other basic works on political economy, historical materialism, and working-class movements. Many members were quickly converted (roughly, in inverse proportion to age), others wavered back and forth, while a stubborn remnant resolutely defended the cherished traditions. Friend parted with friend, long-standing connections were broken, groups underwent constant realignment. The debate engaged the full spectrum of society—from student and underground circles to learned societies and even bureaucratic officials.

The reason for this profound ferment was that Marxism in Russia represented far more than an intellectual fad or a new revolutionary tactic. It posited for the first time a comprehensive scheme for Russia's historical development which went counter to virtually all the hallowed axioms of Russia's intellectual traditions, axioms

---

[22] For this first skirmish of Populism with Marxism see N. K. Mikhailovskii, "O narodnichestve V. V.," *Russkoe Bogatstvo*, No. 10, 1893, pp. 111–35; P. Struve, "Zur Beurteilung der kapitalistischen Entwicklung Russlands," *Sozialpolitisches Central-blatt*, Band III, No. 1 (October, 1893), pp. 1–3; and Nikolai ——on, "Nechto ob usloviiakh nashego khoziastvennogo razvitiia," *Russkoe Bogatstvo*, No. 4 (1894), p. 45.

shared by groups of the most diverse political persuasion. With its irreverent rejection of all notions of the "peculiarity" (*samobyt-nost*) of Russian institutions, such as the commune and *kustar* industry, and of the "special path" of historical development which would spare Russia the tribulations of Western Europe, Marxism offered the Russian intelligentsia for the first time in decades an unreservedly "Westernizing" point of view. It viewed capitalism, not as imported poison from the West, but as a progressive phenomenon rooted in unalterable sociological laws. Unexpectedly, the Populist pamphleteers were forced to break off their campaign to halt the ruin of the peasantry in order to defend the entire intellectual edifice upon which their program rested.

The initial reaction of the Populist authors to the Marxist onslaught was one of outrage bordering on hysteria. They simply could not understand how representatives of the Russian intelligentsia dared offer a rationale for the government policy of protection for industry and forced export of grain, a policy responsible for the famine of 1891 and for all the other ills besetting the countryside. S. Krivenko voiced the alarm of the defenders of the old positions in *Russkoe Bogatstvo*:

> There are authors who uphold the inevitability, indeed, the "historical necessity" of the capitalist process for all countries and all peoples. This process, as is well known, is always accompanied by tearing a significant part of the population away from the land and tools of production, and by the formation of a contingent of free hands. When the inevitable mass dispossession of land occurs . . . [the Marxists] find that this is perfectly natural, and that the size of the proletariat must continue to grow until it matches the proportions of other capitalist lands, etc. Other authors . . . stand for a tie of the population with the land, for protection of the commune and the economic independence of the producers, for the possibility, under certain conditions and efforts, to escape the capitalist process and proceed to a better structure of things—in a word, there are authors who put in first place living people and not just an abstract scheme.

Like other Populist critics, Krivenko attempted to discredit the heretics by saddling them with the moral responsibility for all the unwelcome by-products of capitalism, among which he counted *kulachestvo* (moneylending), the destruction of the commune, the driving of dispossessed peasants into the factory, the opening of pubs and shops, and "other forms of contemptible activity." "For my part," declared Krivenko with pious finality, "I cannot imagine *intelligenty* in such a role."[23] Another Populist author accused the Marxists of "triumphantly destroying those strivings and ideals for which finer Russian people have labored for many years" and suggested that the proper place for new ideas was not in popular polemical literature where it could "inspire turmoil in unprepared minds."[24] The Populists, in short, had evolved a psychology not unlike that of the paternalistic autocracy—they did not wish the susceptible public, particularly young people, to be exposed to "dangerous thoughts."

The Populist arbiters of the press resorted to "censorship" to keep Marxist articles from appearing in the thick journals, channels ordinarily open to intelligentsia authors. Consequently, all the early Marxist works appeared as books, and Struve was obliged to raise the funds to cover his own publishing costs. (It sold out in two weeks' time.) Potresov, who had inherited a private fortune, financed the publication of the equally successful work of Beltov-Plekhanov.[25] All the Populists' efforts to steer the intelligentsia youth away from Marxism through "censorship" and violent denunciations were unavailing. By the end of 1895 at the student "evenings" and meetings of students' organizations, the Marxists had already drawn their ideological opponents into a dialogue on Marxist terms. The older Populist and liberal intellectuals,

---

[23] S. Krivenko, "K voprosu o nuzhdakh narodnoi promyshlennosti," *Russkoe Bogatstvo*, No. 10, 1894, pp. 127 and 129. Krivenko would have been even more convinced that the Marxists and the Ministry of Finance were in league with each other had he known that Struve intended specifically to praise the protectionist policy of Vyshnegradskii and Witte in his book. He was dissuaded by Potresov, who obviously understood its vulnerability to Populist attack. See Struve, "My Contacts," *The Slavonic Review*, XII, 586.

[24] *Russkoe Bogatstvo*, No. 3, 1894, p. 53. From an unsigned review of the book by A. I. Skvortsov, *Ekonomicheskie prichiny golodovok v Rossii* (St. Petersburg, 1894), which, though not explicitly Marxist, used Marxist concepts to subject Populist assumptions to critical scrutiny. It actually was a scientific treatise, and not at all polemical in tone.

[25] See Struve, "My Contacts," *The Slavonic Review*, XII, 581 ff. Potresov and Struve had promoted and financed Skvortsov's book as well. He was a professor of economics whose thoroughgoing "Westernism" and quasi-Marxian economic method attracted Struve even though he was a patriot and not a revolutionary. His works were boycotted by Populist publishers until his young admirers came to his rescue.

however, put up a stubborn defense of the old positions. V. V., Nikolai ——on, and Iuzhakov came out with fresh refutations of the Marxist critique. "Once not so long ago capitalism needed no apology, but did its work silently," Nikolai ——on caustically observed. "Now that its flaws are obvious to everyone, it needs learned apologists."[26] Convinced that they had definitively exposed the "scientific" pretenses of Russian Marxism, the Populists felt confident that this psychic aberration of iconoclastic youth would disappear.

But the Populist faith was soon shaken anew by a series of events which seemed to confirm the Marxist diagnosis of Russian realities. "Society's" flirtation with revolutionary schemes had just received an embarrassing defeat with the collapse of the Party of the People's Rights. In 1895, hopes rode high again with the accession to the throne of the personable young Grand Duke Nikolai and the opportunity of the zemstvos to present addresses. The new Tsar received a zemstvo deputation and mumbled a barely audible speech (from notes supplied by Pobodonostsev) about the futility of "senseless dreams" and his firm intention to uphold the autocracy in the spirit of his "unforgettable father."[27] "Society" again proved itself impotent as the fulcrum of social renewal. Struve and Beltov, as if addressing themselves to these recent blows, characterized the non-class intelligentsia as a mere "heap of idealists" and no social force whatsoever. They held that personality could influence the course of history only to the extent that it aligned itself with "real" social forces—by itself, it was a *quantité négligeable*. It behooved the intelligentsia, therefore, to examine the laws of history to discover by what social forces and through what social processes their ideals were to be realized. Only the "scientific socialism" of Marx, they claimed, provided such a scheme of historical analysis. Despite the manifest injustices of capitalism, Marx had proved that this system of productive relations was a necessary and progressive stage in mankind's conquest of nature, and that therefore all its vicissitudes had to be endured. By virtue of its inner contradictions, capitalism was not only

---

[26] "Apologiia vlasti deneg," *Russkoe Bogatstvo*, No. 1, 1895, p. 154. See also V. V., *Ocherki teoreticheskoi ekonomiki*, chap. 4, and S. N. Iuzhakov, *Sotsiologicheskie etuidy* (St. Petersburg, 1896).

[27] See Stählin, IV, 612.

achieving that "generalization of production" required for the realization of socialism, but of necessity it was giving rise to that social class which would eventually supersede the capitalists, the urban proletariat. The Marxist authors supplied elaborate data and sophisticated arguments to prove that capitalism had already made great inroads in Russian life and that all the Populists' preaching about the viability of the commune and the "impossibility of capitalism in Russia" was being visibly refuted by the facts of social and economic life. The "pivotal task" of the intelligentsia, they conveyed in unmistakable hints, was to "go to the workers" and prepare them for their future historical mission.[28] The scheme was tempting to the intelligentsia on several counts: first, it seemed to be thoroughly scientific (and the intelligentsia desired above all to assess matters "scientifically"); second, it promised firm support for their cause by that class which inevitably was to become the most significant and revolutionary force in society; and, finally, it saw in the relentless expansion of railroads and heavy industry under government tutelage, not the remorseless defeat of intelligentsia hopes, but the assurance of their ultimate triumph.

It was no easy matter for Russian intellectuals to renounce their ideological heritage and adopt a new set of dogmas. Hence, the pained cries at the beginning and the virulent debates that followed. At first the Marxists were able to find many willing listeners, but relatively few resolute converts. The Marxists' position seemed to hinge on the validity of their diagnosis of Russia's economic development, many aspects of which were still far from clear. Nikolai ——on could also muster statistics effectively, and his very denial that capitalism could succeed in Russia made clever use of Marxist analytical concepts. Only an instructed few could penetrate to the real substance behind the abstruse twittings of Struve and Nikolai ——on in the jargon of political economy. In the end, the course of events rather than more lucid arguments determined the outcome in favor of the Marxists. In the summer of 1896 the textile workers of St. Petersburg astounded all of Russia—indeed, all of

---

28 The above is simply a characterization of the major arguments of the two works in question: P. B. Struve, *Kriticheskie zametki k voprosu ob ekonomicheskom razvitii Rossii* (St. Petersburg, 1894), and N. Beltov (G. V. Plekhanov), *K voprosu o razvitii monisticheskago vzgliada na istoriiu* (St. Petersburg, 1895).

Europe—with a remarkably disciplined and co-ordinated strike which lasted for over two weeks. The number of strikers reached into the tens of thousands, an unprecedented event for tsarist Russia. Contrary to its usual policy of forbidding any mention of public disorders in the press, the government released information on the strike and promised publicly to draft a new statute regulating the working day, one of the strikers' chief demands. Although as a matter of principle Witte enjoined the employers from making any concessions to the rebellious workers, many of the firms nevertheless did so inconspicuously to quiet the troubled waters. The working class of Russia had vividly demonstrated that it represented a formidable force in Russian life and could exact concessions from the autocracy, in stark contrast to the recent demonstration of the helplessness of "society." Populist theorizing now seemed bankrupt, and for the balance of the century, neither in the legal press nor in the revolutionary underground, were the Populists able to muster effective resistance to the Marxist tide.

Despite this auspicious turn of events, the Marxists still found it difficult to keep their ideas before the public because of the Populist monopoly of the journals and dailies. It was not easy to come up with frequent book-length monographs, and the Marxists' partially successful efforts to gain a hearing at the sittings of learned societies (such as the Free Economic Society and the Society of Jurisprudence) reached only a limited audience. Potresov's attempt to follow up the first legal Marxist publications with a huge collaborative effort entitled *Materialy dlia kharakteristiki nashego ekonomicheskogo razvitiia* (*Materials for the Characterization of Our Economic Development*) was frustrated by the Tsarist police, who on the order of the censor, burned all but a few of the already printed copies. Finally, in 1897, the Marxists achieved their breakthrough. Krivenko's journal *Novoe Slovo*, a haven of the more Orthodox Populists who had broken away from Mikhailovskii's *Russkoe Bogatstvo*, was foundering from financial difficulties and lack of reader interest. Vladimir Posse, a Marxist on the writing staff (who kept his allegiance hidden), managed to persuade its owner, O. N. Popova, to entrust the editorship to Struve and Tugan-Baranovskii. Under various pseudonyms the entire galaxy of Russian Marxists contributed to the journal: from the Liberation of Labor Group abroad, articles were contributed by Plekhanov (N. Kamenskii) and Vera Zasulich (V. Ivanov); Lenin, Martov, and Potresov (K. T ——n, Egorov, and A. P ——r, respectively) contributed from their places of administrative exile; Maxim Gorkii, just beginning to acquire a reputation, contributed a short novel "Konovalov"; and a host of new authors now made their debut—Bulgakov, Iakovlev-Bogucharskii, Kistiakoskii and Ovsianiko-Kulikovskii. In the ten months of its existence *Novoe Slovo* tripled its circulation and soon became the bible of the partisan youth. In their respective organs Mikhailovskii, Nikolai ——on, and Slonimiskii attempted to match wits with the challenger, but without notable success. In the space of a year *Novoe Slovo* outshone all its rivals in intellectual vigor, popularity, and journalistic respectability.

The new venture, however, was very short lived: in December, 1897 *Novoe Slovo* was closed by the joint order of four ministers. *Zhizn (Life)* and *Nachalo (The Beginning)*, the two Marxist journals which succeeded it after a year's interlude, while popular, did not enjoy the same authority and no longer epitomized the unity of the Marxist camp. *Nachalo*, edited by Struve, was actually planned and promoted by the police agent Gurovich, who posed as a wealthy benefactor. The object of the police had been to keep a close watch on the activities of the Legal Marxist authors, but after three issues the journal proved too daring for them and was closed down. *Zhizn* (edited by Posse), though still a Marxist undertaking, began to patronize some of the figures of the new literary Renaissance and indulgently gave space to articles reflecting revisionist trends in Marxism. In the meantime Marxist articles gained entry into a number of formerly inaccessible journals, including prestigious scholarly journals like *Nauchnoe Obozrenie (Scientific Review)* and *Voprosy filosofii i psikhologii (Questions of Philosophy and Psychology)*. Marxist modes of expression soon edged out Populist clichés in the academic world, in technical literature and even in officialdom. But precisely when the ideological hegemony of Marxism had reached its apex, the monolithic crusade against Populism lost its drive and revealed a spectrum of internal diversities. The writings of Struve, Tugan-Baranovskii, Bulgakov, and Berdyaev showed increasingly heterodox tendencies and eventually these authors left the Marxist camp altogether. Other Marxist authors (Prokopovich and P. A. Berlin)

stopped halfway with Bernsteinian Revisionism. Among party Social Democrats the controversy over "Economism" began to rage.
Militant Populism soon regrouped its forces and *Russkoe Bogatstvo* again became its fighting organ with fresh, more resolute authors like Korolenko, Peshekhonov and Chernov. Some of the
ex-Marxists and Revisionists joined forces with the zemstvo
liberals to form a new bloc of revolutionary constitutionalists, and
Struve later became the editor of their illegal organ *Osvobozhdenie (Liberation)*. The revival of the student protest movement,
the assassination of the Minister of Education Bogolepov, and the
sudden rash of street demonstrations by the radical public in
March, 1901, attracted attention away from the waning strike
movement and demonstrated the existence of other "social forces"
besides the workers. By the end of 1901, the period of Marxist
hegemony was irrevocably past and a new phase in the history of
the Russian revolutionary movement had begun. However, Marxism had fulfilled its historical function in infusing the militant
mood of the radical public after 1891 with a vital ideological content compelling other factions to redefine themselves and mobilize
their forces.

Most important for our purposes, it brought the radical youth
of Russia under the spell of the proletarian masses, whose presence
was increasingly making itself felt with the heady pace of the
Finance Minister's program for the modernization of Russia.

For full titles and bibliographical details on many of the works cited in the footnotes, see the Bibliography (pp. 254–63).

CHAPTER 2

The Breakthrough to Action

Social Democracy first became a significant social and political movement in Russia with the great strikes of the St. Petersburg textile industry in 1896. For the first time in the long history of the revolutionary movement, it could be seriously claimed that the efforts of revolutionaries had drawn the masses—rather than individual converts from the people—into active conflict with the autocracy. This apparent success made the new creed an irresistible attraction for the restless youth and bewildered intelligentsia. The strikes in St. Petersburg, to be sure, did not mark the first time revolutionaries had become enamored of the masses as the agency of social overturn; nor was this the first time that revolutionaries had searched for a formula to draw the masses into the struggle. The Bakuninist *buntari* had become impatient with the slow propaganda work of the first Populist circles and had spurred the great migration of young people to the countryside in 1874. The frustration of their efforts to arouse the masses by tsarist countermeasures had led to the elitist revision of the Populist faith by the People's Will.

It was perhaps no accident that the protest against this revision by the pitifully weak Black Repartition group was articulated by Plekhanov and Akselrod, the future prophets of Russian Marxism. Their protest was based on the notion that any revolutionary effort which bypassed the masses was futile and that the critical problem for the movement was to devise a method for mobilizing the people into an active revolutionary force. Although the dissenting voice of the Black Repartition is an all but forgotten episode, its formula for action was almost identical with the one which was successfully applied by the Social Democrats in the mid-1890's: to begin with agitation among the masses on the basis of their "everyday needs and demands."

The underground Social Democratic circles of Russia, however, were not consciously borrowing from this forgotten leaf in their mentors' past. They rediscovered the technique only after considerable trial and error, during which certain phases of past history had to be repeated. When in 1894 they finally arrived at a definitive formulation of the new strategy in the pamphlet *Ob agitatsii* (*On Agitation*), Akselrod noted with considerable vexation that the young Social Democrats acted as if they had "just discovered America," whereas the whole conception had been worked out long ago and they could have spared themselves many fumbling steps, had they sufficiently acquainted themselves with revolutionary history.[1]

Be this as it may, the Russian Social Democrats' successful drive to the masses was based upon a fundamental reorientation in outlook, habit of mind, and practical endeavor every bit as cataclysmic as the original conversion to Marxism itself. Just how this reorientation came about is perhaps the most important single question requiring elucidation to establish an often contested fact: that the Marxism of the 1890's was not simply the ideological plaything of radical intellectuals, but a significant movement which brought a major sector of Russian society, both workers and intelligentsia, into direct confrontation with the bastions of political authority.[2]

---

[1] P. B. Akselrod expressed these sentiments in his "Preface" and "Epilogue" to Kremer and Martov's *Ob agitatsii* in the edition printed by the *Gruppa Osvobozhdenie Truda* (Geneva, 1896), pp. 1 and 27 ff. Although this was the first version to be printed abroad, *Ob agitatsii* had circulated previously in Russia in manuscript and hectograph form. (The Geneva publication was predated to 1896 for special reasons; it was actually published in late 1897.) See pp. 45–46 of this chapter.

[2] Richard Pipes' short study of the St. Petersburg workers' groups and their relations with Social Democrats bring him to conclusions considerably divergent from my own. He pictures the "labor movement" as largely a product of the workers' own initiative which the Social Democrats attempted rather ineffectually to influence from the outside. Since some of his characterizations have already been

The Social Democrats of the late eighties and early nineties were not entering a vacuum when they first began to indoctrinate small circles (*kruzhki*) of workers with the basic tenets of socialism and Marxism. As early as 1871, the circle of Chaikovskii, one of the first Populist groups, had already conducted propaganda among the factory workers, enjoying considerably more success than their fellow Populists in the villages. In this decade as well, several working-class organizations professing socialism sprang up, the most important of which were the South Russian Union of Workers (Odessa, 1873–77) and the Northern Union of Russian Workers (St. Petersburg, 1878–79). These groups adopted programs which betrayed a trend away from Populism toward Social Democracy. For example, not only did the Northern Union call itself specifically a "Social Democratic" association of workers (reflecting vague familiarity with the German movement), but, contrary to Populist dogmas, it declared that "political freedom" was its immediate aim and ignored the peasantry and the commune. Throughout the 1870's, various Populist groups, frustrated in their endeavors to revolutionize the peasantry, turned to the workers. With the help of a few energetic workers, the groups set up propaganda circles, supplied literature, organized mutual aid funds and co-operatives, and sometimes even encouraged or supported strikes.[3]

During the following decade as well, a number of revolutionary

accepted as proven by other historians, it is hoped that this and the following chapter will demonstrate the possibility of a different interpretation of the evidence. See Pipes' systematized conclusions, *Social Democracy and the St. Petersburg Labor Movement* (Cambridge, Mass., 1963), pp. 117 ff. For reviews of Pipes' book which apparently accept his conclusions, see *Problems of Communism*, XII, No. 4, 1963, pp. 29–32 and *The American Historical Review*, LXIX, No. 2 (January, 1964), pp. 457–58. The first review does note the difficulty in explaining the events of 1905 by a projection of Pipes' scheme. Pipes' book should be credited, however, with being one of the first to add significantly to our acquaintance with the social character of the movement, particularly with the worker contingent, on the basis of fresh materials. On the earliest phase of the movement (where Pipes' command of the sources is best), there are no significant conflicts in our views.

[3] A very detailed and excellent treatment of Populist activities among industrial workers is to be found in Franco Venturi, *Roots of Revolution* (New York, 1960), chaps. 19 and 20. Also of considerable interest is Georgii Plekhanov's autobiographical account of this period, *Russkii rabochii v revoliutsionnom dvizhenii* (Geneva, 1892), reprinted in G. V. Plekhanov, *Sochineniia*, ed. D. B. Riazanov (Moscow, 1924), Vol. III.

Populists, primarily *narodovoltsy* who survived the affair of 1881, continued this clandestine activity. Often the workers were attracted by libraries stocked with appropriate books and pamphlets. These libraries might even be set up by the workers themselves and subsequently turned over to the Populist intelligentsia for safekeeping. Sometimes groups were organized around semilegal "trade schools," which, in addition to technical training, imparted to their pupils the rudiments of advanced education and cautious indoctrination in the teachings of socialism. Since those who directed these activities were usually experienced revolutionaries, highly skilled in the art of maintaining secrecy, they were often able to instruct systematically a fair number of workers for several years before being detected by the police. Thus the number of indoctrinated workers in a major industrial locality might reach a hundred or so. Although occasionally the intelligentsia leaders were swept away by arrests, the groups seldom ceased to exist. The workers themselves simply took over matters until they were able to get in touch with new propagandists and organizers. The exile of those involved in these activities served only to spread the movement to provincial centers. Indeed, the colonies of exiles were customarily centers of recuperation and training for new thrusts of illicit activity. Hence, all through the eighties, the number of workers touched by revolutionary propaganda quietly and inconspicuously continued to increase.[4]

Although this propaganda activity was essentially Populist in orientation, its peculiar ideological makeup should be noted. First of all, the groups conducting it aimed primarily at bringing knowledge and culture to the unenlightened working masses, the

---

[4] A general description of Populist and Marxist groups in the 1880's has been drawn by V. I. Nevskii, *Ocherki po istorii rossiiskoi sotsial-demokraticheskoi partii* (Moscow, 1925), chaps. 3–5. This work is one of the few sound products of Soviet scholarship on the history of Russian Social Democracy. It provides a wealth of information and quotations from now rare sources. Another valuable and more recent work, P. A. Kazakevich's *Sotsial-demokraticheskie organizatsii Peterburga* (Leningrad, 1960), treats only two groups, those of Tochiiskii and Brusnev in St. Petersburg, but sheds much light on the nature of the circles of this period by drawing heavily on unpublished archival material. Another general treatment of early Social Democratic circles by a Soviet scholar, Iu. Z. Polevoi, *Zarozhdenie marksizma v Rossii* (Moscow, 1959), also draws heavily on unpublished materials in the party and state archives, but is far less useful than Kazakevich, due to highly selective use of the sources and rather unimaginative adherence to the canons of party historiography.

majority of whom were illiterate. Negatively, this meant that even though the customary stock of revolutionary *ideas* were sifted into the instruction, the groups seldom engaged in specific revolutionary *action.* In this they did not depart from the prevailing "quiet" of the eighties. This nonactivist approach implied a tacit rejection of the tactics of both the Bakuninists (mass uprisings) and the People's Will (terrorism) and a return to the gradualist teachings of Lavrov.

Lavrov's *Historical Letters,* one of the most widely employed pieces of propaganda literature, accurately reflected the prevailing attitude of both *intelligenty* and "advanced" workers. The revolution and socialism were reserved for an indefinite future, while the intellectuals devoted themselves to the cultural development of the sadly neglected workers. This was accomplished through instruction in small groups or *kruzhki,* and hence the practice, and the era, were appropriately designated *kruzhkovshchina.*

The Populist intelligentsia were impelled along this path of action, often in spite of their own predilections, by the surprising enthusiasm for learning on the part of the more gifted workers. These workers discerned in literacy and enlightenment a way out of their hopeless social situation, and therefore eagerly took advantage of the opportunities afforded by the *kruzhki.* A number of the more perceptive workers not only quickly mastered the basic elements of learning, but displayed a keen interest in "science" and in a scientific understanding of their surrounding world. Darwin's theory on the origin of life was a revelation which soon dispelled their "religious prejudices."

First simple propaganda pamphlets, then advanced works on political economy and sociology by Mill, Chernyshevskii, Mikhailovskii, Spencer and—not uncommonly—even Marx, explained to them the unjust nature of contemporary society, the exploitation of the labor of the working classes, and the necessity for a social revolution which would eliminate all inequalities and place the instruments of production in the hands of the people. The writings of the publicist Shelgunov (which were excerpted for propaganda use from the thick journals of the intelligentsia) familiarized them with the heroic accomplishments of Western European workers, who, unlike Russian workers, were free to organize, to speak and print their views, and even to choose deputies to legislative chambers.[5]

As a result of protracted exposure to the intellectual diet of the socialist world, many workers became almost indistinguishable from the intelligentsia in outlook and in the range and depth of their learning. Occasionally it even happened that persons of working class or peasant origin, following in the footsteps of Khalturin and Obnorskii in earlier Populist circles, became leaders and organizers side by side with embittered *raznochintsy* (those of lower class origin—petty bourgeois, sons of clergy, etc.) and "repentant" sons and daughters of the gentry. Most workers, however, remained bound to their milieu, where they constituted a new identifiable social group, a "worker intelligentsia," marked off from their fellows by a chasm of differences in knowledge, attitudes, values, and even personal appearance and behavior.[6]

When at the end of the 1880's the Social Democrats entered on the scene, they introduced no radical changes in these activities, but merely adapted, supplemented, and deepened them. The experience of the first active Social Democrats in the Moscow region, described by one of its participants (S. I. Mitskevich), differed in no essential respect from their Populist predecessors:

> In this period [1888–90] the intelligentsia maintained here and there ties and acquaintances with the workers, for the most part from the skilled trades: fitters, machinists, lathe operators, etc. These ties bore in general a purely cultural character. They gave the workers "good" books to read and carried on conversations over a cup of tea. . . . This was a time when a noticeable thirst for knowledge began to manifest itself among the workers. They enrolled in libraries, visited municipal reading rooms, attended public lectures, and pooled subscriptions to newspapers, primarily the *Russkie Vedomosti*. Here they valued most of all the foreign reviews in which they

---

[5] Plekhanov was already acquainted with this type of worker in the mid-1870's: "After working at the factory 10–11 hours a day and returning home only in the evening, he would sit at his books until one o'clock at night. . . . I was struck by the variety and abundance of the theoretical questions which concerned him. . . . Political economy, chemistry, social questions and the theory of Darwin all occupied his attention. . . . It would have taken decades for him to assuage his intellectual thirst." ("Russkii rabochii v revoliutsionnom dvizhenii," *Sochineniia*, III, 131.)

[6] The problems posed by the emergence of the worker intelligentsia for the Social Democratic movement are treated extensively in chaps. 4 and 5.

found excellent articles on the workers' movement in the West. Precisely such workers were recruited into the first Social Democratic *kruzhki*.[7]

Convinced Social Democrats and Populists often worked side by side in the same organizations, and their occasional theoretical disputes hindered their active co-operation very little. The Social Democrats simply added Marxist ideas and writings to the intellectual repertory of the *kruzhki* (if, indeed, the Populist propagandists had not already done so). The older Populist propagandists offered little serious resistance to the new Social Democratic teachings. First of all, long before they admitted it to themselves, they had modified their program in practice. Discourses on peasant uprisings and the virtues of the commune, or appeals to terror, had evoked little response from the workers; such themes had long since been softened or dropped entirely.[8] Many propagandists harbored the uneasy feeling that the old Populist programs had become outmoded and were ripe for some "new word." The workers, in turn, responded chiefly to the opening of new spheres of knowledge and to the vision of a social order free from the exploitation of man by man. Although they may have accepted the idea that for the attainment of this order a revolution was necessary, they sensed no urgency in the matter. The combined weight of these pressures gradually modified the content of the inherited propaganda until it approximated that of the Social Democrats.

In the first half of the 1890's, the leadership of the illegal circles passed steadily into the hands of Social Democrats. Not uncommonly, workers and intelligentsia alike became resolute converts upon their first exposure to Marxist ideas. Sometimes an un-

---

[7] *Na zare rabochego dvizheniia v Moskve,* ed. S. I. Mitskevich (Moscow, 1932), pp. 14–15.

[8] The apparent exceptions to this evaluation only prove the rule. It is true that a group of *narodovoltsy* returned from exile headed by M. C. Aleksandrov and took over the *kruzhki* left behind by Brusnev's Social Democratic organization in 1892, and zealously preached terror to the workers. However, the workers of the *kruzhki* made it clear to the new leaders that they were welcome only to the extent that they would continue the work of cultural enlightenment of the Social Democratic propagandists. The result was that over the next few years Aleksandrov's group rendered important technical help to the workers' and Social Democratic groups, particularly in printing their literature, and that most of their members eventually became Social Democrats. References to this group are scattered throughout the sources cited in this chapter on the St. Petersburg movement. See Aleksandrov's own account "Gruppa narodovoltsev (1891–94)," *Byloe,* No. 11 (November, 1906).

attached Marxist intellectual simply took over a workers' circle formerly sponsored by a *narodovolets* who had been removed by arrest. Other groups evolved by degrees toward Social Democracy and manifested conflicting tendencies. At other times Marxists organized their own *kruzhki* in competition with those of the Populists. Occasionally even formal debates were arranged by perplexed workers who wished to hear both Marxists and Populists expound their programs. If the Populists argued in favor of terror (as they sometimes did), the workers invariably decided in favor of the Social Democrats, who seemed more sincerely interested in the workers' cause. In short, the transition was effected in various ways, but evoked little overt conflict and little change in the prevailing forms of activity and organization.

The new teachings of Social Democracy altered only slightly the basic outlook of the worker intelligentsia. Marxism was accepted as a new, more scientific explanation of society which rounded out the formulas of Darwin, Spencer, Lavrov, and Chernyshevskii. With its emphasis on the world historical mission of the proletariat, Marxism perhaps appealed more to the workers' sense of self-importance than Populism; nevertheless, the chief allurement remained as before the prospect of cultural advancement and a scientific understanding of the world order. The workers' attitudes were still more akin to Lavrov's *kul'turnichestvo* than to Marx's notion of the class struggle.[9] The following passage from the memoirs of a worker participant in the *kruzhki* of the late 1880's will perhaps convey the mental horizons and values of this new social type.

> [The Social Democrat–propagandist] acquainted us with the struggle for a better future. He pointed out that our working-class move-

---

[9] One frequently encounters evidences of the Lavrovian outlook of the workers in the sources. A worker addressing his comrades at a secret May First celebration in 1891 declared: "In order for our activity to be fruitful we must try to develop ourselves and others intellectually and morally, and see to it that those around us look on us as intelligent, honest and courageous." (Cited in Vl. Akimov, *Materialy dlia kharakteristiki razvitiia rossiiskoi sotsial-demokraticheskoi rabochei partii* [Geneva, 1905], p. 31.) The official rules of the nominally Social Democratic "Workers' Union" in Ivanovo-Voznesensk defined its membership as "critically thinking individuals seeking to realize progress in mankind" and declared its chief aim to be "propaganda among the more cultured workers of both sexes." ("Ustav ivanovo-voznesenskago rabochego soiuza v 1894-om godu," in the collection *Rabochee dvizhenie v Rossii v XIX-om veke*, 4 vols. [Moscow and Leningrad, 1950–1963], vol. IV, part 1, p. 122). Cited hereafter as *Rabochee dvizhenie v. Rossii*.

ment must traverse the same path as our Western comrades. He acquainted us in broad outlines with socialism as an ideal and with our forthcoming perilous work for the conquest of a better future. He told us that we will attain this future only by the efforts of the working class as a whole. . . . But to be an organizer of the working class, it is necessary first of all to be honest in all relations oneself, secondly, to be a worthy comrade, and finally, a cultivated person to whom others could turn with their questions, and from whom they could receive definitive answers. Therefore, it is necessary to discipline and cultivate oneself. It is necessary to learn by a definite program. . . . A good propagandist must be able to answer such questions as why there is day and night, seasons of the year, and eclipses of the sun. He must be able to explain the origin of the universe and the origin of the species, and must therefore know the theories of Kant, Laplace, Darwin, and Lyell [Sir Charles Lyell, whose geological theories anticipated Darwin's evolutionism]. In the program must be included history and the history of culture, political economy, and the history of the working class.[10]

If faith in the power of knowledge was crucial in the outlook of the worker Social Democrats of this period, it was no less characteristic of the intelligentsia who conducted the propaganda. Before turning to the workers, most early Marxists had spent a relatively long probationary period of disciplined study and intense debate with Populist opponents in intelligentsia circles. For the most part they had taken their task very seriously, working through piles of statistics, mastering complex problems of economic theory, schooling themselves in the dialectical method. When the time came to impart their knowledge to the workers, they tended to begin where they had begun in their own thinking —with the "origin of the universe" and the "origin of the species."

Since there were no immediate revolutionary prospects in the late eighties and early nineties, the first Marxist propagandists had not developed clear notions on revolutionary strategy. They merely espoused the vague conviction that Russia had embarked on the path of capitalism, and that the urban proletariat was the sole force capable of bringing about a social transformation. The outlook of P. N. Skvortsov, one of the earliest Russian Marxists and

---

[10] Nevskii, p. 275. Nevskii takes the quotation from the memoirs of N. M. Bogdanov, excerpts of which appeared in the now rare collection *Ot gruppy Blagoeva k Soiuzu Bor'by (1886–1894)* (Rostov, 1921), p. 40.

founder of the first Social Democratic circle in Nizhni Novgorod, was typical; it has been described by his pupil Mitskevich.

> We had long conversations on the future of the workers' movement. How abstractly we still conceived the future forms of the workers' movement is indicated by the perspectives outlined by Skvortsov: gradually the number of workers studying Marx will increase; they will draw still more members into circles studying Marx; with time all Russia will be covered with such *kruzhki* and then we will form a workers' socialist party. What tasks this party was to perform and how it should conduct its struggle remained unclear.[11]

Such untroubled reliance on the peaceful dissemination of Marxian ideas was characteristic of most of the early Social Democratic groups.[12] Although these attitudes were strongest among those who had matured intellectually before the famine year, they persisted with varying force until the St. Petersburg textile strikes five years later. Thus, although Marxism was a radical departure from the past in theory, its mood and pattern of practical activity at this point differed little from that of the Populist groups of the period.

On the other hand, the younger Marxists, whose convictions had been forged under the impact of the famine year, were not always prepared to "begin from Adam." Many of them sought more concrete methods of revolutionary work which would promise the speedy downfall of the old order. They were inclined to be impatient with the sterile scholasticism of their elders, who, they claimed, dismissed propaganda pamphlets as a "vulgarization of Marx" and insisted that workers must learn to read *Das Kapital* in

---

[11] S. I. Mitskevich, *Revoliutsionnaia Moskva* (Moscow, 1940), p. 144.

[12] Such were the Brusnev organization in St. Petersburg, as well as the circles of Riazanov and Steklov-Nahkamkes in Odessa, and of Abramovich in Kiev. Similar groups existed also in Ivanovo-Voznesensk, Tula, Ekaterinoslav, Kharkov, and Riazan. For information on these groups see Nevskii, chaps. 3–5, and Polevoi, chaps. 3–5. P. A. Golubev, one of the leaders of the Brusnev organization, aptly depicted how the early Marxist circles were influenced by the temper of the times: "We have to admit that even in our propaganda we were caught up in the atmosphere of 'small deeds' which attracted many *intelligenty* during the 1880's, even those involved in revolutionary work. Such a mood did indeed exist. In the desire to perform our practical work we went to extremes in denying party programs and lost our over-all political perspective. Political and socialist propaganda was intermingled with that of a purely cultural content." ("Iz vospominanii V. S. Golubeva," *Rabochee dvizhenie v Rossii*, vol. IV, part 1, p. 123.) Since the present work is concerned primarily with Social Democracy as a mass movement, it does not treat these groups in detail. For a discussion of such groups in St. Petersburg, see chaps. 1 and 2 of Pipes.

the original.[13] The experience of the famine had broken the spell of social quietism of the eighties and aroused more immediate revolutionary hopes. Stirrings of industrial unrest in Poland and the Western provinces (soon, in Russia proper) began to attract attention. Revolutionary tactics, therefore, became a matter of immediate concern.

From various centers of Social Democratic activity came signs that new winds were blowing. Just what new methods of practical work were needed had not yet become clear, but dissatisfaction focused on the apparent fruitlessness of *kruzhkovshchina*. Through long patient labor, the older school of propagandists had nurtured into being a thin layer of cultured worker intellectuals, but the broad working masses remained untouched. The "advanced" workers, coming for the most part from the skilled trades, were almost as alienated from average workers as the intelligentsia. They spoke a more cultivated language than their fellows, prided themselves on book knowledge, and dressed more fastidiously even than the democratically minded *intelligenty*.[14] Since many of them abstained from smoking, drinking and cursing, they were occasionally mistaken for Pashkovites (a Bible tract sect) and made the butts of ridicule from their fellow workers. More alarming, they tended to stand aloof from strikes and other forms of elemental protest, which were becoming increasingly frequent.[15] There was

---

[13] See Mitskevich, *Revoliutsionnaia Moskva*, p. 153. Martov recalled his discomfiture when the older Marxist Stranden (a member of the Brusnev organization), instead of initiating him into the clandestine propaganda work, heaped him with books on primitive culture, ancient history, and the evolution of the species. Martov commented: "Brought up in the previous period of complete social stagnation, Stranden apparently could not imagine any other way of training a revolutionary than having him work out over a period of years a complete theoretical world-view, the crown of which would be admittance to practical work. For us, who had already been touched by the hot breath of the first signs of rebirth, who had already read the speeches of the St. Petersburg workers of May First, 1891, and had been shaken by the bankruptcy of the regime in the face of the famine, it was psychologically inconceivable to condemn ourselves to such a long period of waiting." (Martov, *Zapiski sotsial-demokrata*, p. 92.)

[14] Lydia Dan recalled that if an *intelligent* showed up at a meeting with a stiff collar and tie, his comrades could not restrain their laughter. If the worker Babushkin was thus attired—nobody laughed. (From a private conversation with the author in 1960.)

[15] The above characterization is drawn from numerous passing remarks to be found in the memoirs of both workers and *intelligenty* and no single passage would convey the whole impression. To confirm a few points, see Martov, pp. 278–80 and 286–87.

little prospect that the collective influence of such workers would ever create a serious threat to the autocracy. Consequently, by 1893–94 many Social Democrats were beginning to have second thoughts about the prevailing methods and were exploring new approaches.

Guidance and inspiration in developing more revolutionary forms of activity among the masses were supplied by the Polish and Jewish movements. Greater proximity and sensitivity to influences from Western Europe had fostered a workers' movement and Social Democratic proclivities in the Western provinces a few years earlier than in Russia proper. The Jewish movement anticipated events in Russia by one or two years, the Polish movement by four or five. In Poland, the first wave of industrial strikes occurred in May, 1891, and came to a climax the following year with the general strike of Lodz. In the regions of heavy Jewish population strikes became frequent during the latter half of 1894 and reached a high point early the next year in a textile industry strike at Belostok, which involved no less than 15,000 workers. As for Russia proper, strikes in scattered areas during 1895 were followed by the monumental strike of the St. Petersburg textile workers in 1896, with more than 35,000 workers taking part.

In Poland, extensive propaganda activity had been initiated around 1888 by the group "Proletariat," which had waged a vigorous campaign against the Polish Populists, who were heavily imbued with patriotic separatism. In the following year, a social ferment occasioned by widespread, devastating floods prompted a group of Polish Social Democrats to react against the slow propaganda methods of "Proletariat." The group formed their own "Union of Polish Workers," which began mass agitation among the rank and file workers. In 1890, both groups co-operated to celebrate May First (proclaimed an "international holiday of workers" by the recently founded Second International) by appealing to the workers not to appear for work on that day. During the first year, the response was negligible, but in the following year a similar campaign evoked widespread enthusiasm and occasioned numerous strikes in a number of industries. In 1892 at Lodz, the Russian authorities, hitherto indifferent to strikes (since they affected Poles, not Russians), were obliged to occupy the city with large contingents of troops. Numerous shootings and disorders eventually turned into a pogrom.[16]

The Jewish movement went through the same stages (except for the pogrom) several years later. Engaged in propaganda among the Jewish artisans and factory workers, the Jewish Social Democrats in the Lithuanian border town of Vilna were able to observe the Polish developments closely since they were in contact with Jewish groups in Polish industrial centers and worked side by side with Polish Social Democrats in Vilna. Iulii Martov, in exile in Vilna, recounts how the deliberations of his circle over tactics in early 1894 "drew upon the experiences of the Warsaw Union of Polish Workers, which was well known to us."[17] Sponti, one of the original members of the Moscow *Rabochii Soiuz* (Workers' Union), formed in 1894, had spent a term of military service in Vilna, from 1887 to 1889. There he had instructed a circle of Polish artisans under the sponsorship of Tyshko, who with Rosa Luxemburg later headed the Polish splinter group *Socjaldemokracja Królestwa Polskiego* (SDKP). In 1892, Sponti returned to Vilna to lead propaganda circles, this time, however, under the direction of the Jewish Social Democrats Kremer and Kopelzon. Through his old connections he became acquainted with the latest Polish agitational literature. The following summer he departed for Moscow to pursue his ambition to introduce the new agitational techniques in a major industrial center of Russia.

In Moscow he joined the newly constituted group of Mitskevich, Liadov, and Vinokurov. Mitskevich described as follows the influence of Sponti:

> Sponti told us how propaganda was conducted in Poland—a central group, in strict secrecy, leads the whole work in Poland. This central group heads a series of workers' circles through which it carries on broad agitation, disseminating popular agitational brochures and proclamations among the workers. As a model he brought with him translations into Russian of a few brochures, such as *What Every Worker Should Know and Keep in Mind, The Working Day,*

[16] For a detailed treatment of the early Polish Social Democratic movement, see Ludwik Kulczycki, *Geschichte der russischen Revolution*, 3 vols. (Gotha, 1910–14), III, 195–327. Kulczycki was a member of the group *Proletariat*.

[17] Martov, p. 225. Martov stated that in 1892, during his imprisonment in St. Petersburg, he learned details about the Polish movement firsthand from Polish prisoners.

The Workers' Revolution, and *On Competition.* . . . These brochures were very good—popular, agitational, and easily understandable even for the semiliterate workers. . . . Having exchanged opinions on the information conveyed by Sponti, we decided to set up in Moscow an organization for conducting systematic propaganda and agitation among the Moscow workers.[18]

Takhtarev, who has left the best firsthand account of the St. Petersburg movement, noted that the Polish experience had been stirring the Social Democrats in the capital. "The devil take the *kruzhki!*" he quoted them as saying in the summer of 1895. "They only create intellectual Epicureans. . . . We have to follow the example of the Poles and distribute literature directly in the shops."[19] The Polish leaven had been quietly but forcefully at work in Russian circles during the period 1893–95, although by sheer force of inertia clandestine activity still continued for a time to follow the established patterns of *kruzhkovshchina.*

The Vilna Social Democrats, however, were the first to make a radical break with the past.[20] Until 1894, the Vilna organization had operated no differently from Russian groups, cultivating a minute intellectual elite rather than addressing themselves to the working class as a whole. In Vilna, this work had assumed a distinctive coloration because of the nationality question. In contrast to the Poles, the Social Democratic leaders of Vilna, though of Jewish origin, had become "assimilated." Along with a purely Russian education, they had acquired Russian viewpoints and habits (they employed the Russian patronymic, addressing a friend as "Isaak Moiseevich"), and culturally identified themselves with Russian rather than with Jewish traditions. Correspondingly, they sought to draw the Jewish workers into the Russian move-

---

[18] Mitskevich, *Revoliutsionnaia Moskva,* pp. 147–48.

[19] "Peterburzhets" (K. Takhtarev), *Ocherk peterburgskago rabochego dvizheniia 90-kh godov* (London, 1902), p. 16. (Hereafter cited as Takhtarev, *Ocherk.*) The Brusnev organization greeted the Lodz general strike with a special congratulatory leaflet which was distributed in St. Petersburg, showing that they followed these developments with utmost care. See *Rabochee dvizhenie v Rossii,* vol. III, part 2, pp. 130–31.

[20] Information on the Vilna Social Democratic movement has been drawn chiefly from Martov and Akimov. See also *Materialy k istorii evreiskago rabochego dvizheniia* (St. Petersburg, 1906), and S. Dimanshtein, ed., *Revoliutsionnoe dvizhenie sredi evreev* (Moscow, 1930). The latter work contains many valuable memoir accounts.

ment and to efface any peculiarly Jewish consciousness. In effect, propaganda activity in Vilna, which began with instruction in the Russian language, served to "russify" the worker elite and alienate it from the Jewish milieu.[21] Because of close personal and emotional ties to the Russian Social Democratic movement (a number of their former comrades were now attending Russian universities), the Vilna group was the logical mediator to bring Polish methods to Russian soil.

After thoroughly thrashing the question out during the winter of 1893–94, the Social Democrats in Vilna formally adopted the program of agitation in the spring. Leaders of the intelligentsia decided to broach their ideas on agitation to the workers at meetings of the "mutual aid societies," which had hitherto been their primary means of communicating with the workers. They proposed to turn these collections into strike funds through which the trained worker elite were to carry on agitation among their uninitiated fellows. Unexpectedly, the innovators ran into a storm of resistance. They became the object of incessant harangues accusing them of desiring to keep the workers in intellectual subjection and to use them as "cannon fodder" for the doctrinaire revolutionary aims of the intelligentsia. They were showered with quotations from Lavrov reminding them that the intelligentsia should devote itself unselfishly to the enlightenment of the people, that it should train the workers to be "critically thinking individuals," that it should repay its "debt" to the people without any ulterior motives. The majority of workers had obviously been far more interested in the cultural benefits to be gained from their intelligentsia mentors than in the hazards of fighting for their "class interests."

In the Jewish social milieu, certain factors accentuated the disparity in outlook between the intelligentsia and their pupils. There was only a small factory population in Vilna. The majority of the "workers" among whom the Social Democrats carried on propaganda were actually artisans—tailors, locksmiths, watchmakers—whose forebears had once operated independent work-

21 The "russifying" policy of the Vilna Social Democrats drew bitter denunciations from the nationalistic Polish Social Democrats, who regarded Vilna as Polish territory (although the majority of the population were Lithuanian and White Russian), and the Jews as future Polish citizens. See Akimov, p. 8.

shops. Now, having been ruined by competition from the larger shops, they hired themselves out with their wives and children as sweated labor to "masters." These ruined artisans dreamed of reestablishing their own workshops, and to this end they sought to attain a certain degree of culture and learning—above all knowledge of the Russian language—to deal with their primarily Russian clientele. In the *kruzhki* of the Social Democrats they were able to acquire these rudiments of culture.

Many of the graduates of the *kruzhki,* having carefully saved up a sufficient amount of capital, did not hesitate to set up their own shops. Before long, despite vague professions of allegiance to socialism, they began themselves to employ sweated labor.[22] It was primarily this unwelcome development that had convinced the Vilna Social Democrats of the fruitlessness of circle propaganda. Although the indoctrinated worker adhered to the tenets of socialism superficially, they were not as real to him as the hope of emerging from the miserable ignorance and poverty of the sweatshop. To give up his cultural pursuits and devote his efforts to economic agitation among his untutored comrades meant to be drawn back into the abyss whence he had come. Especially bitter feelings were aroused by the decision of the leaders to replace Russian with Yiddish "jargon" as the language of agitation and propaganda, an innovation designed to widen their impact on the masses. To the incensed worker elite, however, it betrayed the intention of the Social Democratic intelligentsia to keep workers under their intellectual tutelage. That Lavrov had struck more profound roots in the workers' thinking than Marx now became painfully obvious.

In spite of the inflammatory opposition of their best pupils, the intelligentsia benefited from other developments. Unrest among the workers had already cropped up the previous year (1893) when official notices were posted throughout Vilna announcing that henceforward, on the basis of a law dating back to the time of Catherine II, the working day in the craft industries would be limited to twelve hours. This display of "liberalism" on the part

[22] A crisis arose when one of their prized worker Social Democrats, who had become an independent proprietor, boxed the ears of an apprentice for spoiling a piece of work. See Martov, pp. 89–90. Another common solution to the ambiguous social situation of the workers educated in the *kruzhki* was to emigrate to America; such workers were also lost to the Social Democratic cause.

of the Russian bureaucrat who headed the municipal government (*gorodskoi golova*) was in all probability prompted by his antipathy for Jewish (and perhaps other non-Russian) employers. Although little effort was made to enforce his proclamation, it caused considerable stir among the artisans. They circulated petitions and handed them to the authorities, they organized "funds of resistance" in each craft, and, finally, they resorted to sporadic strikes. All this took place without the active intervention of the local Social Democratic organization (although individual intelligentsia undoubtedly assisted).[23]

For a time this spontaneous movement did not conflict with the elaborate propaganda program. The older workers, with the approval of the Social Democratic leaders, took part in the "funds of resistance" with the intention of thereby recruiting new members for the *kruzhki*. However, many younger workers threw themselves wholeheartedly into the strike movement, and when the intelligentsia came forward with their new program, these for the most part uninstructed workers lent them a sympathetic ear. Another source of enthusiastic recruits was found among many Jewish youths of lower-middle-class background who had been prevented from securing a secondary education by the *numerus clausus* affecting Jewish entrants. These largely self-educated *poluintelligenty* (semi-intellectuals), as the workers called them, were very susceptible to Social Democratic influence and were chafing for some practical occupation. During the period of *kruzhkovshchina* they had been considered too immature and uncultured to conduct *kruzhki*. Now, with a better command of Yiddish than their "assimilated" (russified) seniors, they could easily serve as agitators and as translators of propaganda literature into "jargon."

With the aid of these new forces, the innovators were able to circumvent the opposition and assume the leadership of the ever more frequent strikes. Strike fever quickly spread to other localities which had significant numbers of Jewish craftsmen or factory workers—Minsk, Vitebsk, Kovno, Belostok, Brest Litovsk, and Warsaw. Within a very short time, the Vilna Social Democrats

---

[23] Akimov, pp. 9–13. Martov ascribes the utilization of the ancient statute to the ingenuity of the Social Democrats rather than to this accidental circumstance (p. 193). Akimov's version is followed here because it is more convincing.

found themselves riding the crest of a strike movement of major proportions in the entire Western area of the Jewish Pale of settlement.

The movement, without any particular design on the part of the Social Democratic leadership, was rapidly becoming exclusively Jewish. The *poluintelligenty,* with their greater fluency in Yiddish and their more intimate acquaintance with the ghetto milieu, were in a better position to perform day-to-day organizational tasks and above all to conduct verbal agitation. Consequently, they quickly moved into key positions. The older "russified" intelligentsia increasingly turned their energies in other directions—toward establishing relations with other Social Democratic groups in Russia, facilitating communications with émigré groups, securing literature from abroad and smuggling it across the border, and, finally, "colonizing" other industrial centers where Social Democratic work was not yet on a firm footing or had not yet been enlightened by the new word "agitation."

By the summer of 1895, reports of the awakening of militant Social Democracy were pouring into Vilna from the major cities of Russia—St. Petersburg, Moscow, Kiev, Odessa. "All these bits of information," Martov declared, "evoked in us a yearning to emigrate from Vilna . . . to points where the task of revolutionizing the methods of Social Democratic work had just begun."[24] This was the signal for a number of Vilna Social Democrats to "cross over" into the Russian movement. Martov resettled in St. Petersburg, Aizenshtadt in Odessa, and Moisei Dushkan (a trained worker) in Ekaterinoslav. Soon the *poluintelligenty* and experienced workers "departed" in large numbers, especially to the South, where no special "right of residence" was required. Russian Social Democratic organizations came to owe a considerable debt to energetic and talented committeemen who had served their apprenticeship in the earlier strike movement of the Pale.[25]

---

[24] Martov, p. 253. Martov mentions comrades from Vilna who settled in Odessa, Kiev, Belostok, and St. Petersburg. The Vilna organization also had close contacts (mainly through former gymnasium classmates who were now studying at Russian institutions of higher learning) in Moscow, Kharkov, and Ekaterinoslav. Numerous other examples are to be encountered in the literature. See, for example, the short memoirs of V. Tsoglin, A. Ginzburg, and I. Vilenskii in Dimanshtein.

[25] Martov, pp. 196–212 and 250–54. Later chapters will provide many instances of this phenomenon.

The influence of Vilna on the Russian movement was not confined, however, to the force of example and the enthusiasm of its emissaries. The innovators laid down the theoretical arguments for their new approach in the authoritative tract entitled *Ob agitatsii* (*On Agitation*) written jointly by Alexander Kremer and Martov. Although the original purpose for circulating their program had been to answer the charges of the Vilna worker elite, Martov explained, "we sensed that we were serving as innovators in the party and that it was our duty to propagandize those new methods which our experience had developed."[26]

With the ferment for change already brewing in other Social Democratic groups, the document soon became the chief focus for discussions on how best to gain influence over the masses. Mitskevich of the Moscow *Rabochii Soiuz,* on one of his periodic visits to Vilna to fetch literature from abroad (Vilna, not far from the border, served as a point of exchange), chanced upon a session of the central group when the question of agitation was being energetically discussed.

> Our representative [meaning himself] declared that the question of agitation interested the Moscow comrades very much indeed. At this session a resolution was worked out and one of the comrades [Alexander Kremer] promised to compose a theoretical elaboration of the resolution. In a short time the task was accomplished and with the help of our representative the brochure *Ob agitatsii* was edited.... This brochure became our credo.[27]

In April, 1894, Mitskevich brought a manuscript of the new work to Moscow, where it was reproduced by hectograph and immediately sent to other Social Democratic groups with which Moscow was in contact—Nizhni Novgorod, Ivanovo-Voznesensk and Ekaterinoslav. A copy was later sent to St. Petersburg. Other copies soon found their way to nearly all major centers of Social Democratic activity in Russia. It was not long before *Ob agitatsii* gained broad acceptance as laying down the correct course of action for the foreseeable future.

Of course, the swift transition to strike agitation was not even primarily due to the influence of this pamphlet—it merely ex-

---

[26] *Ibid.*, p. 233.

[27] *Na zare rabochego dvizheniia v Moskve*, p. 21.

pressed and hastened an already unfolding process. Nevertheless, until the coming of *Iskra* in 1901, *Ob agitatsii* epitomized the underground work of Social Democracy and served as its theoretical justification. P. A. Garvi, who as a lad of twenty in Odessa began his Social Democratic career only in the fall of 1900, gives this fact striking confirmation in his memoirs.

> Emerging from the narrow confines of secret propaganda circles, the basic tactical problem of Social Democracy was to break through to the masses and embark on the path of leading the struggle of the working class by means of mass agitation. The well-known brochure *Ob agitatsii* clearly reflected the critical moment in the Social Democratic movement in Russia. It exercised on all of us, the party workers of that time, a tremendous influence. The experience of the St. Petersburg strikes, the strike movement in Poland and particularly in the Jewish movement . . . was the best illustration of the correctness of the new tactical position of *Ob agitatsii* which essentially did not "discover" the new strategy, but simply formulated and expressed an empirical change in local Social Democratic work.[28]

The content of the work, therefore, will be of considerable help in understanding the outlook and actions of the Social Democrats of this period.

Addressing itself to the "advanced workers," *Ob agitatsii* prefaced its arguments with the observation that "precisely the worker Social Democrats for the most part support that very preoccupation [circle propaganda] which we condemn as useless."[29] Reviewing the accomplishments of *kruzhkovshchina*, the author argued that "only the superior, more capable workers have thus obtained theoretical knowledge, which they associate in a very superficial way with real life and surrounding conditions." He candidly admitted that "the workers' striving for knowledge, for escape from darkness, was exploited for the purpose of foisting on them the generalizations and tenets of scientific socialism." Such workers tend to "form a distinct group with all the characteristics of the revolutionary intelligentsia, doomed to eternal vegetation in *kruzhki*."[30] While they are preoccupied with their own "self-

---

[28] P. A. Garvi, *Vospominaniia sotsial-demokrata* (New York, 1946), p. 76.

[29] *Ob agitatsii* (Geneva, 1896), p. 1.

[30] *Ibid.*, p. 19.

perfection" the masses go their own way, raise up their own leaders, and devise their own methods of class struggle by trial and error. The elite worker intelligentsia, as a result, finds itself completely alienated from the workers' movement.

The author felt it was high time to cease training "superfluous" worker intellectuals and to do something to overcome their alienation from the masses. This could be accomplished by employing the *kruzhki* to train agitators. The masses cannot be persuaded to adopt socialism and pursue their class interests through an abstract intellectual process. "The broad masses," the author asserted, "are drawn into the struggle, not by intellectual considerations, but by the objective course of events."[31] Hence, the chief task of the agitator was to exploit every petty abuse of employers or authorities to reveal to the average worker his miserable condition and to help him draw the proper generalizations from his experience. "Thus," the author concluded, "the task of Social Democrats is one of constant agitation among factory workers on the basis of their everyday needs and demands."[32]

The notion that the worker's awareness of his social situation progressively develops in the course of his clashes with the powers that be was the leitmotif of the brochure. The workers first see abuses as the machinations of their bosses and supervisors. They send a deputation to the factory inspector to seek redress, only to find that their importunities are "illegal." They stage a walkout, but the government sends in troops to "pacify" them. They call meetings to form unions and collect strike funds, but these are immediately broken up by police; mass arrests and exile to the villages follow. Political tasks and the fundamental irreconcilability of the interests of the workers and employers are driven home by bitter experience. The same basic thought was extended to the whole class struggle as conceived by Marxist theory:

> Spreading out as it progresses, embracing entire industries instead of separate factories, the movement collides with government authority at every step. The lessons of political wisdom occur more frequently, and each time their strict morality is stamped more forcefully into the minds of the workers. Thus their class consciousness matures, their awareness that the people's hopes can only be realized by the efforts of the people itself. The ground is now pre-

---

[31] *Ibid.*, p. 9.   [32] *Ibid.*, p. 16.

pared for political agitation. This agitation finds a class organized by life itself, with a well-developed class egoism, with an awareness of the common interests of all who toil, and of the opposition of these interests to the interests of all other classes. A change in the political structure is only a matter of time. One spark—and the accumulated inflammable material will burst into life.[33]

The prospect of leading a mass movement instead of simply small circles of "advanced" workers was likely to appeal to a generation in earnest quest of "that social force" which would bring about the downfall of the autocracy and the realization of their socialist hopes. It now seemed as if the formula for calling this force into life had finally been discovered.

Indigenous Russian groups soon began to follow Vilna's lead in converting to the new methods. The Moscow *Rabochii Soiuz* set about reproducing and distributing on a wide scale small brochures which were easily comprehensible to simple workers and which explained the necessity for strikes to improve the workers' situation. The Social Democratic leaders frequently called together fairly large groups in woods and meadows outside the city to listen to agitational speeches. Moscow Social Democrats estimated that the number of workers touched by their labors reached about a thousand from thirty different industrial establishments by the summer of 1895.[34]

By fall, reports of the police and factory inspectors were beginning to complain of "unrest" inspired by the circulation of "criminal" leaflets.[35] Although this activity expanded considerably beyond the bounds of traditional *kruzhkovshchina* and attracted the attention of rank and file workers, it failed to apply the formula specifically recommended by *Ob agitatsii* for drawing the masses into the movement—to exploit the workers' "vital everyday needs and demands." The leaflets merely recommended in a general way the formation of mutual aid funds and associations. Hence,

---

[33] *Ibid.,* p. 16.

[34] See Mitskevich, *Revoliutsionnaia Moskva,* p. 221. Information on the early Moscow movement in addition to the works already cited is to be found in M. N. Liadov, *Istoriia rossiiskoi sotsial-demokraticheskoi partii* (St. Petersburg, 1906), I, 101–18, and in a valuable contemporary account in the underground journal *Rabotnik,* Nos. 3–4 (1897), pp. 33–52 and 94–99 (reprinted in *Rabochee dvizhenie v Rossii,* vol. IV, part 1, pp. 396–415).

[35] *Rabochee dvizhenie v Rossii,* vol. IV, part 1, pp. 69–71 and 90–101.

Top: The brothers Moisei (*left*) and Mikhail Lure (*right*), members of the *Rabochee Znamia* group. *Bottom left:* Mark Khinoi, a typesetter for the secret printing presses of a number of Social Democratic organizations. *Bottom right:* I. V. Babushkin, a veteran worker–Social Democrat of St. Petersburg, Ekaterinoslav, and the *Iskra* organization.

Some of the delegates to the First Congress of the Russian Social-Democratic Workers' Party (Minsk, 1898). Members of the Central Committee (*top, left to right*): Stepan Radchenko, Arkadii Kremer, B. L. Eidelman. *Bottom, left to right:* K. A. Petrusevich, Mutnik, P. L. Tuchapskii, Viktor Vannovskii.

A group of veteran worker-intellectuals from Ekaterinoslav

Founders of the underground journal *Iuzhnii Rabochii* (1899–1903). *Clockwise:* Aaron Ginzburg, Moisei Dushkan, Ilia Vilenskii.

the Moscow campaign remained unco-ordinated with the spontaneous outburst of dissatisfaction that *Ob agitatsii* viewed as essential to success. The efforts of the Moscow *Rabochii Soiuz* had already passed their high point when the agitational campaign in St. Petersburg was just beginning. Soon heavy arrests made serious inroads on the intelligentsia leadership and paralyzed Social Democratic activity until the following summer.

In the fall of 1894, the pupils of Skvortsov in Nizhni Novgorod, inspired by reports from the capitals of their former schoolmates Mitskevich and Silvin, formally decided to initiate agitation. The first leaflet pointing out abuses of certain factory administrators and advocating a strike appeared in mid-October, 1894. In the winter and spring of 1895, the Nizhni Social Democrats considerably expanded their contacts with workers, intensified their propaganda efforts, and circulated large quantities of illegal pamphlets which they received from Moscow. Sixty workers participated in a May First celebration in a remote open spot, and were regaled with speeches on the significance of the holiday and exhortations to struggle for improvement in their situation by declaring strikes. The distribution of agitational leaflets at the factories began on a large scale in January, 1896, but was soon cut short by arrests.[36]

Two former members of Mitskevich's circle in Moscow, exiled to Ekaterinoslav in the autumn of 1894, introduced the small Social Democratic group of that locality to the new program. The group was liquidated by the police in the following autumn, but not before the appearance of considerable quantities of popular propaganda pamphlets and several strike leaflets had caused the authorities a certain amount of anxiety.[37]

Even where the question of agitation had not yet been formally discussed, Social Democratic groups were sometimes confronted with the problem of how to respond to the growing industrial

[36] *Ibid.*, pp. 462–83. Most of the above information stems from police reports reprinted in the collection referred to. Because of the dearth of memoirs by participants, the early introduction of agitation in Nizhni Novgorod has been scarcely mentioned in the literature.

[37] *Ibid.*, pp. 158–69. There are a number of brief memoir accounts by participants in this group in the collection edited by M. A. Rubach, *Istoriia ekaterinoslavskoi sotsial-demokraticheskoi organizatsii, 1889–1903 gg.* (Ekaterinoslav, 1923). (Hereafter cited as *Istoriia ekaterinoslavskoi.*) The best of these is by the worker A. Smirnov, "Vospominaniia o pervom rabochem s.d. kruzhke v Ekaterinoslave" (pp. 11–21).

unrest. The widely publicized strike of four thousand cotton spinners in Yaroslavl of April, 1895, during which workers were shot down for stoning government troops, proved to many Social Democrats the dangers of a mass movement without leadership. In the "Russian Manchester," Ivanovo-Voznesensk, a strike involving two thousand weavers broke out unexpectedly in one of the larger firms in October, 1895. The local *Rabochii Soiuz,* which until then had complacently devoted itself solely to secret propaganda work, was suddenly forced to define itself in relationship to spontaneous expressions of the "class struggle."

> As soon as the strike began, a meeting of the active members of the organization was called at Kuklin's quarters to discuss participation in the strike. A strong argument flared up. Makhov and Bagaev hotly defended their proposal that the *Soiuz* should take upon itself the direction of the strike and insisted on distributing leaflets to the strikers. Kondratev and Evdokimov expressed themselves against participation, because they regarded the *Soiuz* as still weak and insufficiently prepared to act openly; putting out leaflets, in their opinion, could only lead to the liquidation of the *Soiuz.*[38]

The *Rabochii Soiuz* resolved the dilemma by permitting Makhov and Bagaev to act on their own, which they did with some energy and success (they actually took over the leadership and prolonged the strike for several days). The *Rabochii Soiuz* was about to reorganize for mass agitation on the basis of this experience when its work was disrupted by the police.

Bearing a manuscript of *Ob agitatsii,* Martov visited St. Petersburg in September, 1894, and proved himself an ardent missionary of the new cause. The document caused considerable stir among the several existing Social Democratic groups. Although a younger group of technological students headed by Chernyshev greeted it with more sympathy at first than the *stariki* (oldsters or veterans) under the leadership of Radchenko and Lenin, both groups had adopted its program, at least in theory, by the beginning of 1895. A few experiments were made with agitational techniques during the first half of 1895, but with few perceptible results. When Martov returned to St. Petersburg in the autumn,

---

[38] M. Bagaev, *Za desiat' let* (Ivanovo, 1930), p. 40. Bagaev was in close touch with Nizhni Novgorod circles and was put in touch through them with the St. Petersburg organizations in 1895. Hence, he was undoubtedly familiar with the debates over agitation and possibly had even read *Ob agitatsii.*

he felt that the *stariki* still maintained a cautious and vascillating posture on the question; nevertheless, he merged his own group with them and when a number of strikes broke out in the autumn they all devoted themselves enthusiastically to the work of applying the new tactics on a large scale. By the end of 1895, the new ideas had struck deep roots in the thinking of Russian Social Democrats and, although they had not as yet matched the achievements of their Polish and Jewish comrades in arousing a mass movement, they had at least made exploratory beginnings.

In spite of the tangible example of the Western border areas and the promising signs of an incipient strike movement in the heart of Russia, the transition to the new phase in the movement was by no means a smooth one. The initial reaction of many experienced Social Democrats and workers was skeptical at best and frequently openly hostile. Martov records that representatives of Social Democratic groups from Kiev and Kharkov visiting Vilna displayed little enthusiasm for the new methods and doubted the advisability of introducing them in the center of the empire. One of them argued that it would constitute an "infraction of the system of strict conspiracy which it had taken years to build up, and upon which the whole edifice of circle propaganda depended"; the other objected that agitation "only touched the surface of proletarian consciousness," whereas the real task of Social Democracy was to train a "class-conscious workers' vanguard" by which, Martov sarcastically remarks, they understood exclusively "well-rounded, educated worker-Marxists."[39]

Such arguments were typical of the old hands who had proudly continued the traditions of the *narodovoltsy* propagandists and felt that the success of their enterprise depended on putting the workers through a complete "university program" without being detected by the police. Agitation in their view could only expose these valuable workers to the eyes of factory guards and police spies, and thus prematurely cut short their ideological preparation. Moreover, arrests would inevitably disrupt the tenuous links which held the network of propaganda circles together. As a precautionary measure based on years of experience, communication with

---

[39] Martov, pp. 250 and 252. These very arguments recur frequently in the literature. See, for example, B. L. Eidelman, "K istorii vozniknoveniia pervago s'ezda partii," *Pervyi S'ezd R. S.–D. R. P.* (Kiev, 1923), p. 45.

the central leadership was maintained solely through key persons known only by their nicknames ("Red Sasha," "Blondie," "Andrei the Hare") and who stored in their memory alone the time and place of secret rendezvous, real names and addresses, passwords, and other vital information. The period of *kruzhkovshchina* had produced genuine virtuosos in this art of conspiracy, such as Stepan Radchenko in St. Petersburg, Sapezhko in Kiev, and Lipkin-Cherevanin (later a famous Menshevik) in Kharkov. Such perfectionists could not reconcile themselves to the rapid turnover in leadership which mass agitation would entail.

Partially these attitudes represented a legitimate concern for the stability and continuity of Social Democratic work, a concern which later developments amply justified. But in them was also reflected a good share of encrusted conservatism which was unsettled by the inevitable psychological and practical readjustment that the new program would demand.

In contrast to the impassioned reaction of the worker dissidents in Vilna, the Russian workers accepted the new method with relative equanimity. The dream of upward mobility had colored the Jewish artisans' response to socialism, whereas their Russian counterparts were primarily "hereditary" factory workers for whom there was no such avenue of escape. Although their ties with the village may long have been severed, they still carried the passports of "peasants" and were subject to numerous social and legal disabilities (such as exile to the "village of origin" for numerous offenses), which precluded rising to a higher station in life. Hence, the Russian workers in general felt they had everything to gain and nothing to lose by engaging in an active struggle against their "exploiters."

Nevertheless, sheer conservatism and the unquenchable thirst for learning engendered mistrust of the innovations on the part of those who had been schooled in the propaganda circles. Moralistic, proud of their cultural attainments, and somewhat fastidious in their habits of life, they were separated by a broad gulf from those workers who were now drawn into the movement by the strikes. Akimov, an early chronicler of the movement, quoted a worker of the former type whom he met in exile. "These leaflets are an idle undertaking. What can you explain in a single leaflet? You have to give the worker books, not leaflets; you've got to teach him. Get him into a *kruzhok*."[40] Akimov cited another example related to him by comrade "E." (probably B. L. Eidelman) from Kiev:

> I came upon one of our female workers and found her in tears. "What's the matter?" I asked. Several of her acquaintances, who had gone through propaganda circles, approached her and began to ridicule her because, not yet having completed circle training herself, she already set about propagandizing other workers. "What's this? They've turned you into a budding Social Democratic agitator? You'd better learn a little yourself first!"[41]

The worker Babushkin from St. Petersburg felt the conflicting motivations of the transitional generation. He had likewise been drawn to the movement by his fascination with books and had zealously helped the Social Democrats organize *kruzhki*. Yet he also burned with hatred for the system which kept him and his comrades in ignorance and poverty, and when disorders broke out in the workshops he immediately joined the fray. Despite his rebellious impulses, however, he feared the results of mass agitation.

> I absolutely rebelled against agitation, though I saw the undoubted fruits of this work in the general upsurge of enthusiasm among the working masses; for I was very much afraid of another such wave of arrests [of most of the *stariki* on December 9, 1895] and thought that now all would perish. However, I proved to be mistaken.[42]

Babushkin's arguments differed little from those of Radchenko and other intelligentsia of the old school. "Here you begin throwing leaflets in all directions," he protested to Martov, "and in two months you've destroyed what it took years to create. . . . The new youth, brought up on this agitational activity will tend to be superficial in outlook."[43] Babushkin looked with contempt on the young, impetuous workers Zinoviev and Karamyshev, who threw themselves into agitational work without precaution and were quickly arrested. However, he soon forgot his earlier qualms and followed their example. When Babushkin was arrested and exiled to Ekaterinoslav, he immediately set about organizing fellow workers for agitational activity. The success of the agitational campaign in

---

[40] Akimov, p. 34. [41] *Ibid.*, p. 73.

[42] *Vospominaniia I. V. Babushkina* (Leningrad, 1925), p. 76. (Cited hereafter as Babushkin.)

[43] Martov, p. 292.

Ekaterinoslav of 1898–99 was in good measure due to his tireless efforts.[44]

Mitskevich explicitly denied that such inner conflicts arose over agitation in Moscow among either the intelligentsia or the workers. "Here we had no traditions of secluded work in *kruzhki* as they did in Vilna," he explained; "indeed, the Moscow factory and industrial workers lived under different conditions than the craftsmen of the petty workshops in Vilna."[45] Moscow was perhaps not entirely typical, since by 1895 few traces were left of the earlier painstaking propaganda work. Large numbers of workers were introduced to the bare essentials of socialism. These relatively loose standards were exemplified by the approach of the worker propagandist, Nemchinov, who illustrated each point of socialist doctrine with a passage from the Gospels![46] Frequent mass meetings took place in the forests featuring speeches and revolutionary songs; simple, graphic literature designed to kindle proletarian enthusiasm was provided in abundance. Only a few leaflets were distributed in the factories, however. The careful, systematic collection of information and its formulation into specific demands corresponding to the mood of the workers as practiced in Vilna and St. Petersburg were absent. So perhaps it can be conceded that "agitation" as practiced in Moscow did not upset any long-standing attitudes and traditions.

Nevertheless, there were older workers in Moscow who displayed a certain reserve toward the new program. In striking contrast to those of his intelligentsia comrades, the memoirs of Prokofev, the only worker member of the *Rabochii Soiuz,* fail even to mention the word "agitation"; on the other hand, he reminisced warmly about the propaganda circles. That his fellow workers were not particularly enthusiastic about the intelligentsia program can be judged from their reaction (in 1895) to the proposed secret May First celebration in the forest by all the organized workers in Moscow.

> When I put this question to my comrades, they decided to celebrate inconspicuously and not raise a ruckus. They were anxious not to spoil our work—they feared arrests. The comrades said: "It's too

[44] See below, pp. 103–7.

[45] Mitskevich, *Revoliutsionnaia Moskva*, p. 191.

[46] See his memoir fragment in *Na zare rabochego dvizheniia v Moskve*, p. 162.

early to speak up, our forces are still too small for open action; the idea of a big celebration—that's an idea of the intelligentsia."[47]

Obviously, Prokofev and his fellows were interested primarily in the undisturbed pursuit of knowledge, and their suspicion of the activities of the intelligentsia reflected the same conservatism noticeable elsewhere.

With the St. Petersburg strike movement of the summer of 1896 and early 1897, Russian Social Democracy entered a new phase. For the most part, groups which had not yet launched a program of agitation accepted the validity of the new tactics in principle. If they hesitated or delayed, only temporary obstacles stood in the way, such as organizational deficiencies, the lack of printing facilities, or the crippling effect of arrests. The fact that the St. Petersburg movement had set a large part of the working population in motion, and won apparent concessions from the government (namely, the promise of a statute regulating the working day), made a deep impression everywhere, on intelligentsia and workers alike. The formula of *Ob agitatsii,* envisaging the welding of the working class into a political force by means of agitation on the basis of "everyday needs and demands," was now felt to have been tested in practice to the satisfaction of the vast majority of active Social Democrats.

Local work was henceforward carried on under entirely new conditions and with new assumptions. Printing and circulating strike leaflets monopolized attention and resources, whereas propaganda was relegated to the background and subordinated to the requirements of agitation. Instead of dealing with a mere handful of literate workers, Social Democrats now addressed themselves to the raw masses, who were becoming more and more receptive to Social Democratic ideas and slogans. The *praktiki* (as the underground workers were called) were subjected to more frequent arrest and harassment by police spies, informers, and plainclothes "shadows." But despite the mass arrests, work was seldom interrupted for long. The appearance of leaflets and the astounding results of the strikes greatly enhanced the workers' veneration for the "socialists" and their secret *Soiuz* (with its official stamp on each proclamation), so that recruitment no longer posed a major problem. As the first generation of polished Marxists were swept

---

[47] *Ibid.,* p. 112.

off the scene by arrests, their places were taken by recruits from the ever-increasing "periphery" of green students who had acquired their enthusiasm for Social Democracy and the workers in the overheated atmosphere of *vecherinki,* all-night bull sessions, and popular expositions of Marx.[48] While the average age of the older generation of leadership had been twenty-four or twenty-five, the newcomers after 1896 averaged scarcely twenty. Radchenko and Babushkin's fear of a debasement in the quality of leadership had not been entirely unfounded. Krupskaia, who belonged to the central group of *Soiuz Bor'by* until the fall of 1896, aptly described the transition.

> After the arrest of Martov, Lakhovskii, and others, the forces of our groups became even more weakened. True, new comrades took their places, but this was a sort less tempered intellectually, and there was no time to engage in self-education. The movement demanded service, it demanded a mass of effort; everything went into agitation and there was little time to think about propaganda. The agitational leaflets enjoyed a huge success. Often they were written hurriedly without sufficient attention to concrete conditions. The strike of the textile workers had been due to the influence of Social Democrats and many became carried away. The soil was being prepared for the flowering of Economism.[49]

Krupskaia put her finger on a connection which was afterward seldom acknowledged by the leaders of *Iskra.* The heresy of "Economism" was the inevitable fruit of the new practice of mass agitation which they themselves had introduced on a broad scale at an earlier stage of their careers. Indeed, many voices had warned against just such dangers, but they had chosen to ignore them.

The subsequent five years were to see repeated attempts in other localities to duplicate the methods and achievements of the St. Petersburg *Soiuz Bor'by* of 1895–97. A reconstituted Moscow group, which tried to arouse the Moscow workers in response to the St. Petersburg strike, kept up incessant agitation until mid-1897, with scattered results. In 1897 the Kiev organization launched a major campaign, as did a group in Nikolaev led by young Trotsky. Ekaterinoslav and Kharkov followed in 1898 and

---

[48] According to Lydia Dan, the best of them seldom got further than the first chapter of *Das Kapital.* (Personal communication.)

[49] N. D. Krupskaia, *Vospominaniia* (Moscow, 1926), p. 25.

1899, respectively; Ivanovo-Voznesensk, Rostov, and Odessa joined in only after the turn of the century. Sporadic attempts were made even in remote provinces, mainly by exiles from the major industrial areas. Sometimes localities undertook the transition in successive waves—arrests would interrupt the promising beginnings of agitation and the surviving comrades would revert temporarily to propaganda work, only to take up agitation again at a more opportune moment. Everywhere, however, agitation was accepted as the appropriate technique for the foreseeable future.

Although the scattered Social Democratic groups introduced agitation at various times, under various influences, and with varying success, the over-all pattern of development was strikingly uniform. First, a group of Marxist intellectuals would organize a small number of advanced workers into propaganda *kruzhki* and impart to them a well-rounded Social Democratic education. At some point, the work would dramatically pick up in tempo, the *kruzhki* would multiply, large numbers of workers would be introduced to the bare essentials of Social Democracy (usually by means of pamphlet literature) and infused with enthusiasm for the new cause. At the first convenient incident or stirring of unrest, the "directing center" would decide to intervene and distribute leaflets at the factories, generating a ferment among the workers. Waves of arrests would follow, temporarily disorganizing the work. Valuable leaders, both *intelligenty* and workers, would be imprisoned and exiled. Finally, new comrades with less experience and background would take over, re-establish broken ties with the workers, set in order the conspiratorial and technical apparatus for printing leaflets, and draw in fresh forces. And then the cycle would be repeated, if not from the beginning, at least in its latter phases.

Not every locality followed precisely these steps, but nearly all at least approximated it. It is instructive to observe that Social Democratic activity in Odessa, described in great detail by P. A. Garvi, although it took place after the turn of the century, differed little in essential details from that in St. Petersburg in 1895–97, in Kiev in 1897, or in Ekaterinoslav in 1898.[50]

---

[50] See Garvi, *Vospominaniia sotsial-demokrata*, chap. 1. For brief descriptions of two other local situations which follow the pattern outlined above, see *Iz rabochego dvizheniia v Odesse i Nikolaeve* (Geneva, 1900), pp. 8–11 and 22–25, respectively.

CHAPTER 3

The Conquest of the Masses

THE emotions accompanying the ground swell of revolutionary impatience at the turn of the century and *Iskra*'s fierce attack on "opportunism" and "Economism" made any reasonable appraisal of the accomplishments of the preceding period all but impossible. Not until the issue of Economism was superseded by the unexpected schism in the party at the Second Congress did a few adherents of the Menshevik faction review their former clichés and formulate more considered judgments. Pavel Akselrod was one of the first to make the attempt. In the December 15, 1903 issue of the new Menshevik *Iskra,* he wrote:

> In the course of this period [of mass agitation] our movement acquired deep roots in the proletariat, revolutionized the mood and even the consciousness of considerable strata of the workers, and aroused them to revolutionary activism. The political significance of the period of economic agitation, a period circumscribed by the narrow limits of trade-union or parochial interests, erupted to the surface in the revolutionary events of the first year of the new century. Workers by the thousands threw themselves into battle against the retinue of the autocracy, but Social Democracy was caught completely unprepared to lead the masses in such tempestuous times.[1]

---

[1] Cited from a collection of Akselrod's articles *Bor'ba sotsialisticheskikh i burzhuaznykh tendentsii v russkom revoliutsionnom dvizhenii* (St. Petersburg, 1907), p. 71. Another Menshevik author, Fedor Dan, made a similar evaluation: "Measured by its practical objectives and the ideology of the working masses, the strike movement of 1896–97 was purely "Economist": the strikers set themselves no sort

For erstwhile partisans of the *Iskra* cause this was a sobering admission that much of their criticism of so-called "Economism" was wide of the mark: the political militancy of the workers was far more a product of the struggle for "every day needs and demands" than of the preachings of *Iskra*. Until the very close of the century the only visible trend in the movement was the spread of the strike agitation technique, worked out by the St. Petersburg *Soiuz Bor'by* during the years 1895–96, to other industrial centers of Russia.

Then in May, 1900, came the unexpected report of an open street demonstration in Kharkov involving thousands of workers. From that point on, the workers rapidly outstripped their leaders in zeal to take to the streets, to defend the students, to broadcast revolutionary slogans, and to engage the forces of the autocracy in tests of physical strength (the "Obukhov Defense" in St. Petersburg of May, 1901, the general strikes in Rostov in 1902, and those throughout the South in 1903). Obviously, a momentous transformation in the psychology of the working masses had taken place since 1895; accumulated discontent and steady exposure to the agitation and propaganda of the Social Democrats had ripened, indeed, overripened them for political protest, and they seized upon any convenient occasion to register their new mood.

Most recent Western accounts of the period, particularly those of Pipes and Keep, have tended to ignore or depreciate this development and treat the workers' movement and Social Democracy as two entirely unrelated phenomena. Perhaps led astray by Anglo-American experience and Lenin's one-sided polemics, they have interpreted "Economism" as a sort of incipient trade unionism striving to liberate itself from the socialist dogmatism of orthodox Marxist intellectuals. It is quite true that strike fever did sometimes cause the workers and their socialist mentors to gloss over revolutionary motifs in practice. However, the pamphlet *Ob agitatsii* had rightly observed in 1894, that the movement was bound to "collide with government authority at every step" and

---

of political aims, nor did they formulate any political demands. Nevertheless, the political significance of the movement proved to be tremendous. In the course of the strike movement, certain political ideas and proclivities penetrated not only the thin layer of advanced workers, but also the working masses themselves, preparing them for that active political role which they were to play in the very near future." (*Proizkhozhdenie bol'shevizma* [New York, 1946], p. 250.)

each time "stamp the lessons of political wisdom more forcefully into the minds of the workers." In the fullness of time, it had averred, a spark would be needed for the "accumulated combustible material to burst into life." Pared of its ideological veneer, this formulation represented a recognition that the prevailing social and political conditions in Russia precluded the evolution of a corporate class spirit based exclusively on economic aims and interests. The dramatic participation of the workers in the emerging nationwide protest would be inexplicable had not Social Democratic ideology provided the workers with plausible formulas justifying the shift from an economic struggle to a political one. All this had been clearly envisaged by the first generation of Russian Social Democrats, and if the preoccupations of the era of politics tended to obscure the logic behind agitation in the minds of some of its own discoverers, a review of the actual spread of agitational techniques should put the original formulas to the test and resolve the issue of whether the Social Democrats of the half-decade 1895–1900 were indeed instrumental in mobilizing the workers for mass political protest.

Ob agitatsii had laid down certain guidelines for the proposed revolution in tactics, but had made very few concrete suggestions for implementing them. The devotees of agitation in scattered localities were obliged to improvise, guided only in a general way by their knowledge of the Jewish and Polish movements. The contrast in social and political conditions made certain features of agitation among minority nationalities inapplicable in the center of the empire. The barrier of language brought about the almost total isolation of the Russian authorities from the population at large and thereby rendered the Polish and Jewish Social Democrats far less subject to police surveillance than their Russian comrades. The former groups could organize and participate in strikes almost with impunity, whereas the Russians could not. The Poles achieved a tightly disciplined, national organization quite early (by 1891), whereas the Jewish Social Democrats were able to establish a network of craft funds through which they led strikes and conducted verbal agitation.[2] Also, there was the fact that the

---

[2] That the craft funds were the heart of the Jewish strike movement is clear from the definition of their function formulated at the First Congress of the Bund in September, 1897: "They [the fund organizations] are to collect data on the situ-

workers in St. Petersburg, Moscow, and Ivanovo-Voznesensk were concentrated in gigantic factories and industrial complexes, whereas the Jewish "proletariat" was scattered in countless petty workshops. This arrangement meant that the Russians were obliged to develop their own casuistry in applying the new precepts. Wherever the innovators attempted to follow the Jewish and Polish models too slavishly, as in the early attempts in Moscow and Ekaterinoslav, their work was quickly destroyed, leaving few lasting traces.

It was the St. Petersburg *stariki*, after joining forces with Martov's circle in the fall of 1895, who successfully developed the techniques which were well-nigh universally emulated by other Social Democratic groups. Their brief agitational leaflets listing immediate grievances and demands were to a large extent substitutes for direct participation; they crystallized the workers' mood and channeled it into co-ordinated action without exposing the Social Democratic leaders to easy observation by the police. The dramatic culmination of their agitational activity in the general strike of textile workers the following summer seemed to confirm beyond all doubt the efficacy of the St. Petersburg methods and won for them imitators in all parts of Russia.

Although the "Vilna program" had been the subject of lively discussion since the autumn of 1894, the St. Petersburg groups did not perfect this technique without a certain amount of trial and error. Lenin's group, the *stariki*, made their first attempt to intervene in disorders at the Semiannikov metal works in January, 1895. A leaflet was prepared in very limited numbers and distributed to a few key spots in the huge complex by the worker Babushkin, who records his disappointment at the lack of response from the workers.[3] A cursory glance at the leaflet removes some of the mystery. In a rather meandering, didactic style it ranged over a wide variety of themes: the advantages of disciplined strikes

---

ation of the workers in this or that craft, workshop, or factory, and to determine on the basis of the acquired data those improvements, the attainment of which can be counted upon; they are to choose the most favorable moment to strike, to select from their number those who are to conduct the agitation on the basis of possible improvements, and to organize aid to the strikers." (*Materialy k istorii evreiskago rabochego divzheniia* [St. Petersburg, 1906], p. 77.) This definition simply summed up what had hitherto been the prevailing practice.

[3] *Babushkin*, p. 65.

over violent disorders, the government's role in the worker's plight, and the accomplishments of the workers in Western Europe. However, it lacked the ingredient discovered later for arousing the interest of the average worker—references to specific abuses and conditions in his own factory or shop which already rankled within him. Instead, the leaflet still appealed to the idealism of the educated worker. "It's the duty of every discerning worker to take up this cause," the leaflet declared. "Struggle and knowledge!—that is what Russian life demands from the Russian worker."[4] A second leaflet, issued shortly thereafter for the benefit of striking workers in the shipbuilding yards of the Admiralty, seems to have enjoyed more success. The strike continued for a few more days and the leaflet aroused comment from police reports—but its style and content were nearly as pallid.[5] The modesty of these efforts indicates that the *stariki* were still feeling their way, uncertain how best to apply the new tactics.

The rival group known as the *molodye* (youngsters) tried their hand that summer when most of the *stariki* were away for the holidays. Akimov states that, upon their return, the *stariki* subjected the efforts of the *molodye* to sharp criticism. He records them as saying:

> This proclamation is borrowed from *Vorwaerts* [the chief organ of German Social Democrats] and is not applicable to Russian conditions. You have to write proclamations about concrete events and conditions of work; there's no point in writing about "syndicates" in Russia.[6]

Thus, the first efforts of the *molodye* seem to have suffered from the same shortcomings as the earlier attempts of the *stariki*—they had not yet discovered how to incite workers to concrete action and had ignored the advice of *Ob agitatsii* to begin with the workers' most keenly felt needs and demands.

When in November, 1895, the *stariki*, now joined by Martov's

---

[4] *Listovki peterburgskogo "Soiuza Bor'by," 1895–97 gg.*, ed. S. N. Valk (Moscow, 1934), p. 6. (Hereafter cited as *Listovki*.) The possibility of Lenin's authorship of this leaflet, not recognized in Soviet publications, is discussed by Pipes, p. 66.

[5] See *Rabochee dvizhenie v Rossii*, Vol. IV, part 1, pp. 2–5. Most of the leaflets included in *Listovki* and cited by the author have been reprinted in this collection.

[6] Akimov, *Materialy*, p. 37. It should be noted that Akimov is the only source for these early efforts of the Chernyshev group.

group, finally embarked on their campaign of agitation, they applied the principles of *Ob agitatsii* with great energy and consistency. As soon as they heard rumors of unrest at a certain factory, one of their groups was dispatched to find out the exact causes of dissatisfaction—non-observance of the quitting time, bullying and threats of discharge by shop stewards, repeated delays in the pay roll, spoiled goods and high prices at the company stores, arbitrary deductions from wages, unfair differentials in the piece rate for various types of cloth, and so on. As far as possible, the *stariki* tried to get the workers themselves to formulate their grievances. These, with very little embellishment were itemized in a leaflet and quickly distributed. The leaflet invariably concluded with a summons to walk off the job until the demands were met.

The effect was frequently quite dramatic. Here, in neatly summarized form, the worker found the expression of misgivings which he could articulate for himself only with difficulty. The day a leaflet appeared in the shop, the atmosphere immediately registered it. One can imagine that the workers, instead of engaging mindlessly in routine tasks, excitedly conferred in whispers: Who had seen it? What did it say about the fines? Who had a copy? Would there be a *bunt* (outbreak of violence)? Wherever they were able to escape the eyes of factory guards, stewards, or known stool pigeons (the most convenient place being the "club"—the factory toilet), they gathered in small groups while one of their number read it aloud. " 'Neatly said!' " and " 'Absolutely right!' " one account records as the reactions. " 'To the director! Send it to the director!' "[7] In a very short time, rumors about the leaflets circulated throughout the factories of St. Petersburg. Soon the intelligentsia no longer needed to seek out the workers, who avidly inquired after the "students" and requested leaflets.

The heavy arrests of December and January, sweeping away most of the *stariki* including Lenin and Martov, caused only a tem-

---

[7] Takhtarev, *Ocherk*, p. 24. Descriptions of the fall campaign of 1895 are also to be found in Martov, pp. 275–94 and Akimov, pp. 34–38. Other sources attest to the excitement which invariably accompanied the first appearance of leaflets. The following describes Nikolaev in 1897: "Such a leaflet does not go unnoticed: it only needs to be posted on the factory walls or in the shops, stuffed in the pockets of coats hung in the entranceway or slipped into lunch buckets. Someone—and probably more than one—will read it aloud to those who can't read. It will set fly rumors and stir up thinking about things." (*Iz rabochego dvizheniia v Odesse i Nikolaeve* [Geneva, 1900], p. 24.)

porary interruption in the agitational campaign. Splinter groups merged with the survivors to form a new unified "Union of Struggle for the Emancipation of the Working Class" (hereafter *Soiuz Bor'by*), which found many willing hands in the periphery of sympathizing students. In the early months of 1896, a dozen or so new leaflets appeared in almost as many factories and industrial plants. Although no significant strikes resulted, one thing is clear from the evidence: the *Soiuz Bor'by* had acquired a considerable reputation and had struck a responsive chord among the St. Petersburg workers. In a casual conversation with a worker previously untouched by propaganda, an *intelligent* was treated to the following impromptu declaration:

> "Just think of the times we live in! . . . We used to work and work and never see daylight. You could see with your own eyes how they swindled us, but what could you do about it? But now! Now comes the factory inspector, the military, and stick their noses in everywhere—the management has to stay on its toes. Marvelous! It used to be you'd see an abuse or a gyp, but you wouldn't even pay attention to it—you had gotten used to it. But now we have our boys who notice everything, everywhere and take it down. Tell it to the *Soiuz*, you hear, we have to let them know about this."
> "Who passes out the leaflets?"
> "Students, I suppose. God grant good health to those people who print the leaflets."
> Thereupon the worker fervently crossed himself.[8]

Events were soon to show that this receptive frame of mind had affected a large segment of St. Petersburg workers.

For an understanding of precisely how the Social Democrats sought to work on the minds of the workers, the agitational literature of this period must be examined with care. The heart of the agitational leaflet was a list of immediate bread-and-butter demands followed by an exhortation to strike. Beyond this, however, in calculated words and phrases, certain basic attitudes and ideas were implanted in the reader's mind. These recurring motifs and their method of presentation were reflected in the large number of leaflets distributed by *Soiuz Bor'by* in the agitational campaigns

---

[8] Takhtarev, *Ocherk*, p. 25. Takhtarev's account is particularly valuable for this period because of his direct involvement all through 1896 and the fact that he wrote his account with the events fresh in his mind (in 1897).

of 1895–97. With rare exceptions, these leaflets made use of the same slogans, the same circle of ideas, the same "jargon," no matter who had written them or when they appeared. Slightly more sophisticated ideological concepts were introduced only after the great textile strike of 1896; bold assaults on the social-political structure were not ventured until after the second major textile strike of early 1897.

First of all, the workers were repeatedly exhorted to act in a spirit of unity and comradeship, since, it was argued, only resolute collective action could force concessions from their employers. Exhortations such as the following were typical: "Stick together, comrades, and manfully defend your interests," or "Therefore, comrades, let us act in a spirit of solidarity and not surrender to new outrages."[9] The authorities try to persuade the workers to voice their complaints individually, the leaflets asserted, because individuals pose no threat and their requests can be safely ignored. But the authorities fear the strength of workers acting in concert and would be forced to give in to collective resistance.

> We can only count on success when we all act together harmoniously. Look at the Thornton workers. As long as they acted separately, each one individually bowed and scraped and begged the owners for an extra kopeck. They were squeezed at will until they got together last November and presented their demands—then they got concessions.[10]

The *Soiuz Bor'by* therefore called upon the workers to prove their solidarity with their fellow workers by responding at once to the call to strike.

The second noticeable emphasis was the admonition to break off work peacefully and without violence. One leaflet framed it thus: "Let us prove that the working people can pursue their demands . . . calmly and resolutely, without uproar or violence. . . . Another enjoined: Let's keep calm and show the government that they are not dealing with ruffians, but with conscious and courageous workers."[11] The reason for this appeal was sometimes made explicit: "In order not to give the authorities an excuse for inter-

---

[9] *Listovki,* pp. 23 and 31.

[10] *Rabochee dvizhenie v Rossii,* Vol. IV, part 1, pp. 200–201.

[11] *Listovki,* pp. 55 and 127.

vention with crude military force, let's conduct our struggle calmly, without disorder and violence."[12] The Social Democratic agitators were keenly aware that the customary mode of workers' protest had been not disciplined strikes, but random destruction and disorders, such as smashing machines and windows, pummeling unpopular shop stewards, burning administration buildings, or looting company stores. The outbreaks at the Semiannikov works in January and at the Laferme tobacco factory in November of 1895 had been of that sort. On such occasions the government quickly summoned Cossacks or infantry regiments to pacify the rioting workers, who were subjected to severe beatings and punishments. "Ringleaders" and "instigators" were sent back to the villages. There were even some instances—for example, at the Yaroslavl cotton mills in 1895—when the troops opened fire, inflicting many casualties.

The Social Democrats were not necessarily trying to prevent military intervention; they only wanted to make sure that the onus of resorting to violence would fall, not on the workers, but on the government. Only in this way, they felt, would the workers learn the important lesson that the government invariably upheld the interests of the employers, no matter how peacefully the workers conducted themselves.

On the whole, the strategy of the St. Petersburg Social Democrats worked quite successfully. It was typical of official reports to observe that "no disorders occurred during the strike," or that "the workers are conducting themselves calmly."[13] When Witte reportedly inquired of the military commander of St. Petersburg, General Kleigls, whether he could get the striking workers back to their jobs, the latter was supposed to have replied: "If the workers mill in the streets and violate peace and order, I know how to take care of them; but if they simply sit at home, I can't do anything with them."[14] That the need for disciplined restraint and order in

---

[12] *Ibid.*, p. 19.

[13] "Iz istorii rabochego dvizheniia kontsa 90-kh godov," *Krasnyi Arkhiv*, No. 93 (February, 1939), pp. 126 and 135. The former quotation is from a police report of November 9, 1895, and the latter from a letter of the Minister of Internal Affairs Goremykin to Nikolai II of January 4, 1897.

[14] Takhtarev, *Ocherk*, p. 54. One would be inclined to dismiss this exchange as apocryphal were it not included in a very detailed account of a session of the

the conduct of strikes was so well instilled in the workers was one of the greatest achievements of the Social Democrats of this period. Unfortunately, during the turmoil of the Revolution of 1905 and the ensuing period of reaction, much of this good work was undone.

The images which agitational literature devised for employers and government authorities indicate how well the leaflets were adapted to the narrow horizon of the untutored worker. Seldom did they resort to tendentious socialist epithets or phraseology. The employers (not "capitalists") were blamed for being "mercenary" (*korystoliubivye*) or "greedy" (*alchnyi*), but only occasionally for "defending their class interests." They were found guilty of "niggardly tricks" (*prizhimki*), "oppressions" (*pritesneniia*), "swindling" (*naduvatel'stvo*), and "outrages" (*nadrugatel'stva*), but almost never of "exploitation." Occasionally there were bitter complaints over the lives of luxury which the "moneybags" (*bogachi*) enjoyed in contrast to the workers' honest struggle for daily bread. Clearly socialist formulations such as the following were exceptions: "Remember that the employers' interests are always irreconcilable with those of the workers."[15] Rather, the leaflets assumed the rhetorical pose that the employers were guilty of selfishness and obvious injustices which the factory inspectors and police could easily correct if they would simply do their job.

Strictures against the police, the military, and the factory inspectors for siding with the employers were applied much more frequently than against government authority in general. In such situations, no appeal was made to attack the representatives of political authority per se, but only to continue the struggle for justice in spite of their interference. For example, one leaflet stated "Neither the government nor crude military force will intimidate us," and another commented, "No sort of police is going to drag us to work."[16] It was made clear to the workers that it was futile for them to reason with the authorities to secure their demands, and that they would win concessions only when they confronted employers and the government alike with the solid phalanx of

---

Imperial State Council. Through sympathetic liberal bureaucrats, Social Democrats were sometimes surprisingly well informed of proceedings inside the government and frequently reprinted documents marked "secret" in their underground publications.

[15] *Listovki*, p. 28. [16] *Ibid.*, pp. 59 and 64.

their combined efforts. "The government, the inspectors, the police, everybody is 'concerned about' the workers' welfare. Don't believe it! Nobody is going to help us if we don't take the sacred cause into our own hands."[17]

Thus, during this period, even the *stariki*, Lenin and Martov included, avoided introducing political, or even mild Social Democratic slogans and concepts into their agitational writings. The writers of leaflets consciously adapted themselves to the level of understanding of the most backward workers and confined themselves only to those notions which were most certain to evoke from the workers an immediate response and touch their most visceral concerns. There is no doubt that the *stariki* were conscientiously applying the formula of the Vilna program for securing leadership over the spontaneous workers' movement as spelled out by *Ob agitatsii*:

> In order to get hold of that trifling issue capable of rallying the workers to the struggle, it is necessary to understand which abuses most easily excite the workers' interests, to choose the most auspicious moment to begin, to know what methods of struggle under the given conditions of time and place are the most effective. Such knowledgeability demands that the agitator be in constant touch with the working masses, that he continually follow developments in a given branch of industry. In every factory there are countless abuses and the worker may be interested in the most trivial details; to discern just when to advance a given demand, to know ahead of time about possible complications—such is the real task of the agitator. . . . Knowledge of the conditions of life, knowledge of the feelings of the masses . . . will make him their natural leader.[18]

One could not find a better summary of the program carried out by the St. Petersburg Social Democrats during the years 1895–96. Although the St. Petersburg *stariki* were slow to accept the position of *Ob agitatsii*, they ultimately adopted it without reservation and carried it out to the letter. The critic of *Iskra*, Akimov, appears to have some justification for his insistence that "The first 'Economists', and the only genuine 'Economists', were none other than the members of the *Soiuz Bor'by* of 1895, subsequently the found-

---

[17] *Ibid.*, p. 92.   [18] *Ob agitatsii* (Geneva, 1896), p. 17.

ers of *Iskra* and zealous unmaskers of Economism."[19] Lenin's later claim in the heat of the controversy over "Economism," that by 1895 the *stariki* had already advanced the "broadest historical tasks of Social Democracy" and had engaged in political agitation, is thoroughly at odds with the available evidence.[20]

On the other hand, neither the *stariki* nor *Ob agitatsii* held that Social Democrats should simply reflect and articulate the mood of the masses. They confidently anticipated that Social Democrats would soon be able to *lead* the masses. *Ob agitatsii* thus elaborated this conception:

> It is understood that the Social Democratic views of the agitator will determine the path along which he will lead the crowd. He must always be one step ahead of the masses, he must illuminate their struggle for them, explaining from a more general point of view the irreconcilability of their interests [with those of the employers], and thus he must expand the horizons of the masses.[21]

Therefore, *Ob agitatsii* by no means simply idealized "spontaneity," as was later often asserted, nor did it disparage Social Democratic "consciousness." Indeed, it stressed the obligation of Social Democrats to "expand the horizons" of the masses and thereby prepare them for conscious political action. It was as-

---

[19] Akimov, p. 41. Of course, it is inaccurate to imply that only the *stariki* in 1895 consciously avoided the use of ideologically slanted terminology in their agitational literature, but Akimov rightly established that they were much more consistent practitioners of "Economism" than many groups later excoriated by *Iskra* for their Economism, including *Rabochaia Mysl'*.

[20] "The first Social Democrats (fully taking into account in this regard the truly useful propositions of the manuscript brochure *Ob agitatsii*) *zealously practiced economic agitation*—but not only did they not regard this as their sole task, but on the contrary from the *very beginning* advanced the broadest historical tasks of Russian Social Democracy in general, and the task of overthrowing the autocracy in particular." (Lenin, *Sochineniia*, 3d ed. [Moscow and Leningrad, 1931], Vol. IV, p. 385. Italics in original.) The only agitational leaflet known to have come from Lenin's pen merely denounced the "venality" of the employers and exhorted the workers to struggle "with comradely solidarity" for the typical petty economic aims. *Ibid.*, I, 449–51. A few leaflets (a very few) departed from this general pattern, as for example the following of November 12, 1896: "The hour will strike when the workers will cast off the despicable yoke of the employers and the government! . . . We need unions, we need strike funds, but all this is forbidden because the government supports the employers." (*Listovki*, p. 97.) The author of this leaflet, however, was not one of the future adherents of *Iskra*, but Katin-Iartsev, a "workerphile" opponent of Lenin in 1897 and later an adherent of *Rabochaia Mysl'*.

[21] *Ob agitatsii*, pp. 17–18.

sumed that the very involvement of workers in a direct clash with the authorities would force on them practical conclusions which subsequent agitation would be able to formulate.

To pursue this goal in the prescribed manner, the *Soiuz Bor'by* periodically distributed leaflets of a more general nature, typically addressed to "all the workers of St. Petersburg." These leaflets gave information on strike developments, summed up losses and gains, listed the names of discharged or arrested comrades, boasted of the concessions granted, exulted in the discomfiture of employers and authorities, and urged the workers to further mutual aid and support. A typical proclamation of this kind appeared in December, 1895. "The past month has been full of events," the leaflet began. "Three times . . . the workers of St. Petersburg rose up against the oppressions of their masters; three times they struggled for better conditions of life."[22] A straightforward chronicle of the strikes followed. Another leaflet of December 15 noted that the agitational leaflets continued to appear despite the mass arrests (of December 9, 1895), proving that the *Soiuz Bor'by* remained intact. "The police got the wrong address," it boasted. "By arrests and banishments it is impossible to stamp out the workers' movement."[23] Another such didactic proclamation declared: "Comrades, on the side of the robber-employer is the strength of his capital, to his service come the factory inspectors and the police, on his side are our Russian laws, which forbid the workers to consult together about their own affairs and to cease work when work becomes no longer bearable."[24]

In all, about a dozen such leaflets were put out by the *Soiuz Bor'by* by the end of 1896. These leaflets, of course, did not yet formulate definite political or Social Democratic goals, but they did lead the worker a step further than the day-to-day leaflets by summarizing and broadly interpreting his experiences, and by enhancing his sense of solidarity with his fellow workers. The employers' abuses were perceived with growing frequency, not as individual foibles, but as the calculated pursuit of class interests; the hostility of the government was presented increasingly, not as fortuitous, but as a necessary consequence of prevailing social conditions.

---

[22] *Listovki*, p. 16.   [23] *Ibid.*, p. 15.   [24] *Ibid.*, p. 22.

Such cautious molding of the thoughts of the masses was well designed to create a receptive frame of mind for the implantation of more explicit ideological motifs. The next logical step was to draw as many of the newly converted workers as possible into propaganda circles and supply them with appropriately simple edifying literature. Previously, propaganda circles had enjoyed the leisure to dwell for months on short passages from Marx, but the new era required that indoctrination be considerably condensed and popularized. It was logical, therefore, for the introduction of agitation to increase many-fold the demand for pocket brochure literature that was written in a popular style.

The *stariki*, Lenin in particular, had been preoccupied with this problem since early 1895, when the decision to undertake agitation had been made. In pursuit of this aim they initiated negotiations with the People's Will group to make use of its excellent underground press in Lahti, Finland. The main purpose behind the respective trips of Lenin and Sponti to Switzerland in the summer of 1895 was to secure agreements with Plekhanov and Akselrod on the printing of simple literature for workers. Lenin returned with a huge suitcase full of booklet and pamphlet materials, most of which were earmarked for the indoctrination of workers. He also worked out an arrangement by which Akselrod was to edit a journal for workers entitled *Rabotnik* (*The Worker*), and the St. Petersburg group was to supply the appropriate material.[25] Sponti was allowed to print several manuscripts of worker literature on the printing press of the *Gruppa Osvobozhdeniia Truda*, but without the latter's official imprint.[26]

From the autumn of 1895 onward, the police reports noted a considerable increase in the circulation of illicit literature, which they ascribed to the Lahti press and to Lenin's trip abroad.[27] The most frequently recorded titles were *The Working Day*, *Who*

---

[25] See Krupskaia, *Vospominaniia*, pp. 19–21. Pipes's account of this trip fails to note this well-substantiated fact (see p. 81) and thus portrays Lenin as a budding Marxist author totally unconcerned with the underground movement at this time. On the contrary, the chief purpose of the trip was to secure the help of the veteran émigrés in meeting the anticipated increase in demand for illicit literature, once the agitational campaign was underway.

[26] See E. I. Sponti, "Vstrechi a Leninym," *Zapiski Instituta Lenina*, III (1928), pp. 73–75.

[27] See *Rabochee dvizhenie v Rossii*, Vol IV, part 1, pp. 32 and 35–36.

Lives with What?, The Clever Trick, Tsar Hunger, and *The Weavers.* Some of these pamphlets were new editions of old Populist works; others were translations of Polish agitational materials.

The Populist admixture did not matter, since the primary purpose of such literature was merely to make the worker aware that he was being exploited and to provide him with arguments and concepts that would justify organized protest. Some of the pieces, such as *The Weavers* and *The Clever Trick,* simply told instructive stories from working life. Others more or less systematically developed elementary Marxist concepts, buttressed by impressive statistics and examples. For example, *Who Lives with What?* elucidated the labor theory of value by calculating how much "value" in crystallized labor terms the laborer receives back as wages from a yard of cloth and how much the employer retained as profit. It led up to the conclusion that "all masters and factory owners hire workers, all purchase *labor energy,* only in order to make a profit from the workers' labor, i.e. to enrich themselves."[28] Workers weaned on such literature were far less sophisticated than their predecessors, but far more of them were reached. Many who formerly were suspicious of the illicit publications of "atheists" and "socialists" were now anxious to examine the teachings of the secret *Soiuz* which championed their cause. The *Soiuz Bor'by* circulated large quantities of this literature in addition to their leaflets in the winter and spring of 1895–96. (From January on, the secret press in Lahti was operating incessantly.)

In mid-April, following the Polish precedent (and hoping to duplicate the results), the *Soiuz Bor'by* printed and distributed two thousand copies of a May First proclamation to over forty factories and enterprises (April 18 of the Russian calendar corresponded to May First in Western Europe). The text of this proclamation struck the theme that "all the wealth of the world is created by our hands, at the expense of our sweat and blood," and that in turn "we" are treated as slaves. In addition to the expected appeals for unity and "unflagging resistance" against the "conscienceless exploiter-employers," the leaflet called for "total liberation from their power." By offering vivid descriptions of the movement in other European countries, the proclamation promoted a sense of international

---

28 S. Dikshtein, *Kto chem zhivet?* (Geneva, 1898), pp. 11 and 15.

solidarity and awareness of the Russian workers' need for political rights. In France, England, and Germany, it affirmed, the workers march along the main avenues of the city and the bourgeois governments dare not interfere; uncensored speeches at mass assemblies openly bruit the goals of the movement, such as the eight-hour working day. The leaflet closed with an exultant flourish. "Let us raise our mighty hand and the shameful chains of slavery will fall, the working people of Russia will rise up and the hearts of the capitalists and the government, which always serves and aids them, will tremble!"[29]

Although such passages implied a revolutionary transformation of society and sought to infuse a more militant spirit of class consciousness, it should be noted that they still maintained a somewhat diffuse emotional appeal and avoided the clear formulation of political tasks: the main theme was still the direct struggle with employers, a struggle merely complicated by the interference of the government. Many pieces of agitational literature subsequently put out by so-called "Economists" were far more explicitly "political."

Nevertheless, the reaction to this proclamation was perhaps the best indication that the previous agitation had taken effect. Takhtarev, the best contemporary witness, reported that "many workers subsequently claimed that had it not been for the May proclamation, the summer strikes would not have occurred," although he cautiously notes that "this opinion is probably exaggerated."[30] Professor Pipes, in discussing the textile strikes of 1896, accurately points out that the beginning of the strike took the *Soiuz Bor'by* by surprise, but he goes on to draw the unwarranted conclusion that the role of the Social Democrats in the entire affair was marginal, if not innocuous, and that the workers simply followed their own lights. This is to misunderstand the reciprocal relationship between the two groups almost entirely.[31] It is true that the *Soiuz Bor'by* had little to do with the direct instigation of

[29] Lenin, *Sochineniia*, I, 452. This leaflet was formerly ascribed to Lenin, but M. A. Silvin in his posthumously published memoirs (*Lenin v period zarozhdeniia partii* [Moscow and Leningrad, 1958], pp. 138–40) claimed the authorship for himself. Recent Soviet publications seem to accept this claim. For accounts of the preparation and distribution of this proclamation, see *ibid.*, pp. 138–44 and B. I. Gorev, *Iz partiinago proshlago* (Leningrad, 1924), pp. 20–21.

[30] Takhtarev, *Ocherk*, pp. 25–26.   [31] Pipes, pp. 102 ff.

the strike, which erupted unexpectedly over the question of pay for the coronation days of the new Tsar, or with its rapid spread, which was accomplished mainly by roving bands of workers who by means of pleas, shouts, and hails of stone persuaded workers in other factories to close down. However, the Social Democrats must still be credited with a considerable contribution both in preparing the ground for the strike and in influencing its outcome. First of all, even though the textile workers had been less affected by Social Democratic propaganda than other workers in the capital, leaflets had in fact been distributed in a number of textile plants (the firms of Thornton, Voronin, Lebedev, and Kenig), and rumors of them had certainly circulated in others. As factory inspectors' reports bear out, a large number of textile workers moved frequently from plant to plant and constituted a "restless element."[32] Further, the May First leaflet was distributed in at least seven textile plants; a report from one of them, the New Cotton-Spinning Works, claimed that "because of your May leaflet the workers here began to stir and think about things."[33]

Irrefutable evidence of Social Democratic influence on the workers' demands found its way into a factory inspector's report, which described an incident occurring on the first day of the strike, before the Social Democrats were able to intervene. From a crowd of striking workers an unidentified voice cited, for the benefit of the factory inspector, data from England, Lodz, and the metal plants of St. Petersburg, in support of the demand for legislation to regulate the length of the working day![34] The knowledgeability of the speaker could only have been due to his familiarity with the propaganda pamphlet *Rabochii Den'* (*The Working Day*), which had been widely distributed by the *Soiuz Bor'by* in the early months of 1896. It is quite probable that the circulation of this pamphlet contributed more than any other single factor to the transformation of a disorderly protest over non-payment for

---

[32] See the report of June 7, 1896, in *Rabochee dvizhenie v Rossii*, Vol. IV, part 1, pp. 234–35.

[33] Cited in *Rabochee dvizhenie v Rossi*, Vol. IV, part 1, p. 839 from unpublished archives of the *Soiuz Bor'by*—in all probability the very materials upon which Takhtarev formed the judgment cited above (n. 30). For a list of textile factories where the proclamation was distributed, see Silvin, pp. 141–42.

[34] See Public Prosecutor's report of June 25, 1896, *Rabochee dvizhenie v Rossii*, Vol. IV, part 1, p. 258.

the coronation days into a remarkably coordinated general strike seeking government regulation of the hours of work. The pamphlet submitted graphic "proofs" that low wages, inadequate educational opportunities, child and female labor, poor health, high accident rates, premature mortality, invalidism, and many other ills were "all direct consequences of the length of the working day," and concluded that it was imperative to "bend all our efforts toward attaining shorter working hours." It specifically recommended a ten-hour day (the chief demand of the strikers) and declared that strikes were "the sole means of compelling the government to pass a factory law limiting the hours of work."[35] Consequently, it can be safely stated that *Rabochii Den'* supplied the program for the summer strikes.

The pamphlet was widely circulated not only before, but during the strike from the third day on. Fedor Dan gave a batch of four hundred to representatives of the workers along with the first mimeographed leaflets on June 1 (O.S.); on the following day, another representative of the *Soiuz Bor'by* read it aloud to an assembly of factory representatives and delivered more copies. From June 2 on, representatives of the *Soiuz Bor'by* met almost daily with the strike committee, each time bringing huge piles of leaflets and pamphlets, doling out contributions from sympathizers, and reading aloud instructive propaganda literature.[36] A

---

[35] *Rabochii Den'* (Geneva, 1897), pp. 25 and 31. The pamphlet had been printed in several different versions, most recently by the press in Lahti, Finland at the request of the *Soiuz Bor'by*. For the examples cited by the worker mentioned, see *ibid.*, pp. 7–8 and 30. For references on the wide distribution of this pamphlet in the first half of 1896, see *Rabochee dvizhenie v Rossii*, Vol. IV, part 1, pp. 33, 35, 321, 325, 326, 332 and 334.

[36] *Ibid.*, pp. 330–32. These details, though not to be found in accounts of the strike, are irrefutably established by police reports which give dates, locations, and names. The contacts of the *Soiuz Bor'by* with the strike committee were primarily through Fedor Dan, S. A. Gofman, M. N. Leman, and F. V. Lengnik (the last two were *narodovoltsy* cooperating with the *Soiuz Bor'by*). Constant indirect contact was also maintained through experienced worker Social Democrats from the Putilov works. These points are worth emphasizing because Pipes's account conveys the impression that the role of the *Soiuz Bor'by* was marginal except for printing leaflets, which he claims affected the strike very little (pp. 103–4). He also claims that the agitation of the Social Democrats did little to prolong the strike or to affect its course, which seems to me at variance with both the evidence and logic. Pipes's dates are thoroughly confused, partially due to incorrect transposition from Old Style to New Style, which causes him to telescope the major events considerably (five weeks from the May First leaflet to the end of the strike instead of eight; five days for the strike instead of two weeks). At least the public prosecutor would have disagreed with Pipes: "During the first days of the strike the direct participation of

worker from the Kozhevnikov mill bears witness to the impact: "The more well-read of us got together frequently during the strike in groups of five or more and in some unobtrusive spot read *The Working Day, What Every Worker Should Know,* and *Tsar Hunger.*"[37] There is no doubt that the almost daily appearance of leaflets and the news that monetary support was forthcoming encouraged the workers to remain steadfast in spite of the many stratagems of the government. When a factory inspector showed an assemblage of workers an official telegram enjoining them to return to work, someone shouted from the midst of the crowd: "We don't believe that written stuff! We have our own, and printed at that!"[38]

Thus there are many indications that the *Soiuz Bor'by* made its influence felt and considerably enhanced its reputation in the course of the strike. Although after two weeks hunger obliged the workers to return to work without having gained serious concessions, their spirit was far from broken. The government had promised to review their claims, particularly with respect to the length of working hours, and, in spite of Witte's strict orders to the contrary, many employers hastened to mollify their employees with minor concessions. The workers had clashed repeatedly with the police and troops, they had turned a deaf ear to the appeals of factory inspectors and other government spokesmen urging them to return to work, and they had greeted with derision Witte's leaflet, imitating the *Soiuz,* which claimed that the workers' needs

---

anti-government intelligentsia agitators was not observable, but the rapid spread of unrest among the working masses, embracing the greater part of the textile manufacturing industry of the capital, the uniformity of the demands presented by the workers, the identical pattern of development of each individual strike . . . and finally, the remarkable outward tranquillity of the masses despite their excitement, all point to the fact that the strike grew out of soil prepared by previous criminal propaganda among the workers." (*Rabochee dvizhenie v Rossii,* Vol. IV, part 1, pp. 314–15.) Official government reports repeatedly make this point. See *ibid.,* pp. 237, 254, 615, and 618.

[37] *Ibid.,* p. 285. Cited from "A Worker's Story," an eyewitness account by a participant, originally cited in full by Takhtarev (*Ocherk,* pp. 51–56).

[38] *Rabochee dvizhenie v Rossii,* Vol. IV, part 1, p. 84. Typical of the government's stratagems were: police incursions into the workers' barracks with the liberal application of truncheons; disguising soldiers and policemen as workers and having them file toward the factories at the whistle to give the impression that the strike was over; interrogating and intimidating workers in small groups; luring the workers to choose representatives and then arresting the latter. All this is taken from the above-cited "Worker's Story."

were "just as dear to us" as those of the manufacturers. The agitational leaflets now openly mocked the displays of official helplessness. They boasted that the St. Petersburg workers had stood up to the combined strength of the capitalists and the government, and noted with satisfaction that their strike had won the attention and sympathy of the workers of Western Europe, who were collecting large contributions for their Russian comrades.

In spite of arrests, the impromptu strike committee tried to organize itself on a permanent basis, build up new strike funds, and keep up its connections with the *Soiuz Bor'by*. The worker leaders had been profoundly influenced by their contacts with Social Democratic ideas and sought more permanent, formal identification with the *Soiuz Bor'by*. In the middle of August, however, a series of new arrests removed all the more active workers and intelligentsia, and prevented the realization of these ambitious plans.[39]

The persevering spirit of the St. Petersburg workers became evident when they called for a new strike in the middle of winter (January, 1897) because the government showed no signs of reviewing their demands. Although the government quickly announced that beginning in the middle of April the working day would be limited to 11½ hours, the strike spread and continued for another week, winning additional concessions. A few leaflets were issued, but the *Soiuz Bor'by* had been too weakened by the arrests of the previous autumn to intervene energetically. Even the worker leadership had suffered severely, and as a result coordination and discipline were weaker than in the summer strike. Nevertheless, this new incident served to demonstrate that the government could be forced into concessions by the mere threat of a strike.

The agitational leaflets now made sport of Witte's assurances that the government was "deeply concerned to improve the lot of the workers" and that they should present their demands in a "legal" form. "Ask and it shall be given you," he was mercilessly parodied. "Ask one by one, each for himself; ask the inspector, the

---

[39] For the activities of the *Soiuz Bor'by* and their relations with the new worker groups until the mass arrests of August 11, see Silvin, chap. 10, especially pp. 153–58. That the rosy anticipations of the workers and the *Soiuz Bor'by* were not entirely compatible and that this led to incipient conflict is demonstrated in the following chapter. Here we are simply concerned to establish the marked shift in the workers' psychology as the result of the summer strikes, in general moving along the lines anticipated by *Ob agitatsii*.

police; ask me, your minister."[40] By pointing out that a new law covering working hours had been promised only under the pressure of the first strike, and that a definite date had been set only after the second strike, the leaflets could plausibly argue that "the government only makes concessions to our strength" and that persistent strikes were the only logical means to gain other favorable laws that were patterned after those of advanced European countries and guaranteed the right to strike, to collect funds, and to form unions. Henceforward, the agitational leaflets could attack the government, including the Tsar himself, with impunity, and count on a favorable response. A leaflet of March 6, 1897, drew up an open indictment of the existing political structure.

> The last strike showed us that we have more than one enemy: on the side of the capitalists is the Tsar with his *chinovniki* [bureaucrats]. The tsarist government passes only laws which favor the capitalists. . . . [It] holds in its hands the laws, the courts and the troops with which it prevents all attempts of the workers to cast off the yoke of the factory owners. We need freedom of assembly, speech and press. Our representatives should participate in framing laws to defend our interests. . . . Against the strength of the government we must pose our own strength, the strength of united workers.[41]

This political agitation was kept up intensively during March and April, 1897. The objective was to stage on May First a general strike and mass street demonstration with open revolutionary aims. Once again arrests forestalled these ambitious plans, which in any event would not have succeeded on the desired scale. Nevertheless, the workers of the capital had undergone an extraordinary shift in temperament in space of a single year. Having overcome their awe of the authorities and their mistrust of socialists, they were now prepared to risk direct clashes with the full force of government authority for what they felt to be their legitimate aspirations.

Police reports, memoirs, and "correspondence" published in various illegal organs bear witness to agitational campaigns in other industrial centers of Russia in the ensuing years, although the fragmentary nature of the sources makes it impossible to trace

---

40 *Rabochee dvizhenie v Rossii*, Vol. IV, part 1, p. 545.
41 *Ibid.*, p. 568.

them in as much detail as was possible for St. Petersburg. Typically, such campaigns, after an initial period of trial and error, gained momentum suddenly, continued at a high pitch for a few months, and then waned because of an abatement of strike enthusiasm and the crippling effect of arrests. The available information suggests that for the most part the methods employed in these strikes conformed, consciously or unconsciously, to the St. Petersburg model, even though none of them achieved the spectacular dimensions of their prototype.

At the outset, strike campaigns invariably concentrated on minute issues of factory life and merely inspired general feelings of indignation and comradely solidarity. For example, a Moscow leaflet of July, 1896, exclaimed: "Comrades, we can ease our heavy lot only by our own efforts, by taking up the struggle against the oppression by our bosses."[42] A leaflet of the same year, aimed at the workers of a machine construction plant in Nizhni Novgorod, asserted that "our oppressors humiliate us at every step" and queried rhetorically: "What are we, comrades—serfs or freemen?" It counseled that "if we stick together as comrades, we will get what we want."[43] A police report described the activity of the Moscow *Soiuz Bor'by* during 1897 and 1898 in this way:

> The practical activity of this group conforms to the rules of agitation laid out by the brochure *Ob agitatsii*, which has been printed by the *Soiuz* on hectograph. Pursuing the basic agitational strategy to operate exclusively on the basis of petty needs and demands, the members of the group, having contacted workers of different factories and shops, and having attempted to find out the particular needs of each factory and enterprise, wrote them down as dictated by the workers and then worked them up into a proclamation.[44]

In Nizhni Novgorod, the police report complained that agitation was undertaken, not out of sympathy for the workers, but "exclusively to incite the workers to form a workers' Union, workers' funds, and in general to strike, which was the chief recommendation of the leaflet."[45] The underground newspaper *Rabochaia Gazeta* reported that leaflets, beginning to appear in Kiev in large numbers early in 1897, were creating "quite a stir among the

---

[42] "Iz istorii rabochego dvizheniia," *Krasnyi Arkhiv*, No. 93, p. 142.

[43] *Rabochee dvizhenie v Rossii*, Vol. IV, part 1, pp. 464–65.

[44] *Krasnyi Arkhiv*, No. 93, p. 163.   [45] *Ibid.*, p. 167.

workers" and that "the gendarmes and police spies" were unable to do anything about it.[46] The Geneva publication *Listok Rabotnika* reported on the numerous petty demands, the philippics against the "bosses," and the appeals to concerted struggle of the first agitational leaflets to appear in Ekaterinoslav in the fall of 1898. "More than once we stuck together," said one leaflet, "and more than once we were victorious." The Geneva report commended "the moderation and caution of the Russian Social Democrats" in avoiding political themes in their proclamations, since this was "the right path for the present."[47] Similar reports from Odessa, Tiflis, and Rostov, and minor ripples from still more remote regions (Yaroslavl, Kostroma, Tver, Saratov, and Tula) during the next two years complete the impression of the uninterrupted diffusion of the technique of economic agitation to all corners of the Empire.[48]

Although most of the strike campaigns followed the above pattern, the latent political thrust of the movement can be discerned in the increasingly bold use of Marxist phraseology in the leaflets. This could not have been ventured if it had not been based to some degree on advances in the thinking and mood of the readers. The Moscow proclamations of 1896, for example, made more copious use than St. Petersburg counterparts of terms like "capitalists," "exploiters," and "the tsarist government." Moscow leaflets sometimes pointed out explicitly that Russian laws deprived the workers of the right to strike, to form associations and collect funds, and to print and distribute literature on their needs, whereas the capitalists freely enjoyed such rights. A leaflet of November, 1896, declared that "besides the capitalists we have another enemy—the government, which is the faithful defender of the ruling class."[49]

---

[46] *Rabochaia Gazeta*, No. 1 (August, 1897), reprinted in *Pervyi S'ezd R.S.D.R.P. Dokumenty i materialy* (Moscow, 1958), pp. 248–49. About a dozen such economic leaflets are reprinted in *Rabochee dvizhenie v Rossii*, Vol. IV, part 1, pp. 739–71.

[47] *Listok Rabotnika*, No. 8–9 (November, 1898), p. 17.

[48] The progress of the strike waves can be traced, albeit very imperfectly, in the underground journal *Rabochee Delo*, Nos. 1–10 (November, 1898–March, 1902), which supplanted *Rabotnik* after the break of the young émigrés in the Union of Social Democrats Abroad with Plekhanov and Akselrod.

[49] *Rabochee dvizhenie v Rossii*, Vol. IV, part 1, pp. 381–82. For the text of other Moscow proclamations see *ibid.*, pp. 338–82 and 619–48, and *Krasnyi Arkhiv*, No. 93, pp. 141–53 and 160–63.

In 1897, the Moscow agitation seems to have reverted to pure economics, but by 1899 the leaflets were again stating that the aim of strikes should be not merely higher wages and better working conditions but also the conquest of political rights.

Kiev seems to have introduced political notes into its agitation quite early. A leaflet of March, 1896, declared "we know that the police are just as much our enemies as our employers";[50] and another of 1897, that "the interests of capitalists and workers are irreconcilable." The latter pointed out that the Tsar's troops had shot down workers in Yaroslavl, Lodz, and, most recently, in Dombrovo, Poland, concluding: "Let such a government, stained with blood and violence, rather die. Let the hour strike when we shall be liberated from the yoke of the Tsar's bureaucrats and from the slaughter of his 'glorious troops.' "[51] Another Kievan leaflet of 1897 clearly formulated the issue. *"In addition to the struggle with our employers, the economic struggle, the workers are forced to engage in a struggle with the government—the political struggle."*[52] The strictly economic proclamations of 1898 in Ekaterinoslav were followed by others in 1899 expressing more militant sentiments.

> Comrade workers! Prepare for battle! Organize unions! . . . It will be no easy matter to withstand the attack of both our oppressors, the capitalists and the government.

and:

> Our every struggle with the employers must at the same time be a struggle with the government. We will not lay down our arms until we win: the right to strike, to assemble, to declare our wishes freely, and to defend our interests without fear of being thrown into prison or shot down by soldiers.[53]

Consequently, in spite of reversals and inconsistencies, an unmistakable trend can be observed: first, the emphasis on the struggle for common interests and the need for unity; next, the appeal

---

[50] *Listok Rabotnika*, No. 1 (November, 1896), p. 23.

[51] *Ibid.*, No. 5 (January, 1898), pp. 16–17. After the Yaroslavl disorders were quelled by a regiment of infantry, Tsar Nikolai reportedly sent an ecstatic telegram in which he praised the valor of his "glorious troops."

[52] *Ibid.*, No. 6 (February, 1898), p. 12. (Italics in original.)

[53] *Krasnyi Arkhiv*, No. 93, pp. 182 and 187.

to class consciousness and solidarity against all exploiters; and, finally, the open declaration of specific political goals in the class struggle. These steps had been carefully outlined by *Ob agitatsii:*

> The [economic] struggle . . . teaches the worker to stand up for his own interests, it elevates his courage, it gives him confidence in his own strength and consciousness of the necessity for unity, it places before him more important tasks demanding solution. Prepared thus for a more serious struggle, the working class proceeds to come to grips with these vital questions. The class struggle in this more conscious form creates the soil for political agitation, the goal of which is to change the existing political conditions to the advantage of the working class. The further program of Social Democracy becomes self-evident.[54]

Although *Ob agitatsii* did not specify what changes in the "existing political conditions" should be promoted through political agitation or what form they would assume in the minds of the workers, the practice of Russian Social Democrats led to a very clear answer, formulated in the Ekaterinoslav proclamation cited above: "the right to strike, to assemble, to declare our wishes freely, and to defend our interests without fear of being thrown into prison or shot down by soldiers."

To the extent that political demands were introduced into the agitational literature of this period, they were limited to those specific political and civil rights required to carry on the battle with employers more effectively. Only rarely did they call for the right to elect representatives who would treat with the government or participate in the framing of legislation. The battle cry "Away with the autocracy!" and demands for a democratic constitution were rarely heard until after the "swing to politics" in 1901.

Since the sample of agitational leaflets which are available is so unrepresentative, one might argue that it does not supply a very reliable index to the complexion of the Social Democratic movement as a whole. Moreover, it is not always clear, even from memoir accounts and police reports, how decisive the role of Social Democratic agitation was in stimulating the workers' expressions of protest. The sources do not indicate that on many occasions Social Democratic organizations actually instigated or supervised the conduct of the strikes. It seems evident, however, that,

---

[54] *Ob agitatsii,* p. 16.

contrary to the views of Pipes, Keep, and others, Social Democratic agitational activities helped to give coherence, force, and direction to the otherwise diffuse dissatisfactions of the workers and eventually influenced the latter's whole outlook. Such was the design laid out by *Ob agitatsii* and such was the aim of most groups which sponsored "agitation."

Perhaps the clearest evidence of the success of the Social Democrats in shaping the workers' thinking and preparing them for revolutionary action was the spread and popularization of the celebration of May First.[55] Since the May First campaigns were calculated to demonstrate openly the strength and class solidarity of the workers, they were an inherent challenge to autocratic authority and necessarily reflected the extent to which the workers had absorbed and were prepared to act upon the ideological principles of the Social Democrats. Since the founding of this holiday by the Second International in 1889, small groups of Social Democrats and "advanced" workers had frequently held secret celebrations of the occasion. However, the May First proclamation circulated in St. Petersburg in 1896, the first of its kind in Russia, proved an effective method for promoting the workers' "class consciousness" and encouraging them to open defiance of the political authorities. Henceforward, the technique rapidly spread to new localities and soon became the universal practice of Social Democratic groups. The proclamations themselves assumed ever sharper political—and eventually outright revolutionary—tones; from 1900 on they were invariably accompanied by attempted demonstrations and clashes with the police.

The May First proclamation in St. Petersburg of 1897, in contrast to the calculatedly diffuse belligerence of the previous year's proclamation, explicitly demanded "those basic rights without which a broad struggle is impossible: the right to strike, to assemble, to form unions, and to speak and write openly about our needs, i.e., the freedom of speech and press."[56] In Kiev and Nizh-

---

[55] May First in Russia is treated most extensively by Akimov in a series of articles "Pervoe Maia v Rossii," *Byloe*, Nos. 10, 11, and 12 (October, November, and December, 1906). Additional information is to be found in V. I——n (Ivanshin), "Maiskii prazdnik v Rossii v 1899 g.," *Rabochee Delo*, No. 2-3 (August, 1899), pp. 13–34, and "Pervoe Maia v Rossii v 1900 godu," *Listok Rabochego Dela*, No. 1 (July, 1900), pp. 2–6.

[56] Akimov, *Byloe*, No. 10, p. 177.

ni Novgorod the same year leaflets were distributed explaining in general terms the significance of the "great international holiday of the workers"; in Kiev for the first time in Russia, a group of 530 railroad workers walked off their jobs in recognition of the day.[57]

Two May First proclamations were circulated in St. Petersburg in 1898. The first merely repeated the previous year's call for basic civil liberties: the right to strike "so that every time we don't lose our best fighters" and the right to assemble and organize unions "in which we can confer about our own affairs."[58] The demand for that modicum of political freedom necessary to carry on more effectively the economic struggle against the employers remained for the time being the principal "political" content of the May First agitation in Russia.

The second proclamation, however, did not observe these limits. It was headed by the slogans: "The Eight-Hour Working Day!" and "Political Freedom!" The content was devoted exclusively to contrasting the political freedom enjoyed by the workers in the West with the disabilities suffered by the workers in Russia. Not once did it fulminate against employers—only against the tsarist government. It included among the civil rights to be demanded freedom of conscience and religion, equal rights for all nationalities, and a representative parliament elected by universal, secret, direct, and equal suffrage. It concluded: "By our solidarity we will create a mighty hammer under the blows of which the ancient chains of the autocracy will be shattered."[59] Although this proclamation departed radically in tone and content from the current agitational literature, it anticipated to a remarkable degree the popular slogans of a few years later. At this time, however, it far outstripped the level of political awareness of the majority of workers, and Akimov observed that it evoked little reaction, whereas its companion proclamation, and others of purely economic content, succeeded here and there in precipitating walkouts and strikes.[60] Although 1898 was a difficult year for the Social Democrats because of the nationwide arrests following the First

---

[57] Ibid., p. 179.

[58] Full text in Listok Rabotnika, No. 8 (June, 1898), pp. 15–18.

[59] Full text in ibid., No. 9–10 (November, 1898), pp. 41–43.

[60] Akimov, Materialy, p. 52.

Congress of the party, May First proclamations are known to have appeared in Tiflis and Ekaterinoslav.

The St. Petersburg proclamation of 1899 (printed by *Rabochaia Mysl'*), although it mentioned political rights in passing, reverted primarily to bread and butter demands, the chief of which was regulatory legislation protecting the health and welfare of the worker. In the meantime, however, a number of provincial groups —in Kiev, Kostroma, Saratov, Moscow, Ekaterinoslav, Rostov, and Kharkov—had taken up the precedent of the capital in stipulating political demands. In addition a special May number of the new émigré underground organ, *Rabochee Delo,* was circulated in many localities. The May campaign in Kharkov was probably representative in its impact:

> The success was tremendous: at many factories they talked about quitting early, they gathered in small groups and conferred. They even tried to stop those who wanted to keep working, but no one took the decisive initiative. May, 1899, was also marked by meetings outside the city numbering up to 150 participants; there were speeches on the significance of May First and the special problems of the workers' movement. Discussions arose on tactical questions, on workers' funds, libraries, circle propaganda, agitation, etc. These assemblies reverberated with the singing of revolutionary songs and left a deep impression on all who were present.[61]

The Kiev Committee of the party (a designation assumed since the abortive First Congress of March, 1898) for the first time in Russia made preparations for a mass street demonstration. Although the attempt was forestalled by arrests on the eve of the planned event, heavy patrolling of the streets and industrial districts by mounted Cossacks advertised the cause with sufficient eloquence. The Kievan organ *Vpered* gave the following account:

> May leaflets, distributed in huge quantities at literally every factory and industrial firm and even in the craft establishments of the city and its environs obliged the authorities in spite of the many arrests to take additional measures in case the workers should attempt to celebrate May First. In the city rumors circulated about an unheard of "workers *bunt*," occasioned, as it turned out, by the police. A declaration of Dragomirov [the police chief] posted at the time

---

[61] *Rabochee dvizhenie v Rossii,* Vol. IV, part 2, p. 616. Reprinted from *Rabochee dvizhenie v Kharkove* (Geneva, 1900).

of the student disorders [a few weeks earlier] that it was forbidden to congregate on the streets . . . was reposted. Day and night the streets were patrolled. . . . On May First itself patrols were assigned to each factory.[62]

In the western border regions of the Empire, the Polish, Jewish, Latvian, and Lithuanian Social Democratic groups succeeded in staging street demonstrations of ominous proportions. In Vilna, over a thousand workers gathered in a public park to unfurl a red banner and chant "Away with the autocracy! Long live political freedom!" In Warsaw, a similar demonstration drew several thousand participants, and in Libau it initiated a general strike lasting ten days.[63]

Henceforward, mass arrests and elaborate security measures by the military were to characterize the approach of May First in the major industrial centers of Russia. In 1900, the days leading up to May First in Kiev, Rostov, and Ekaterinoslav were marked by hectic activity: proclamations were printed in huge quantities, signals and marching plans were drawn up, and placards and red banners bearing slogans were hastily fabricated. The authorities responded with searches, mass arrests, and Cossack patrols in the streets.

The tone and slogans of the May First literature were now considerably more militant and tinged with class sentiment. In St. Petersburg, for the first time in Russia proper, a leaflet circulated in five thousand copies raised the cry: "Away with the autocracy! Long live political freedom!"[64] Other proclamations continued to call for the right to strike and freedom of assembly and the press, sometimes adding a demand for some form of representative government. Solidarity with the aims and achievements of the workers' parties of Western Europe was repeatedly emphasized. Although the focus still remained on the workers' cause, the language was becoming increasingly that of a fiercely disaffected class acutely aware of its potential strength and spoiling for an open battle with the prevailing order. The St. Petersburg proclamation gave voice to the new spirit:

---

[62] Cited in *Rabochee dvizhenie v Rossii*, Vol. IV, part 2, pp. 147–48.

[63] All this information is from works referred to in note 55, above.

[64] Akimov, *Byloe*, No. 11, p. 79.

Our factory owners and their obliging government are deathly afraid every time our May holiday approaches. . . . The government is not disturbed in vain: over the entire Russian land the Russian worker is rising to do battle. Now here, now there we celebrate our bright holiday. Our Polish comrades have celebrated it in Western European style three times [i.e., with street marches], the Jewish and Lithuanian workers also. . . . Comrades, let's show the capitalists and their despicable government that we are a real force, that the St. Petersburg worker has awakened and understands that he must do battle; the best proof of this will be our celebration of May First. . . . Let them hear from the workers' own lips a spirited indictment of their deceits, oppressions, robberies and violence.[65]

It was quite clear that the movement had arrived at the threshold of a new phase of its existence.

In Kharkov, where the local Social Democratic organization had made few or no preparations, the workers took matters into their own hands. Several thousand of them marched from factory to factory around the outskirts of the city, singing and proudly bearing improvised red banners. The arrest of some of the demonstrators touched off a general strike which closed down most of the factories in Kharkov and involved 11,000 workers. A demonstration in front of the jail persuaded the flustered Governor-General to release the workers, after which the movement subsided.[66] This was a harbinger of what was to happen all over Russia in the next few years. Its significance was well understood by the police official who drew up a report of the affair:

> These particular qualities of the factory worker [his permanent status as a city dweller, cut off from the "healthy influence" of the village] make it easy to arouse in him dissatisfaction with his situation and with the social structure, which the enemies of the existing order have recently exploited, regrettably with considerable success. . . . An investigation of the disorders revealed that the workers acted as a result of the influence of proclamations which have been widely distributed of late by various Social Democratic circles, since they have followed the program which these circles recommended. The investigation also indicates that the workers in the present case were by no means the blind tool of evil-minded

---

[65] *Listok Rabochego Dela*, No. 1, p. 2.

[66] See accounts in *Rabochee Delo*, No. 7 (April, 1900), pp. 35–39 and *Listok Rabochego Dela*, No. 1, p. 3.

persons, but that many of them [workers] had consciously thought out what they wanted, firmly adopted a program of action, and exhibited perseverance and discipline in executing it. This, I venture to say, is a very dangerous symptom.[67]

The review of May First agitation in Russia offers a very important perspective on the development of Social Democracy in this period. The workers' movement grew steadily in numbers, geographical scope, and political and class self-consciousness. In the course of five short years all industrial centers of any consequence had undergone the first throes of economic agitation, and had given birth to a mass workers' movement susceptible to the ideological and political influence of Social Democracy. Even the group enjoying the worst reputation for Economism, *Rabochaia Mysl'*, had by 1901 accepted agitational slogans which would have seemed too radical to the St. Petersburg *stariki* of 1895.[68]

The years 1899 and 1900, the blossoming time of "Economism," according to Lenin's periodization, saw no abatement of this process. The proletarian "giant" had indeed been aroused and provoked to do battle with the forces which bound him. But was he the creation envisaged by the Marxist theoreticians? Would he of his own accord play the historical role that this generation of Russian revolutionaries anticipated? The Social Democratic intellectuals regarded themselves as the conscious vanguard of an ineluctable historical process and the legitimate leaders of its driving social force, the proletariat. By articulating the "class interests" of the latter, the intelligentsia assumed that the position of "leadership" was assured to them. This was true enough when the worker was taking his first steps, but what would he do when he discovered his ability to walk on his own? What would be the role of a "heap of idealists" once hundreds of thousands of workers became aware that the liberation of the working class was to be a task for the working class itself? To such questions *Ob agitatsii* provided no answer. The next two chapters will be devoted to the painful encounter of the intelligentsia with the reality of this dilemma.

---

[67] "Pervomaiskaia stachka 1900 g. v Kharkove," *Krasnyi Arkhiv*, No. 93, pp. 193–94.

[68] See pp. 149–50.

CHAPTER 4

The Workers'
Bid for Self-Liberation

THE Russian Social Democratic movement encompassed two distinct social elements: a segment of the disaffected educated classes, the Marxist wing of the traditional intelligentsia, and a new worker elite or "worker intelligentsia" trained by the former in propaganda circles. In theory, these two groups shared a common world view and were engaged in a common task which allowed of no social or hierarchical distinctions. "Democracy" implied that an individual's rights and obligations within the movement were to be determined solely by his talents and his commitment to the goals and ideology of the movement irrespective of class origin.

Nevertheless, differences in social background and unexpressed nuances of aims and values could not be so easily effaced. In a quite genuine sense the two groups were "exploiting" each other. The restless radical intelligentsia sought "roots in the masses" to overthrow absolutism and achieve their socialist Utopia; the workers sought a means to enter the broader world of culture and break the shackles of their social position. In the era of *kruzhkov-shchina*, the intelligentsia's adopted role as *Kulturträger* among the masses and the workers' Promethean longing for the oracles of "science" had complemented each other in such a way that the

89

inherent tensions between them tended to be glossed over. Similarly, when agitation was introduced, the workers were disarmed by the intelligentsia's concern for their immediate grievances and its categorical avowal that the liberation of the working class was the task of the workers themselves.

Such agreement on a program of action, however, could not remove the underlying division: expressions of workers' distrust of the motivations of the intelligentsia marked the entire history of relations between the two groups and frequently took on an embittered tone. Workers' groups were constantly springing up in opposition to the regular Social Democratic organizations; hardly a single local situation remained unaffected. At precisely the moment when the Social Democratic intelligentsia achieved maximum success in shaping a politically-oriented class psychology among the great mass of workers, the worker leadership's reaction against the tutelage of the intelligentsia reached crisis proportions, threatening a permanent rupture. By the end of the *Iskra* period in 1903, the rupture was a fact: workers either tried to do entirely without intelligentsia support or left the movement in despair. Many workers succumbed to the allurements of Zubatov's police socialism and later of the Gapon movement. Both the Mensheviks and Bolsheviks in the period 1903–5 maintained only tenuous contacts with workers, and then principally with younger, more hotheaded types rather than with the tempered veterans of the movement.[1]

The roots of the chronic tension between the *intelligenty* and the workers become clear when one examines the social and structural context of their mutual association. The first and most salient fact to be observed is that, even for the Populists before the advent of Social Democrats, the conditions of underground propaganda work imposed a certain natural division of labor between worker and intelligentsia participants. The workers assumed those tasks which they could perform most easily without attracting the attention of the police—recruitment, safekeeping of books and literature, handling of funds of mutual aid, and furnishing secret quarters for propaganda sessions. The intelligentsia, for their part, served as propagandists, supplied and reproduced literature, com-

---

[1] For references on this point, which is likely to meet with objections, see notes 58 and 60, pp. 251 and 253.

municated with groups from other localities, raised money, and secured subsidiary help from sympathizing outsiders. Enjoying relatively more leisure and mobility, the intelligentsia performed tasks requiring special technical capacity or the coordination of efforts, whereas the workers confined themselves primarily to smoothing the path for intelligentsia propaganda in their own milieu. Initiative and decision-making roles devolved quite naturally upon the intelligentsia; at the best the workers served in an advisory capacity, but more often they simply carried out the directives of the leaders of the intelligentsia. The imperative of maintaining secrecy prevented workers and *intelligenty* from meeting together except at propaganda sessions; they therefore communicated only through designated representatives who observed the prescribed conspiratorial precautions.

As long as the scale of operations was small, this division of functions seemed normal and evoked no conflict. The workers regarded their teachers with veneration and quite spontaneously looked to them for guidance. As the work grew in scope and the number of *kruzhki* multiplied, the intelligentsia leaders were faced with ever more complex organizational problems. The result was that local groups periodically developed elaborate organizational hierarchies with subdivisions into factory districts and separate collegia with specialized functions (literary commissions, propaganda staffs, fund-raising groups, technical groups for printing). The shift to agitation brought no basic differences into this pattern, but simply added new elements of complexity, such as agitators' assemblies and special groups for turning out leaflets.

Despite infinite variations in different localities or at different times, the fundamental structural pattern or "constitution" which had evolved in the Populist era was almost universally carried over by the Social Democrats. The most characteristic feature was the formation of a "directing center" by a relatively small number of the more experienced *intelligenty* who perpetuated themselves solely by co-optation. Occasionally an experienced worker was included, but more often not. The activities of the center and its make-up were kept strictly secret from the "periphery," that is, not only from the workers, but also from the countless students and intelligentsia sympathizers who served in auxiliary capacities. Often an individual might be performing an important function, such as raising funds or directing several propaganda circles, and remain totally ignorant of the scope of the organization, or of the participation of his best friend. Each person from the center kept his finger on a certain operation and bore full responsibility for it without confiding details to his comrades.

The counterpart to the intelligentsia center was always a "workers' committee" composed of *kruzhki* or factory district representatives (again depending on the scale of operations). The worker representatives on this committee were usually not elected, but "selected" by the directing center from the more experienced workers. This method was felt to be necessary to ensure the caliber of the committee and as protection against police informers. The policy did not necessarily lead to conflicts, since in the majority of cases a particular worker obviously stood out from his fellows and was easily acknowledged by both parties as their spokesman. Communications were almost universally maintained by an intelligentsia representative on the workers' committee. That the workers were seldom granted representation on the intelligentsia center underscored their subordinate position. The normative "constitution" of local Social Democratic organizations, therefore, came to be a "bicameral system" vesting all decision-making authority in a highly restricted, self-perpetuating "upper house." The "lower house" remained at best advisory and more often was treated along with other special groups of the "periphery" as a mere "executory" organ.[2]

No matter how it may have been justified for reasons of maintaining secrecy, this sealing off of the directing group from its subordinate counterpart became with the passage of time a major source of conflict. The *intelligenty* of the periphery, if they performed their appointed tasks faithfully and well, could count on being eventually co-opted into the center; workers, on the other hand, could entertain no such hopes. Any grievance or misunderstanding, therefore, could easily spill over into resentment over their inferior status. Despite the pretensions of the intelligentsia

---

[2] The language of the author–participants often reflects their attitudes. For example, the notion that *rukovodstvo* (leadership, direction of policy) was the natural function of the intelligentsia will find repeated confirmation in this chapter. For the terms "advisory" (*soveshchatel'nyi*) and "executory" (my rendering of *ispol nitel'nyi*) as applied to workers' organizations, see Martov, p. 272, and "Rabochee dvizhenie v Moskve," *Rabotnik,* No. 3–4 (1897), pp. 35–36.

center of "directing" the workers' movement, the more active workers were necessarily better acquainted with their fellow workers' mood and conditions in the factories. Although one of the duties of the workers' committee was to collect information and forward it to the center, the center frequently misunderstood it and made miscalculations. Consequently, the workers became impatient with intelligentsia fumbling and attempted to penetrate the inner circle for more direct influence on the course of events.[3] Added to this was the danger that the workers would appeal to the "periphery," which, anxious to become more directly involved in affairs, might turn a willing ear. The very structure of local organizations, therefore, invited rebellions from below, which indeed often occurred.

A passive role could not in the nature of the case satisfy the workers for long. Even if they were inclined at first to look on the *intelligenty* as the bearers of enlightenment and the final authority in all things, unpropitious arrests often left them as sheep without a shepherd. The Moscow worker Prokofev describes the panic which broke out among neophyte workers when their intelligentsia leaders were suddenly arrested in 1894: "I was depressed, sick, and ashamed. I was left without leaders. This was an irreparable blow. When I told my comrades we groaned and sat around as at a funeral."[4]

The arrests of their leaders forced the workers to be more self-reliant and resourceful. Gradually they came to realize that they could perform many tasks themselves without depending on the *intelligenty* for guidance, that despite temporary interruptions the "center" would eventually get in touch with them and things would function normally again. (There was always one person, relatively above suspicion, who was entrusted with all the vital information concerning the organization; in the event of arrests he simply put the survivors back in touch with each other.) Prokofev and his comrades concluded that "there was nothing to do but to

---

[3] The following is a typical instance of worker dissatisfaction with the intelligentsia's leadership: "We sometimes received strike instructions from the center, but they were very vague, and did not always take into account the particular conditions of a factory; so the workers carried out their own plans according to their own experience." (From a memoir fragment of a worker, N. Nemchinov, in the Moscow organization; in *Na zare rabochego dvizhenie v Moskve*, p. 169.)

[4] *Ibid.*, pp. 112–13.

hold out and continue the work ourselves. So we set out and began to work on our own." Once they had become accustomed to "working on their own," workers were far less inclined to submit unquestioningly to commands from above.

The periodic absences of intelligentsia leaders because of arrests, the threat of arrests, or simply semester vacations at the university, allowed the workers periodically the free exercise of their organizational talents. The most typical expression of the workers' own initiative was the organizing of funds of mutual aid, the *kassy*. Although references in the memoirs to the origin of the *kassy* are few, the evidence suggests that the workers usually founded and managed them separately from the funds of the intelligentsia center, sometimes without the latter's foreknowledge or approval.

These funds became quite popular among the workers and served as a convenient means of recruiting new members into the *kruzhki*. Each worker in a given *kruzhok* or group of *kruzhki* would contribute so many kopeks per ruble of his monthly earnings to a "kitty" which served his particular factory or industrial district. This kitty was then administered by an *elected* cashier. When a workers' committee or some equivalent was sufficiently firm, a given share of these local funds might be pooled into a central workers' fund and specific "regulations" worked out for their use. The workers' *kassy* sometimes contributed to the treasury of the intelligentsia and vice versa. During the period of *kruzhkovshchina*, the funds were employed chiefly to purchase literature and to aid the families of discharged and arrested workers. With the introduction of agitation they were easily converted into strike funds, which considerably enhanced the workers' ability to wrest the initiative from the intelligentsia.[5]

The *kassy* easily became the focus of workers' attempts to liberate themselves from the tutelage of the intelligentsia. In the spring of 1894, the St. Petersburg workers decided to establish a citywide "United Fund" that apparently was to supplant the Workers' Organization, which had maintained a precarious existence since the dissolution of the Brusnev organization. Babushkin gives the following account of its inauspicious beginnings.

_____

[5] For the texts of the regulations of several workers' funds see Nevskii, *Ocherki*, pp. 655–58, *Rabochee dvizhenie v Rossii*, Vol. IV, part 1, pp. 122–24, and *Listok Rabotnika*, No. 9–10 (November, 1898), pp. 51–52.

I well remember the resolution on the St. Petersburg Workers' Fund, which was to become the chief organ of all the district workers' funds, and which was composed of a certain percentage of their collections; the aim was to give money to the arrested and, in the case of need, to come to the rescue of the poorest district funds. A big argument broke out over the fact that the intelligentsia had plenty of financial means, whereas the workers' *kassy* were empty, and we had plenty of urgent needs with no funds to cover them. Many workers insisted on getting money from the intelligentsia and became rather worked up about it, which somewhat surprised me. . . . Finally, it was decided to take 100 rubles from the intelligentsia and put it into the workers' fund.[6]

The hapless representative of the intelligentsia apparently had no alternative but to yield to the will of the workers.

The distrust bred by such differences easily led to outbursts of hostility against the intelligentsia. Babushkin describes how at a meeting in a forest the following summer the intelligentsia leadership was roundly upbraided for leaving on summer holidays just when things were beginning to stir. One of the orators launched into a diatribe against the *burzhuaznost'* and "upper class habits" of the intelligentsia:

Imagine, gentlemen, that tomorrow representatives arrive from abroad or from another city and ask for our *intelligenty*, the leaders of our movement. . . . Excuse us, gentlemen, our leaders have left for the holidays, because in winter they became worn out and must recover their health—oh yes, and to store up more knowledge at their holiday leisure.[7]

The absence of the intelligentsia was all the more tactless because they had talked a good deal in the spring about setting the work on a new footing through agitation at the factories and thereby had imparted a sense of expectancy to the propagandized workers.

The intelligentsia, for their part, heartily distrusted the *kassy*, regarding them at best as means to an end, not as ends in themselves. When the workers displayed too much independence in handling the *kassy*, the intelligentsia tended to detect in them ideological shortcomings of one sort or another. Consequently, the leadership often attempted to intervene and control the *kassy*

---

[6] Babushkin, p. 57.   [7] *Ibid.*, p. 68.

operations, particularly with respect to how the funds should be disbursed. Such interference could only occasion hard feelings on the part of the workers, who had come to view the *kassy* as peculiarly "theirs." When the center of the Moscow *Rabochii Soiuz* decided early in 1896 to unite all regional *kassy* into one central fund under its own direction, a few regional groups raised strong objections, especially those representing the skilled workers. The Bolshevik Liadov, who in his early days took part in this controversy, interprets it retrospectively thus:

> Here two irreconcilable world-views met head on. The defenders of the local funds stood for trade-unionism; they regarded the funds, not as instrumental to the class struggle, i.e., as an organizational and agitational weapon, but as an end in themselves.[8]

When Martov inquired upon his arrival in St. Petersburg why no workers had been drawn into the center, his comrades replied that the older workers grouped around the United Workers' Fund opposed the new methods of agitation and were preoccupied with their intellectual development, whereas the younger ones, eager to introduce agitation, were as yet too inexperienced to maintain the necessary conspiratorial precautions.[9] The *intelligenty* were probably somewhat biased in their assessment of worker attitudes, for Babushkin recalls that many workers were in favor of the new ideas. The leaders of the United Workers' Fund, for instance, "talked about how the movement was proceeding too quietly and that it was necessary to strengthen it by some new method as yet untried and on a much broader scale."[10] Sometime later, when the *stariki* were about to embark on their agitational campaign, they called together representatives of the *kruzhki* to secure their cooperation. The workers apparently listened to the intelligentsia's plans with interest, but when the question arose of how best to organize the workers for the new mode of activity, the conflict in organizational conceptions and attitudes erupted to the surface.

> They [the representatives of the Neva Gate district] insisted on the organization of a united independent workers' fund and in support of it declared it to be the most effective means of bringing together

---

[8] Liadov, I, 53. For another account of this same incident, see "Rabochee dvizhenie v Moskve," *Rabotnik*, No. 3–4, pp. 36–37.

[9] See Martov, pp. 270–72.   [10] Babushkin, pp. 68–69.

the workers from the outside. Representatives of the intelligentsia, rejecting the idea that this was a suitable way of uniting the workers, suggested that all money should be turned over to them and put into a Social Democratic Fund out of which it would be disbursed to district groups when needed for a certain purpose.[11]

The workers in this case were overruled; individual districts were allowed to have their own strike funds, but the "Workers' Committee" was to confine itself to collecting information for the center and otherwise assisting in agitation.

In the wake of the strikes of 1896 and 1897, *kassy* again became very popular among the workers of St. Petersburg. (By that time, the old United Fund was gone, most of the leaders having been arrested.) The idea was revived of using the *kassy* to mobilize the entire working population of the capital. Several projects along these lines found their way into the archives of the *Soiuz Bor'by*. The characteristic argument was this:

> We must press relentlessly forward, gathering around us a huge force, but for this we must attempt to make use of those atoms of freedom already in our possession and enlarge them with the least possible sacrifices. How can we achieve this? . . . The first and foremost step in this direction must be the organization of workers' *kassy*.[12]

The workers drafted such a plan and requested the *Soiuz Bor'by* to print it for them. This unexpected development put the intelligentsia leaders on the spot, since their own plans were hardly compatible with those of the workers. In the workers' scheme, the *kassy* were to constitute the framework of the entire organization. Representatives from the *kassy* and the intelligentsia were to form one responsible body supervising all the work in St. Petersburg, whereas the intelligentsia as a separate group were to perform purely technical functions as directed by the worker-dominated whole.[13] Debates over these organizational issues dragged out into

---

[11] Takhtarev, *Ocherk,* p. 21.

[12] *Ibid.,* pp. 64–65.

[13] By this time both the intelligentsia and workers' groups had undergone nearly a complete turnover since the previous winter, and thus the "organizational" problem had to be faced anew. In the summer of 1896, because of the strikes, the guiding spirits of the *Soiuz Bor'by*, Silvin and Lengnik, were faced with the problem of a large influx of active workers. They apparently were willing to sanction the workers' demands, even to the extent of vesting leadership of the *Soiuz Bor'by* in

the fall and winter. A few members of the directing center of the *Soiuz Bor'by*—Iakubova, Takhtarev, and Katin-Iartsev—supported the aspirations of the workers (within certain limits); Gorev, Radchenko, Potresov, and others rejected the proposed innovations and upheld the "old constitution."

While locked in bitter wrangling over this question, the central group managed to arrange a meeting with the *stariki* (Lenin, Martov, and others), who were freed for a few days early in 1897 to "settle their affairs" in St. Petersburg before departing for their Siberian exile.[14] Lenin, chief spokesman for the *stariki*, subjected the workers' proposals to sharp criticism. According to Martov, who supported Lenin, the critics feared that the workers' project would "bind the directing core in all its attempts to expand the channel of its revolutionary activity beyond the limits of a purely trade-union struggle." Leadership of the "professional workers' movement" by the Social Democratic intelligentsia, they reasoned, was not an end in itself, but a "strategical formula to bring about in the most expeditious manner a direct struggle with the autocracy."[15]

Gorev, who presided over the proceedings, represented as follows his own and Lenin's position:

> In my report I touched upon the incipient controversies within the *Soiuz*—the tendency toward "worker-philism" and playing at democracy; these questions were evoking considerable discussion, not to say passion. Lenin, the chief spokesman of the *stariki*, pounced on these "innovations" very sharply and decisively. Already he displayed all the peculiar traits of his character and thinking: on the one hand, confidence in the validity of his own position and, on the other, faith in the revolutionary-theoretical infallibility of a self-perpetuating group of professional revolutionaries, which he regarded as the nucleus of the future party. Lenin was against any sort of autonomous workers' organizations as such; [he was] against

---

a body of elected representatives of the workers. This is instructive, considering the fact that Silvin later became a Bolshevik and a blind admirer of Lenin. See Silvin, pp. 153–60. Arrests in August of that year precluded the realization of these plans, and the vexing question was left open.

[14] In addition to the versions cited below, there are references to these controversies in Lenin's *Chto delat'?* (*Sochineniia*, IV, 387) and in N. Katin-Iartsev, "Teni proshlago," *Byloe*, No. 25 (1924), pp. 116–17.

[15] Martov, pp. 316–17.

allowing the workers any function of control, etc. He said: "If there are any conscious individual workers deserving of confidence, let them come into the central group and that's all. No other *Arbeiter-politik* is necessary."[16]

The Bolshevik Gorev was perhaps overanxious to see in this early episode the historical Lenin in full stature; however, the "worker-phile" Takhtarev also discerned here the outlines of Lenin's later ideological physiognomy:

> She [Iakubova, his future wife], like myself and several other comrades, was of the opinion that the *Soiuz Bor'by* must serve the workers' movement with all our strength, but not necessarily lead it at every step. Vl. Ilich, on the other hand, saw the chief aim of the *Soiuz Bor'by* in just that, i.e., in unquestioned "leadership." In this instance, as always, he was thoroughly consistent.[17]

Unlike Gorev and Radchenko, Lenin did not oppose the admission of workers into the central group per se; he simply insisted that such workers be well-informed Social Democrats in basic agreement with the policies of the Social Democratic leadership and that they be "selected" for their role by the center itself.

The "worker-phile" faction not only strongly favored worker participation in the center, but argued that many workers now displayed organizational capacities on a par with the intelligentsia and were therefore entitled to manage their own affairs. While acknowledging that the workers were very much attached to the name of the *Soiuz Bor'by* (because of the previous summer's strikes) and by no means wished to desert its banner, they pointed to a suppressed resentment against the *Soiuz's* leadership by the more capable workers. If their aspirations were not met half way, the "worker-philes" warned, then "in the near future we may have to reckon with the deplorable fact that some of the most conscious workers will desert the *Soiuz* and operate independently."[18] Their suggestion was to draw several representatives chosen by the

---

[16] Gorev, p. 37.

[17] Takhtarev, "Lenin i sotsial-demokraticheskoe dvizhenie," *Byloe*, No. 24 (1924), pp. 14–15. Takhtarev's account is based on the testimony of Iakubova (his wife), who was present at the confrontation. Takhtarev had already fled abroad to avoid arrest. In his *Ocherk*, he includes a long account of the affair which was undoubtedly written by Iakubova herself.

[18] Takhtarev, *Ocherk*, p. 68.

workers' committee into the center immediately, and to make the workers' project for a network of *kassy* the basis for further discussions on organizational reforms.

An immediate radical solution to the dilemma proved to be unnecessary. Shortly after the departure of the *stariki,* the center decided to co-opt two of the ablest workers, but the workers' project as such was rejected. It is doubtful whether this compromise would have satisfied all parties, but once again mass arrests intervened, crippling normal activities for some time. The entire proworker contingent in the center was swept away, and the center's plan to co-opt the workers was dropped.

Although it left no immediate traces, this episode unveiled two diametrically opposed attitudes toward the goals and character of Social Democracy which eventually crystallized into the well-known divisions within the movement. In retrospect, nearly all the participants expressed such an opinion. To be sure, Takhtarev and Iakubova contested Lenin's claim that the controversy foreshadowed the later one between *Iskra* and the Economists. Their view was that "political" as opposed to "economic" goals were not at issue here, but rather organizational democracy and encouragement of the workers' initiative, to which, theoretically, all Social Democrats were committed.

However, Lenin's characterization (in *Chto delat?*) of the "two basic tendencies" in Russian Social Democracy was much broader than the issue of "Economism." The one he described as the "adulation of spontaneity" and the pursuit of the "tail-end" of the workers' movement (*khvostizm*), which he specifically equated with the position of the "worker-philes" of 1897. Inevitably, in Lenin's view, such a viewpoint resolved itself into narrow trade unionism. The other viewpoint, that of *Iskra* and its followers, upheld the principle of "consciousness," which to him implied the imperative to maintain leadership over the workers' movement for the theoretically disciplined Social Democratic elite, the "professional revolutionary" vanguard.[19] It can scarcely be disputed that precisely these two opposing attitudes found their expression in the controversy under discussion. The *stariki* and Gorev were seeking to preserve an organizational structure which would en-

---

[19] For the pertinent passage from *Chto delat?*, see his *Sochineniia,* IV, 387 ff.

trench the Social Democratic intelligentsia in a position of leadership and to this end were prepared to thwart the aspirations of the more ambitious workers. The faction represented by Takhtarev, Iakubova, and Katin-Iartsev, on the contrary, assumed that the spontaneous course of events would follow the channel marked out by Marxist analysis, and therefore the leadership could be surrendered without qualms to democratic control by the workers. Bolshevism was to carry on with Lenin's banner of elitism, whereas Menshevism, albeit with considerable vacillation and inconsistency, eventually became the champion of "worker initiative" and party democracy.

The deep-rooted sociological basis of the conflict was borne out by the frequent recurrence of such incidents. An almost identical controversy had arisen earlier in the Moscow movement, in the autumn of 1894. Mitskevich offers the following version:

> Several comrades felt that a central workers' committee, composed of representatives of all factory *kruzhki* and supplemented by a few *intelligenty* who engage directly in propaganda work should serve as a collective to lead the whole workers' movement in Moscow. This central circle should gather material for agitational leaflets and brochures and give directives for the whole organization. . . . Others objected that the workers were insufficiently prepared, and that it would be particularly questionable to surrender the conspiratorial part of the enterprise to such a large circle. . . . They even considered the formation of such a central circle to be unconspiratorial, since it might lead to the complete liquidation [by arrest] of the whole organization. The affairs of the organization, according to these comrades, should be directed by a central *kruzhok* of fully tested people, who would co-opt the most well prepared and experienced comrades, both workers and *intelligenty*.[20]

Mitskevich also believed that these differences foreshadowed the subsequent differences between *Iskra*-ites and Economists, and between Mensheviks and Bolsheviks. He observed that Sponti, a partisan of the former view, left the Social Democratic movement entirely, whereas the proponents of the latter view, Mitskevich, Liadov, and Vinokurov, remained Bolsheviks and members of the party to the end of their days. Mitskevich's account reduces the conflict to purely theoretical terms, to differing viewpoints on the

---

[20] Mitskevich, p. 175.

organizational question among individual members of the intelligentsia center. The hostility of Prokofev's circle to intelligentsia leadership and Liadov's suspicion of workers' *kassy*, however, suggest that here, as in St. Petersburg, the theoretical controversies reflected pressure from below on the part of the workers. The basic source of the difficulty in these disputes was not the peculiar "elitist" conception of Lenin and a few other proto-Bolsheviks, but an inherent contradiction within the Social Democratic movement itself. Social Democratic "consciousness," which even Plekhanov conceded should be an offspring of the class struggle itself, could be maintained only by violating the commitment to "democracy." The intelligentsia covertly feared that the "elective" principle would bring the less "conscious" workers into positions of leadership, but few of them were hardy enough to explicitly recognize the source of their fears. (Lenin was an exception.) Thus the upsurge of initiative from below could only provoke ambivalent reactions on the part of the most Social Democratic committeemen, as the Gordian knot could be cut only by deciding in favor of either "socialism" or "democracy." The Social Democratic intelligentsia projected an image of the movement and their own role within it which simply did not correspond to historical reality.

So far, the problem of worker-intelligentsia relations has been presented as it appeared in the critical years 1894–97. This approach violates historical perspective somewhat, as it could easily be demonstrated that the basic sociological problem in all its dimensions had already arisen in Populist circles and had vexed the groups of Tochiskii and Brusnev, and probably other early Social Democratic groups as well.[21] Although interesting details might come to light, such a demonstration would not essentially alter the

---

[21] See Franco Venturi, *Roots of Revolution* (New York, 1960), chap. 19, and Pipes, chap. 1. Pipes deserves credit for being the first of present-day scholars to examine this interesting sociological question. However, as previously noted, he is inclined to exaggerate the independence of workers from intelligentsia tutelage. On the other hand, that is far less serious an error than to overlook the phenomenon of worker initiative entirely, of which nearly all accounts by both Soviet and Western scholars have hitherto been guilty. Impressed by the phenomenon, Pipes tends to view the "labor movement" as entirely independent of the Social Democratic movement all the way through the 1890's, although he has difficulty maintaining a consistent picture on the basis of his own evidence. Part of his problem is that he draws general conclusions from the rather restricted scope of his own investigations, which cover only the St. Petersburg movement and break off arbitrarily at the beginning of 1897.

image of the problem at the beginning of the period under investigation. The same is perhaps true of the incidents and crises which recurred in never-ending waves in numerous localities for the balance of the century. However, a brief survey of some specific local situations will help to formulate general conclusions for the period as a whole. In Ekaterinoslav, Kharkov, and Odessa, conditions may be studied rather closely because good documentation is available.

Ekaterinoslav

Social Democratic activity in Ekaterinoslav during the years 1898–99 was typical for the rapidly expanding industrial centers of the South. Here the intelligentsia and worker "centers" were built up independently by the arrival of exiles from older industrial areas. In 1897, the forces of the intelligentsia were still suffering from the effects of arrests which had liquidated the group of Leiteizen and Mandelshtam in 1895; the survivors were barely able to keep in touch with a few individual workers and helpful outsiders. In the meantime, workers who had participated in Social Democratic organizations elsewhere streamed into Ekaterinoslav and lost no time in putting their experience to work. One group, consisting of Jewish artisans and *poluintelligenty* from Vilna and Vitebsk, quickly organized a network of craft funds, transplanting the techniques familiar to them from the Jewish movement.[22] Babushkin from St. Petersburg needed no instructions from the intelligentsia on methods of organizing agitation. He soon grouped around himself a small core of veteran Social Democratic workers employed in the gigantic new industrial plants and set about finding the local Social Democratic intelligentsia for help in printing leaflets and securing funds. (He did not doubt for a minute that the latter group existed.) This aid was not long in coming; by early 1898, Babushkin's group had established a smoothly-functioning apparatus for distributing agitational leaflets, which soon stirred the workers of Ekaterinoslav to life.

---

[22] See the memoirs of I. I. Vilenskii, "Iz vospominanii partiinago tipografa" in *Istoriia ekaterinoslavskoi sotsial-demokraticheskoi organizatsii*, pp. 78–93. Craft workers in Ekaterinoslav, as in many other urban areas of southern and southwestern Russia, were primarily Jewish.

Babushkin and his Workers' Committee maintained a rather self-assured, condescending attitude toward the handful of local *intelligenty*. In his reminiscences he casually remarks that "the *intelligenty* were a rather unstable lot, easily carried away; but that could do harm only to them, not to our workers."[23] He often derided their carelessness in habits of conspiracy or their rosy socialist convictions.

> I inwardly had to smile at the naïveté of this overzealous *intelligent*, an impetuous but superficial socialist, who was prepared to sacrifice himself without reservation for the sake of his ideas. Nevertheless, there was no point in shaking his faith, as he was a valuable man in Ekaterinoslav.[24]

Obviously Babushkin and his comrades regarded themselves as masters of the situation; they simply made use of the services of the well-meaning intelligentsia for their own, the workers', cause.

Meanwhile, the intelligentsia succeeded in forming their own organization with its own "center."[25] Several exiled Social Democrats, including Petrusevich from Kiev, Orlov from Poltava, and Lalaiants from Penza, came to the aid of two young comrades, Zelikman and Dunaevskaia, who had kept a few former ties intact. It was not long before the question of the relationship of their group to the existing workers' organizations became the topic of lively discussion. As in St. Petersburg and Moscow, the intelligentsia divided into opposing camps over the issue. The veteran Social Democrats, Lalaiants and Orlov, insisted on the "complete subordination of the workers' groups to the common tasks of the *Soiuz*" by which they meant the abrogation of the workers' existing autonomy. Zelikman and Dunaevskaia favored encouraging the workers' initiative and independence.[26] Petrusevich and a few

---

23 Babushkin, p. 89.

24 *Ibid.*, p. 98.

25 Babushkin's account of the Ekaterinoslav movement is nicely supplemented by M. Zelikman, "Ekaterinoslavskii Soiuz Bor'by za Osvobozhdenie Rabochego Klassa 1895–98 gg.," *Letopis' Revoliutsii*, No. 6 (Kharkov, 1924), pp. 171–81. Zelikman was a participant in the intelligentsia group whose inner sanctum Babushkin was unable to penetrate. The memoirs of Babushkin's fellow workers G. Petrovskii and I. Shevchenko add little except to note that Babushkin exercised a "firm dictatorship" over his small group and that they knew very little of affairs outside of it. See *Istoriia ekaterinoslavskoi*, p. 53.

26 See Zelikman, *Letopis' Revoliutsii*, No. 6, pp. 175–76. A thoroughly schooled Marxist theoretician, Lalaiants, like many of the older generation, was preoccupied

others favored a mediating position and contrived a compromise arrangement. Their formula for reconciliation, as in St. Petersburg, was that two workers should be co-opted into the directing center. Such an agreement was apparently worked out with the Jewish workers' group, because two representatives from it were accepted into the intelligentsia circle.

Relations with Babushkin's group, however, continued to be tense and undefined. At the First Congress of the party (March, 1898), Petrusevich alone represented the Ekaterinoslav organization, even though the invitation recommended two representatives from each locality, one *intelligent* and one worker. In his memoirs, Babushkin vented his indignation over this slight.

> It was clear to me that the intelligentsia had committed an impropriety and had acted in bad faith, even criminally, toward the workers in sending a representative only from the "city" [the intelligentsia center], since previously not a word had been breathed to the workers about representation at the congress.[27]

Although as a matter of "discipline" Babushkin made no protest at this time, it is clear he considered his group as the official "Committee" of the Ekaterinoslav organization and the intelligentsia as the "periphery." Arrests following the First Congress again threw his workers' group on their own resources, but before long the arrival of a new contingent of exiled Social Democrats resurrected the issue anew. Babushkin's account of the situation is worth quoting in full.

> It turned out that a group of such *intelligenty* [newly arrived Social Democrats] formed their own committee in the city. Our committee at first knew nothing about the new organization, which, of course, wanted to take the leadership of the work on itself. It seemed rather strange when the old (I will call it workers') committee functioned well, when it met every week, discussed various questions and put out leaflets, that another separate committee should be formed which refused to be satisfied with fulfilling the directives of the workers'

---

with conspiratorial secrecy and systematic propaganda (like Radchenko in St. Petersburg). Lalaiants' own memoirs, *U istokov bol'shevizma* (Moscow, 1934), are singularly uninstructive for this period of his career.

27 Babushkin, p. 89. He could not know that the Jewish group had been offered representation, but had surrendered their vote to the *intelligent* Petrusevich. Had he known, he would have been even more indignant. See *Istoriia ekaterinoslavskoi*, p. 90.

committee, such as securing literature and funds and printing leaflets which we had drawn up. . . . The *intelligenty* wished to take over the writing or at least the editing of leaflets and the leadership of the movement in general. On these grounds various incidents arose in the workers' committee, provoked by the representative of the "city," i.e., of the intelligentsia committee. The incidents at first were trivial and quickly settled; but gradually they took an unpleasant turn. . . . I remember that the *intelligenty* often criticized the unliterary language of the leaflets, and finally one was shortened and somewhat altered by the "city" committee. This provoked a direct clash, which threatened to lead to a complete break between the workers and the intelligentsia. The intelligentsia declared that they might refuse to perform the technical work of printing leaflets, to which the workers replied that they would run off leaflets in their own quarters and thus would no longer need the services of the intelligentsia.[28]

After prolonged negotiations, a compromise was worked out which, in effect, recognized the entrenched prerogatives of the Workers' Committee. The idea of a unified committee consisting of equal numbers of workers and intelligentsia was rejected by the intelligentsia group as too likely to attract the attention of outsiders. The existing "bicameral" system received formal sanction, but to balance the intelligentsia representative on the Workers' Committee, a representative of the Workers' Committee was entitled to attend sessions of the intelligentsia group. Both committees were entitled to "originate legislation," that is, to compose leaflets, but approval of the final text and the determination of its appropriateness belonged to the Workers' Committee. Also the intelligentsia representative in the Workers' Committee could not be changed without the latter's consent.

These elaborate arrangements reestablished peace and removed friction for the time being, but only at the price of surrendering to the importunities of the workers. However, this formalization of the "constitution" brought about but a brief interlude in the conflict between the "two principles of government." Several even more virulent clashes were to take place in Ekaterinoslav in the years to come.[29]

---

[28] Babushkin, p. 110.   [29] See pp. 220 and 242–44.

There was a curious sequel to this crisis. After the normalization of relations with the intelligentsia, Babushkin became a strong partisan of party regularity. However, as the work grew in scope in the following two years, splinter groups inevitably formed, including a new "workers' opposition" with a fierce anti-intelligentsia bias. The delicate mission of persuading them to submit to "party discipline" fell on Babushkin. Ironically, he was greeted by them, not as a fellow worker, but as an emissary of the intelligentsia. Although in this situation he managed to reconcile the dissidents, it proved how even the most careful efforts to arrive at constitutional stability could not arrest the undertow of worker independence and hostility to intelligentsia leadership. In his efforts to establish "regularity," Babushkin also felt the lash of this undertow.[30]

Kharkov

The Kharkov movement has been illuminated by only fragmentary documentation. The early organization of "morally perfect" Social Democrats headed by Lipkin-Cherevanin (later a famous Menshevik) was still a typical provincial intelligentsia group of Social Democracy's period of gestation.[31] The introduction of agitation was not attempted until 1899, when this sleepy provincial backwater was suddenly transformed into a booming industrial center.

As in Ekaterinoslav, the impetus toward large-scale activity among the masses came from Social Democrats and workers exiled from other centers. O. A. Ermanskii (Kogan), one of the newly arrived *intelligenty*, describes in his memoirs the difficulties of the intelligentsia committee with workers of the "Ivanovo-Voznesensk type," who, in his words, "reflected the low level of cultural and political development of the textile workers of that region."[32] Thus he explains their inclination to "Economism" and "trade unionism." Ermanskii's account is marred by his obvious attempt to exonerate himself retrospectively for his reputed opposition to *Iskra's* "political" tendency and bears little relation to

---

[30] See Babushkin, pp. 136–37.

[31] See Nevskii, pp. 473 ff.   [32] Ermanskii, p. 50.

historical reality. Fortunately, other sources reveal the inaccuracy and superficiality of his characterization.[33]

An early account of the Kharkov movement touches briefly on the "workers' opposition."

> The distinctive feature of this organization was its negative attitude toward the intelligentsia, which it reduced to a purely subordinate role. "It's your job to supply literature and money, the real work we will do ourselves," the worker leaders told the intelligentsia.[34]

To a second group it attributes similar views, "compounded with other traits—in particular, with the cult of the 'strictly workers' movement.'" These brief references would exhaust our knowledge of the Kharkov situation, had the police not employed an effective network of agents and informers. According to these sources, the worker Makhov wrote to an old acquaintance from Ivanovo-Voznesensk, who had been trying to persuade him that even seasoned workers needed guidance from the intelligentsia:

> The question of the relations of workers and the intelligentsia is no small matter—it is a question of principle which it is impossible and unforgivable to ignore. We have to realize that our interests and those of the intelligentsia are not one and the same; and if there is a common element (political freedom), then this is not the main thing. We must not be taken in tow by them, but go along of our own free will only to the extent we find it expedient. Otherwise we will be led along a path contrary to our own interests.[35]

The worker socialist Makhov was simply drawing a logical inference from the principle of class egoism which he had learned in propaganda circles to justify his ingrained suspicion of the intelligentsia's motives.

Makhov and another worker, Ioffe, were credited by the police with working out a "program," a set of organizational regulations, a course outline for the propaganda *kruzhki*, rules of conspiracy,

---

[33] Two of the workers concerned, Evdokimov and Makhov, were thoroughly schooled in the propaganda circles of Ivanovo-Voznesensk which acquainted their pupils not only with the doctrines of Marx, but also those of Darwin, Spencer, and Kant. See M. Bagaev, *Za desiat' let* (Ivanovo, 1930), p. 36 and *passim*.

[34] *Rabochee dvizhenie v Khar'kove* (Geneva, 1900), p. 10.

[35] "Delo khar'kovskogo sotsial-demokraticheskogo rabochego Soiuza remesliennikov," *Letopis' Revoliutsii*, No. 4 (Kharkov, 1923), pp. 207–8. From a police document dated March 15, 1900.

and an order of business for an "Assembly of Workers' Representatives."[36] The police recorded meetings of fifty to sixty workers in
the forest, where speeches were delivered on the workers' life in
Western Europe and on the necessity of political rights and freedom. Makhov and Ioffe were also suspected of distributing the
leaflets which began to appear in the Kharkov factories, but proof
was lacking. If the police sources are accurate, the workers were
doing quite well without the benefit of "leadership" by intelligentsia. (To be sure, they undoubtedly received some help from
individual *intelligenty*.)

Nevertheless, the inevitable debate arose in the intelligentsia
center over the necessity of supervising the workers' activities.
Young students from Kharkov University were dissatisfied with
merely conducting propaganda circles and executing technical
commissions; they claimed the right to direct strikes and offer guidance to the workers. "One of the accused," a police document reported, "expressed the opinion, on the basis on facts known to him
from the life of Western European and Russian workers, that they
[the workers] are incapable of formulating their own demands by
themselves." "Everywhere," it cited the conclusion of the speech,
"the workers are guided by the intelligentsia."[37]

Doctor Trutovskaia, the experienced old hand who held the
reins of secret communication in her hands, defended the workers'
prerogatives and forbade any interference in their affairs; the students, of course, accused her of "despotism." Thus she exercised a
role that was parallel to, but the reverse of Stepan Radchenko's
role in St. Petersburg. The "Grand Conspirator" in Kharkov was a
"worker-phile," and the "youngsters" sought to assert the leadership of the "revolutionary intelligentsia."[38] In the winter of 1900
the "workers' revolution" in Kharkov was totally successful, and

---

[36] Iasha Ioffe was a Jewish artisan from Vitebsk who had departed from his
native region in order to become involved in the Russian movement. He later became
active in the Odessa organization where his abilities were highly valued. Garvi gives
a detailed sketch of his character and life in *Vospominaniia sotsial-demokrata*, pp.
101–3.

[37] *Letopis' Revoliutsii*, No. 4, p. 204.

[38] The shift in roles was not accidental. Kharkov was beginning "agitation" just
as the ferment in the universities was marking the revival of "politics." The students were anxious to draw the workers directly into the revolutionary struggle
against the autocracy. This new atmosphere, paving the way for *Iskra's* dramatic
success in winning the loyalty of party *praktiki*, is discussed in chaps. 7 and 8.

the organizational structure of the St. Petersburg *Soiuz Bor'by*, the pioneer Social Democratic organization in Russia, was stood upon its head. The Kharkov Committee was so out of touch with the situation at the factories that the first mass workers' political demonstration in Russia, the May First demonstration in Kharkov of 1900, took them completely by surprise.[39] Somehow the workers were able to keep pace with intelligentsia leadership in advancing the "pivotal new tasks" of the movement.

Odessa

Although Odessa Social Democrats boasted of one of the first organizations to establish extensive ties among the workers (the group of G. Tsyperovich and Iurii Steklov-Nekhamkes) and in principle endorsed agitation very early (through the efforts of the Vilna missionary Aizenshtadt), they suffered throughout the nineties from provocateurs and frequent arrests. Hence, they were unable to undertake anything more than intermittent propaganda work, primarily among the Jewish artisan class.[40] By 1900 the prerequisites for full-scale Social Democratic work based on agitation were at hand—a large contingent of experienced workers who had participated in the movement in other parts of Russia, a rich reservoir of organizational cadres among the frustrated, young Jewish *poluintelligenty*, and widespread economic discontent due to the recession which had hit this port city particularly hard.

When P. A. Garvi entered the newly formed Odessa Committee of the party late in 1900, work was being carried on at a dizzy tempo. Odessa was quickly catching up with the most advanced centers of Russia in the diversity and scope of its activity—extensive propaganda work, frequent strike campaigns, funds of mutual aid, elaborate security arrangements, regular communications with other party centers, and even preparations for a local party newspaper (*Rabochee Slovo*—only one number of which appeared in late 1901). The Odessa organization which directed this pro-

---

[39] See Ermanskii, pp. 51–52.

[40] On the Odessa organizations in the early 1890's see Nevskii, *Ocherki*, pp. 316–20 and Polevoi, pp. 477–89. On the mid-1890's there are short memoirs by several participants in the collection *K dvadtsatipiatiletiiu pervago s'ezda partii (1898–1923)* (Moscow, 1923).

fusion of effort conformed to the normative pattern of Social Democratic groups at the peak of their development. The highly secret "Committee" perpetuated itself by co-optation, presiding over a staff of propagandists and a "periphery" for technical functions and reserve members. The workers were organized into two "Agitators' Assemblies," one for craft workers and another for factory workers. The Committee kept the assemblies under its control by hand-picking their membership and by delegating one of its own number to attend the assemblies' sessions.[41]

Soon after his admission to the Odessa Committee, Garvi was invited (unofficially) to attend a celebration by the workers of one of the Agitators' Assemblies in honor of a departing comrade. The only *intelligent* present, he was dumbfounded as, one after the other, the workers rose up to denounce the intelligentsia:

> The speeches began with rather transparent references to the "dictatorial habits" of the Committee and of *intelligenty* in general; they emphasized that in a workers' movement the workers should be the leaders, and that such an outstanding worker as their departing comrade, Leo the tailor, couldn't get along with the Odessa organization.[42]

It turned out that the workers were thoroughly dissatisfied with their subordinate position and were preparing a "revolution." The meetings of the Agitators' Assemblies became very stormy—the workers demanded no less than a total reorganization of the local structure on the "elective" principle. The Committee first agreed to allow the representative of the Committee in the Agitators' Assemblies to be elected by the latter, but this did not satisfy the opposition.

The Committee pleaded the necessity of strict conspiracy, which in its view made the election of worker representatives inadvisable. The situation seemed to have reached an impasse, when clear evidence of a provocateur in the workers' midst strengthened the arguments of the intelligentsia. The workers agreed to abide by the old order of things. Garvi's reflections on the incident undoubtedly expressed the thinking of many intelligentsia participants of the period.

---

[41] For the organizational structure of the Odessa Committee, see Garvi, pp. 23–25.

[42] *Ibid.*, p. 109.

The Committee emerged the victor in this conflict. But we weren't overjoyed with our victory—we knew that the conspiratorial practices of the underground, forced on us by the prevailing police regime and constituting for us a sort of "categorical imperative," stood in contradiction with our cherished conviction that "the liberation of the working class must be an affair of the working class itself," and that a Social Democratic party, even at the early period of its development, must be constructed on the principles of initiative and worker autonomy.[43]

The existence of a chronic workers' opposition making use of the most cherished slogans of Social Democracy was a source of continuous embarrassment and qualms of conscience for the Social Democratic *praktiki*.

St. Petersburg, 1899–1900

Following the crippling arrests of August, 1896, no citywide workers organization existed in St. Petersburg for nearly four years. The St. Petersburg *Soiuz Bor'by* consisted of a never-ending succession of groups whose motley history will be touched upon in later chapters. Some of these groups, in particular those associated with the underground newspaper *Rabochaia Mysl'*, adhered to the "strictly-workers'" ideology. Although *Rabochaia Mysl'* was founded by two splinter worker groups in late 1897, these groups were soon liquidated, and "worker-phile" elements of the intelligentsia took over both *Rabochaia Mysl'* and the leadership of the *Soiuz Bor'by*. About a year later a proclamation appeared in the underground press in the name of a St. Petersburg group called "The Self-Liberation of the Working Class'" (*Samoosvobozhdenie Rabochego Klassa*). Although few data of significance are available on the group, its temper is very clear from the content of the proclamation:

The ardent revolutionaries honor themselves by mistake with the title "Ideologue of the proletariant." . . . Into their organization, their *Areopagus* so to speak [i.e., the Committee], least of all are admitted the very ones whose interests [they] presume to "defend."

---

[43] *Ibid.*, p. 112.

. . . The workers must finally take their own cause into their own hands.[44]

Ironically, at precisely this time the intelligentsia Committee was dominated by professed "worker-philes," and *Rabochaia Mysl'* was its official organ.

In the winter of 1899–1900, the St. Petersburg movement reached a low point: nearly all the existing groups were liquidated by mass arrests. However, when in the autumn of 1900 the few surviving *intelligenty* began cautiously piecing together the slender organizational threads, they discovered that the workers had indeed "taken their own cause into their own hands." In the course of the summer, a Workers' Organization had come into being that had drawn up a set of by-laws and an elaborate plan of organization and action; by winter, one of its participants claimed, it embraced the majority of the "conscious" of St. Petersburg workers.[45]

According to the plan, leadership was to be exercised by a "Workers' Committee" made up of representatives of district committees (the Obukhov, the Narva, the Vyborg, and so on), which in their turn were to represent numerous workers' *kassy* in the factories. The memoirist of the group avowed that the Workers' Organization aimed at strict autonomy and sought to make use of the intelligentsia only for specific services. Although an *intelligent* was allowed in their midst for purposes of communication with the *Soiuz Bor'by*, the workers accepted no "directives" from him; on the contrary, they used him to deliver their requests to the intelligentsia. This representative, a convinced "worker-phile" and Economist, obligingly forwarded their demands.

The group was further distinguished by its emphasis on strict

---

[44] "Vozzvanie gruppy samoovobozhdeniia rabochikh," *Nakanune*, No. 7 (July, 1899), p. 80. To my knowledge, the only references to this group in the literature are a polemical barb by Lenin in *Chto delat?* (*Sochineniia*, IV, 394 ff.), and a brief passage in N. P. Paialin, *Zavod imeni Lenina 1857–1918* (Moscow, 1933), pp. 78–80, which does little more than list the names. Of course, several members of the group were "worker-phile" students.

[45] Most of the information on this group is taken from K. Semenov, "Pervyi god peterburgskoi 'Rabochei Organizatsii'," *Minuvshie Gody*, No. 7 (December, 1908), pp. 264–95. For a parallel account of the St. Petersburg *Soiuz Bor'by* of this period, less well informed on the Workers' Organization, see A. V. Logacheva-Piletskaia, "Soiuz Bor'by za Osvobozhdenie Rabochego Klassa v 1900–1901 gg.," *Byloe*, No. 27 (1925), pp. 93–107.

conspiracy, its insistence on the elective principle, and its antipathy to the intelligentsia. *Rabochee Znamia* and the other St. Petersburg groups of "political" hue were roundly taken to task.

> The second number of *Rabochee Znamia* we regarded as the perfect embodiment of fine-sounding intelligentsia verbiage, which completely fails to take into account the interests and level of development of the workers.[46]

The ideology of the Workers' Organization was summed up by its chronicler in this way:

> The workers must construct the organization themselves, they must run their own affairs, since "the liberation of the workers is a task for the workers themselves." . . . It is necessary to maintain the purity of the workers' movement from any influence by "fellow travelers" [*poputchiki*], with whom the workers have "a common path from St. Petersburg to Moscow," but beyond that their ways part. . . . Genuine ideologists of the working class from the bourgeois milieu are as rare as "white crows."[47]

The author confessed, however, that the actions of the group did not follow the original design in practice. With the deepening industrial crisis of 1900–1901 and accompanying unemployment, it became increasingly difficult to persuade workers of the value of the *kassy*, the pivotal point of the organizational structure. It was not always possible to follow the principle of strict elective democracy because of the frequent interruption of communications and lack of initiative from below. In such situations, the Workers' Organization appointed the regional representative, who might be not a worker but an *intelligent*. The Committee soon became aware of the dangers of infiltration by provocateurs, who never failed to display initiative. With the lull in strike fever, the workers' program of action became outmoded, and involuntarily they followed the lead of the intelligentsia in staging political demonstrations.

Their only success seems to have been their discipline in matters of conspiracy. After the events of March, 1901, most of the intelligentsia organizations were severely hit by arrests, whereas the Workers' Organization remained intact. The fever of political protest which had seized the intelligentsia now overtook them.

---

[46] Semenov, p. 269.   [47] *Ibid.*, p. 267.

Scathed by *Iskra* (the first issues were just appearing) for refusing to participate in the March demonstration, they attempted to make up for it by planning an ambitious May First campaign. Mass arrests on the eve of the anticipated demonstration swept away the Workers' Organization, but the preliminary agitation had stirred up enough feeling to provoke a series of disturbances climaxing in the famous "Obukhov Defense," in which workers for the first time in Russia erected barricades and defended themselves by force.

In the course of six or seven years the workers' movement had grown from a handful of isolated propaganda circles in scattered localities to a mass movement fully prepared for revolutionary action. The underlying disparity between the workers' aspirations for self-liberation and the intelligentsia's pretensions to leadership, however, had found no resolution. The experienced workers had proved that they were perfectly capable of replacing the intelligentsia in mobilizing the workers for large-scale strikes and May First processions—indeed, in this matter the intelligentsia groups had become almost superfluous by 1901—but their attempts to form an effective "opposition" seldom proved self-sustaining. The unending flux in organizational arrangements imposed by the contingencies of police harassment meant that old battles had to be fought ever anew. And the intelligentsia organizations, however pitiful in numbers and talent, could not be cured of the impulse to monopolize the "leadership."

The worker elite, despite their sallies of proletarian chauvinism, were never able to sever entirely the umbilical cord which linked them more to the intelligentsia than to the untutored masses. The intelligentsia had brought them into being, created them in their own image, and hovered over them as relentlessly as a jealous parent who refuses to acknowledge that its progeny has matured. The worker had proved his competence in the sphere of the practical day-to-day conduct of the struggle, but in the sphere of values and further perspectives for the movement he still needed to replenish himself at the wellsprings of socialist ideology. Moreover, this ideology viewed the workers' movement in essence as an international political movement, expressed through representation in the Socialist International. But the organizational and co-ordinating efforts needed to make this a reality were beyond the capacity of even talented workers, who were physically and mentally bound to the factory milieu. Even when the workers showed themselves capable of completely replacing the intelligentsia in local work, party statesmanship and all larger ventures had to be left up to the intelligentsia.[48]

In the changed political atmosphere of 1901, the mutual alienation between workers and intelligentsia became ever more acute. Even those *intelligenty* who sympathized with the workers' aspirations deserted them to join the general assault of "society" on the autocracy. The workers, though also supporting this assault, lost the reputation they had formerly enjoyed as the sole revolutionary force whose cause was equated with that of the nation. On the contrary, their own identity was obliterated in the wider national effort.[49]

Furthermore, the new era altered the character of intelligentsia groups: the return flood of exiles from Siberia, the increased harassment by police, and *Iskra's* advocacy of the concept of "pro-

[48] I have treated above those instances which are best illuminated by the sources. However, there is hardly a single center of Social Democratic activity which did not encounter similar tendencies. Dissident workers' groups and controversies over the "worker question" arose at various times in Kiev, Tiflis, Ivanovo-Voznesensk, and Tula. The references are: "Doklad Kievskogo komiteta," *Vtoroi S'ezd R.S.-D.R.P. Protokoly* (Moscow, 1959), pp. 644–45; S. T. Arkomed, *Rabochee dvizhenie i sotsial-demokratiia na Kavkaze* (Moscow, 1923), pp. 81–84; *Rabochaia Mysl'*," No. 8 (February, 1900), p. 1 (Proclamation proposing an all-Russian congress of workers' organizations to be represented exclusively by workers); and "Otchet Tulskogo Komiteta," *Vtoroi S'ezd*, pp. 603–4. The same phenomenon is observable in the history of the Bund. B. Frumkin described the Jewish movement around 1897 as follows: "A great change took place in the relations between the Jewish masses and the leading instances of the movement. . . . The demand for [applying] the elective principle to all institutions, responsibility before the organized masses, and for overturning of the sway of the intelligentsia were the slogans of the day. . . . In a short time this opposition assumed a mass character. . . . It embraced all cities and localities where the movement existed." ("Ocherki iz istorii evreiskago rabochego dvizheniia," *Evreiskaia Starina*, No. 5 [April–June, 1913], sec. II, p. 260.) In the early Social Democratic circles of Georgia the upholder of the "old constitution" was quite possibly Stalin. Trotsky attributes to him the following speech (cited from Arkomed): "They [those who favored admission of workers into the Committee] flatter the workers; I ask you, are there among you one or two workers fit for the Committee? Tell the truth, placing your hand on your heart!" (*Stalin: an Appraisal of the Man and His Influence* [New York, 1941], p. 30.) I agree with Trotsky that the style, at least, is that of the man whom Deutscher describes as the "committee-man *par excellence*."

[49] For further discussion of the worker question in the *Iskra* period, see chap. 8, pp. 218–21 and 241–44.

fessional revolutionaries" gave rise to a new type of underground figure, one who moved from place to place, used a false passport, constantly changed lodgings, and subsisted on "party" funds. This meant that the local committees became the property of small bands of conspirators who entered and left the organizations with scarcely a whisper, never remaining long enough to develop attachments, or even to acquaint themselves with the local workers' groups. These conspirators devoted all their energies to winning support for the *Iskra* line, distributing its literature, and attacking the dead horse of "Economism." The workers' organizations, often commanding a membership of several hundred, grew increasingly hostile to the impenetrable intelligentsia committees, which often consisted of not more than a half a dozen persons. Once more there were rebellions, vigorous denunciations of the high-handed Committees, and attempts to "go it alone," but again for the most part the efforts foundered. Confused and embittered, many experienced workers drifted out of the movement, surrendering their places to younger comrades who were caught up in the tense political atmosphere, but only vaguely conversant with Social Democratic ideas.

After the Second Congress of the Party in 1903, the Social Democratic intelligentsia became ever more absorbed in its intramural squabbles and remained almost totally unaware that it had lost the ties that once firmly bound it to the working class. It had foolishly squandered the rich capital which had been accumulated through years of dedicated efforts. A certain amount of sensitivity and tact could undoubtedly have done much to ease the breach; but this would have required yet another reorientation in the psychology of Russia's wandering fraternity of social renegades. This was not to come until after the upheaval of 1905, and then only in the Menshevik camp.

CHAPTER 5

The Journal
of Workers' Thought

THE workers' attitudes examined in the previous chapter manifested themselves in sporadic outbursts and only rarely achieved sustained organization or expression in print. It was not that the workers had no such ambitions, but that the worker groups lacked the resources, connections, and leisure time of their intelligentsia counterparts, while at the same time suffering as much as the latter from periodic arrests. The workers could hope to succeed in the enterprises they initiated only if they were aided by friendly elements of the intelligentsia.

Although the necessary ingredients were present in varying proportions in other localities, only *Rabochaia Mysl'* in St. Petersburg brought them into fruitful combination. Not only was it easily the most successful undertaking of the underground press in this period (from 1898 to 1902, sixteen issues appeared with a fair degree of regularity), but by and large it can be taken for what it purported to be—an "organ of the St. Petersburg workers," a sounding board of their feelings and discontents. It is true that the technical and editorial functions from the third issue on were taken over by sympathizing *intelligenty*. The project had been initiated and set on its feet by workers, however, and even under intelligentsia patronage the voluminous correspondence from the

118

industrial districts of the capital imparted to the publication its characteristic stamp. Moreover, the contributions of the intelligentsia diligently sought to mirror the temper and wishes of their readers. Within limits, *Rabochaia Mysl'* was a monument to the striving of the workers of this period to register their own thoughts and find their own orientation in their surroundings, unhampered by the "guidance" of the intelligentsia.

No recounting of the history of *Rabochaia Mysl'* can ignore the fact that it already occupies a fixed place in the conventional image of the early Social Democratic movement. This has been largely due to the fact that Lenin seized upon it in his polemics of the *Iskra* period (especially in *Chto delat'?* of 1902) as a symbol of the "opportunistic tendencies" in the movement. Lenin's astute oversimplifications have entered unretouched into nearly all available historical treatments of this period. This is unfortunate, not only because certain of his distortions have been uncritically accepted, but also because some of his genuine insights have been insufficiently appreciated. (Lenin should be credited with more, not less, historical acumen than Western scholars ordinarily accord him.) Sweeping generalizations, particularly those propounded for political effect, are bound to skirt certain historical issues and do violence to others. Therefore, this chapter aims not so much at "refuting" the Leninist version (though this will be done where necessary), as at reconstructing the story of *Rabochaia Mysl'* more fully in the hope that such an account will facilitate sounder, more enlightened judgments.

The very origin of *Rabochaia Mysl'* validates its credentials as a workers' enterprise. Two worker groups loosely connected with the St. Petersburg *Soiuz Bor'by* were involved in the beginings of *Rabochaia Mysl'*. The initiative probably belonged to a circle of workers headed by Vasilii Poliakov at the Obukhov Ingot Steel Works, whom Takhtarev characterized as dissatisfied with the leadership of the *Soiuz Bor'by*. Little is known about this Poliakov group except that its members were very hostile to the intelligentsia and that they were encouraged in their endeavors by a few students on the periphery of the *Soiuz Bor'by,* among them two medical students from Takhtarev's former circle (N. A. Alekseev and N. A. Bogoraz), and a teacher at the Obukhov Sunday School

(N. Korsak–Kulazhenko).[1] With their help, the Obukhov workers managed to put out a proclamation in late 1896 advising their fellow workers to "stop getting drunk and start fighting for improvement in our situation."[2]

Concerning the second group, a few interesting data have been preserved. Early in 1897 a handful of workers who had participated in the St. Petersburg strikes of 1896 resettled in Kolpino, a sprawling industrial complex outside St. Petersburg administered by the Admiralty where they formed a group of their own. Arrests of the preceding year had effectively severed their relations with the Soiuz Bor'by, except that two intelligenty holding positions as clerks in the factory administration provided the Kolpino group with occasional leaflets and literature, although they did not otherwise become involved in Kolpino activities.

In view of its isolation and meager resources, the vigor and improvisations of this new group were remarkable. They won the respect of their fellow workers by staging an audacious celebration of May First under the very noses of the authorities. Several hundred workers boldly marched through the Kolpino settlement singing revolutionary songs and displaying a makeshift red flag. To be sure, the procession dispersed quickly when the unsuspecting guards recovered their senses and seized some of the demonstrators. The reputation of the workers' group was solidly established by the ensuing police investigation, which, in spite of lengthy interrogations, failed to uncover the ringleaders.[3]

Encouraged by this success and the influx of new recruits, the daring conspirators sought new ways of stirring up the masses. The guiding spirit, I. A. Andreev, asserted that they soon could count on dependable adherents in every shop or division of the

---

[1] S. Zavialov, Istoriia izhorskogo zavoda (Moscow, 1934), p. 171.

[2] Ibid., p. 157.

[3] There are two excellent accounts of the Kolpino group by worker participants: Ia. A. Andreev, "1897–98 gg. v Kolpine," Proletarskaia Revoliutsiia, No. 14 (March, 1923), pp. 77–85 and I. K. Mikhailov, Chetvert' veka podpol'shchika (Moscow, 1928), pp. 8–20. The Zavialov, a secondary account, also supplies many interesting details drawn in all likelihood from police and factory inspectors' records and interviews with old-timers. However, its usefulness is marred by the complete lack of references to sources and heavy interlarding with Stalinist glosses. See pp. 150 ff. See also brief references in Akimov, Materialy, pp. 47–64 passim.

huge complex.[4] He guided a number of study circles himself according to a prescribed program of readings (probably worked out by helpful intelligentsia), which included the writings of Marx, the legal journal *Novoe Slovo,* and an ample supply of popular pamphlets. One of Andreev's fledglings, I. K. Mikhailov, claimed that drunkenness and fighting in the settlement were soon a thing of the past—a doubtful assertion, but characteristic of the new climate.[5] A member of the Andreev circle was deputized to sound out contacts at the Obukhov works in the city and soon he brought back the leader of the Obukhov circle, Poliakov, who outlined to them his own group's plan for a worker newspaper. The newspaper was to be organized and staffed only by workers, so that they could voice their own concerns and inform each other about conditions at their particular factories.

The Kolpino group readily volunteered to co-operate; they agreed to handle the collection of material, while the Obukhov group was to take care of the editing and printing. Although pursuit by the police held the project up for a few months, it was completed by the end of 1897. Andreev zestfully recounts their venture.

> Such as we were, so was our newspaper. We set about it unsystematically and impulsively, totally ignoring the prevailing Social Democratic tendency. Our approach to reality was purely pragmatic without a scrap of scientific evaluation. The *Soiuz Bor'by* apparently did not then have the resources to extend their influence over us, and we were a stubborn group of self-styled bumpkins [*samorodki*]. And this was the character of our newspaper. It combined revolutionary ardour with an everyday common sense judgement as to how the workers should struggle for a better existence. We lived and thought with incorrigible self-assurance, and, of course, wrote in the same way.

> The first number of *Rabochaia Mysl'* came out in such bad condition that it was hard to read even for those who wrote it, and the public for which it was intended could could scarcely make it out. The theme of the articles and remarks was that the heavy lot of the workers had to be alleviated, taking into consideration, of course, that we had to deal with both the capitalists and the Tsarist regime.

---

[4] Andreev, *Proletarskaia Revoliutsiia,* No. 14, p. 78.
[5] Mikhailov, p. 14.

The reading of the newspaper, of course, had to be done by the "authors" themselves.

I should not fail to mention comrade Vlasov, then a sixteen-year-old youth and a very gifted chap. He helped a lot in distributing the first number of the paper. He made friends with a vagabond guitarist; they sat together in the most crowded places of the settlement, where he read the newspaper in sing-song fashion to the accompaniment of the guitar, interspersing our weighty considerations with his brilliant wit, which the workers readily appreciated. For two weeks they toured in this fashion all the populated places of Kolpino and its environs, until rumors about them reached the police, who took measures to arrest them.[6]

The one hundred and fifty or so illegible copies were quickly exhausted, fetching a price, according to Andreev, as high as forty rubles apiece.

A second issue was soon run off and distributed in the same primitive fashion, while material for a third was assembled. In various parts of St. Petersburg, workers already expected the regular appearance of their "own" newspaper. The police were soon on the trail of the clandestine operators, but several new incidents occurred before they could close in. In one, a leaflet was circulated declaring that Admiral Verkhovskii was the anti-Christ because he refused to close down work on religious holidays. (The numerous official holidays in Russia had been reduced by the law of 1897).[7] In another incident, factory guards seized a few participants of an improvised demonstration; the workers were beaten unmercifully and locked up in the local guardhouse. According to Andreev, the workers outside resolved that "they can't treat 'our boys' like that." After a skirmish, they managed to free their comrades and "arrest" the unfortunate guards and the local police officer. "In a word," Andreev gloated, "our little revolutionary swoop came off without a hitch."[8] This impudence put an end to the patriarchal ways of the factory settlement and brought in the ruthless efficiency of the Department of Police. In January, 1898, about two hundred "unreliable" workers, including all the leaders, were arrested; about forty of these were eventually exiled. With

---

6 Andreev, *Proletarskaia Revoliutsiia*, No. 14, pp. 82–83.

7 See Zavialov, p. 171.

8 Andreev, *Proletarskaia Revoliutsiia*, No. 14, p. 84.

this, the "strictly workers" phase in the history of *Rabochaia Mysl'* came to an end.

Although the first issue of *Rabochaia Mysl'* has not been preserved, the program article was reproduced in *Listok Rabotnika* and has been reprinted many times since. This article served as the basis for Lenin's later claim that the organ propagated bread-and-butter trade unionism, ignoring the political tasks of the movement. The appeal to the workers was framed as follows:

> Let the workers conduct their struggle knowing that they are struggling, not for future generations, but for themselves and their children; let them remember that every victory, every square inch of territory wrested from the enemy represents one more rung on the ladder to their well-being.

This candid appeal to narrow class interests was buttressed by the author's highly individual version of the laws of economic materialism.

> The struggle for economic interests represents the most stubborn, the most powerful means . . . by which the average person defends his right to existence. Such is the law of nature. The political always obediently follows the economical, and in the final analysis political chains are burst asunder in passing. *The struggle for economic betterment, the struggle with capital in the sphere of everyday vital interests, and strikes as the means of this struggle*—such is the motto of the workers' movement.

As if to incriminate himself further in the eyes of his critics, the author attributed the success of past year's strikes to the fact that "the worker himself finally took his own fate into his own hands, wresting it from the hands of the leaders." The movement was alien to the workers, he averred, as long as it was merely a "means to salve the guilty conscience of the repenting *intelligent*"; economic goals had been neglected by the intelligentsia "out of anxiety never to forget the political ideal."[9]

In Lenin's view, such sentiments enshrined the principle of "spontaneity"; they amounted to riding the "tailend" of the work-

---

[9] Cited in full in *Listok Rabotnika*, No. 9–10 (November, 1898), pp. 49–50. The author was not a worker but Takhtarev's fellow medical student N. A. Bogoraz; however, he was one of those self-effacing "worker-philes" who made it a point of sacred honor to voice the workers' sentiments as exactly as possible. See Zavialov, p. 171.

ers' movement, blindly encouraging the most primitive aspirations of the masses. *Iskra* and revolutionary Social Democrats, on the contrary, upheld the principle of "Social Democratic consciousness," that is, the leadership of the masses by a vanguard of professional revolutionaries who were thoroughly imbued with the insights of scientific socialism and willing to submit to "party discipline." However, Lenin was using *Rabochaia Mysl'* as an abstract ideological target for his polemical thrusts; he skirted the issue of whether or not it could be regarded as a genuine expression of worker sentiments.

Lenin's cutting remarks on Social Democracy's own "V.V.'s" (to Marxists, "V.V.," author of *The Fate of Capitalism in Russia*, epitomized the effete Populism of the 1890's), and on the vogue of "critical" literature on Marx seem to blame these heresies upon certain misguided *intelligenty*.[10] Very few Social Democrats then or later acknowledged the existence of a visceral revolt against intelligentsia leadership by the more active workers; hence, few observers understood the real import of the appearance of *Rabochaia Mysl'*. The fulminating of the program article against the intelligentsia was dismissed as the ravings of a guilt-ridden worker-phile, the Social Democratic equivalent of the Populist "soil worshippers" of the 1880's. The crucial point, however, is not whether the author was a misguided *intelligent* (as indeed he was), but whether the sentiments he voiced were genuinely characteristic of the workers for whom he wrote. The worker editors would hardly have printed his article had they not substantially approved its content. The numerous examples in the previous chapter support adequately enough that such thoughts were stirring in the workers' minds.

The bluntness with which the author attacked the intelligentsia and insisted on strictly bread-and-butter issues proved an embarrassment even to some of the workers' friends. An enthusiastic review of *Rabochaia Mysl'* in *Listok Rabotnika* noted cautiously that this program article "does not fully and accurately reflect the general tendency and character of the organ."[11] Takhtarev, re-

---

[10] For the relevant passages from *Chto delat'?*, see Lenin, *Sochineniia*, IV, 387–94 *passim*.

[11] *Listok Rabotnika*, No. 9–10, p. 49. The author of this review was the ultra-economist Ivanshin, co-editor of *Listok Rabotnika* and a short time later a contributor to *Rabochaia Mysl'*.

counting the history of *Rabochaia Mysl'* in 1902, expressed the same view and adduced as proof a second article from the first number which he felt was more typical of the adherents of *Rabochaia Mysl'*.[12] The article (probably written by Poliakov) stressed many of the same points as its companion piece: the workers' impoverished situation, the advantages of funds of mutual aid, the appeal for tighter organization and solidarity of effort. However, in other respects the articles differed, if not in principle, then certainly in emphasis and outlook.

In the second article, overt expressions of hostility to the intelligentsia were completely absent. In contrast to the first, which insisted that funds be spent "not for propaganda, not for books, but for daily bread in times of strikes," the second defended systematic learning in circles as essential to the normal development of the movement and paid scant attention to strikes per se. While offering tribute to "economic materialism," it appealed to the idealism of the worker as well, to his sense of historical mission.

> Our historical situation is such that in working to achieve our own well-being we are fulfilling a social task. We are the final class. After us comes no one. The victory of the working class is universal victory, or, better yet, universal equality, the attainment of which we must work for; only then can we say that we have not lived in vain, and our children will live to confirm it.[13]

Finally, the two articles differed in their assessment of the relative importance of political as opposed to economic aims. The first advanced exclusively economic goals, convinced that political change would be achieved "in passing," presumably without conscious effort. It pointedly ignored the prevailing political structure and did not so much as acknowledge that a struggle with the capitalists might involve conflicts with the police or other organs of government. The second, on the contrary, did not hesitate to brand tsarism and the "monarchial structure" as the chief obstacle to the workers' movement. Its formulation of the organ's purpose was not unlike the one later adopted by *Iskra*: "To illuminate the

---

12 This article is reproduced in full in his *Ocherk peterburgskago rabochego dvizheniia*, pp. 81–85. Its author was probably Poliakov, the worker mentioned above, whose schooling in socialism and general culture, like that of his fellow workers Norinskii and Bogdanov, was almost on a par with the intelligentsia.

13 *Ibid.*, p. 85.

life of the workers in its true context, to arouse their interest in their surroundings . . . and to brand with words of scorn and ridicule our *oprichnina* [that is, the tsarist regime]."[14] Thus, the second article was far more imbued with the spirit and overall goals of the Social Democratic movement than the first.

It would be idle to argue which of the two articles was more representative of *Rabochaia Mysl'* at this stage. As Andreev pointed out, the thought that a newspaper should have a definite "tendency" did not enter the heads of these pioneer worker-publicists. The workers of the capital displayed a whole spectrum of attitudes, depending on what time and under what circumstances they had entered the movement: older workers with families differed in outlook from younger unmarried ones, urbanized "hereditary proletariat" from those with recent ties to the villages, skilled from unskilled workers. *Rabochaia Mysl'* simply registered these diversities as if oblivious to their incompatibilities. It is true that rather primitive sentiments frequently appeared on its pages, but just as often it printed the thoughts of mature worker socialists who openly expressed their disenchantment with religion and their hostility to the priesthood and the Tsar. The second article articulated the feelings of this latter group, who were well represented at the Obukhov works. The first article reflected the enthusiasm of those workers who had been drawn into the movement by the strikes and had not undergone a long period of circle training.

Paradoxically, there were even younger workers, Andreev's successors, at Kolpino, who were deeply disturbed by the bread-and-butter emphasis of the first two numbers (apparently they were unimpressed by Poliakov's contribution). "How can you win the eight-hour day," they reasoned, "when the government posts its spies and gendarmes everywhere, when the priests at confession ask whether you have sinned against established authorities or read anti-Christian books?"[15] These workers soon switched their loyalty

---

[14] The lead article of *Rabochaia Mysl'*, No. 2 (1898), could be accused even less of "trade unionism": "On the banner of the enemy camp the words 'Tsar, faith, and fatherland' are inscribed in golden letters. . . . Under the red banner of the proletariat is a slowly but relentlessly gathering force. . . . If the capitalist is defended only by monarchical power and the priests [*popovshchina*], then anyone who values life and not the grave will join the workers." (Cited in *Listok Rabotnika*, No. 7 [April, 1898], p. 19.)

[15] Mikhailov, p. 13. On contacts with *Rabochee Znamia*, see Zavialov, p. 178.

from *Rabochaia Mysl'* to *Rabochee Znamia* whose literature they avidly read when it began to appear in 1898; still they continued to place their correspondence regularly in *Rabochaia Mysl'*.

With the arrests following the second issue, the workers' groups which had organized *Rabochaia Mysl'* ceased to exist. Manuscripts for the third issue and the fate of the enterprise itself fell into the hands of a group of sympathetic *intelligenty*, for the most part students, several of whom had been active in reconstituting the *Soiuz Bor'by* after arrests in the summer of 1898.[16] It is unlikely that these students alone would have been able to cope with the technical problems of a "workers' newspaper," but help came from an unexpected source. A certain August (by other sources Karl) Kok arrived in St. Petersburg with credentials from Buchholtz, the Social Democrats' contact man in Berlin, and through Radchenko got in touch with representatives of *Rabochaia Mysl'*. He informed them that he could provide both the technical and financial means to print the workers' organ abroad. The offer was gladly accepted, and the two parties hastily made arrangements for regular communications and the secret delivery of the completed issues to Russia.

Henceforward, Kok was to be the chief inspiration and driving force of *Rabochaia Mysl'* and his personal idiosyncracies determined to a large extent its peculiar ideological stamp.[17] Born in 1873 in a small Estonian community in the Caucasus, and a skilled machinist by training, Kok developed even as a youth an insatiable curiosity for his surrounding world. He wandered over the face of Russia supporting himself by occasional labor, until in 1891 he settled in Tiflis, where he took part in one of the early workers' *kruzhki* of mixed Marxist and Populist composition.[18] Under the

---

[16] There is no firsthand account of this new group of worker-phile *intelligenty*; both Takhtarev and Akimov supply rather vague second- and thirdhand information. The participants are known through an otherwise not very useful police account "S. Peterburgskoe okhranoe otdelenie v 1895–1901 gg. (Trud chinovnika Otdeleniia P. Statkovkogo)," *Byloe*, No. 16 (1921), pp. 122–24. It was written years after the events described (1912) to further the career of the author in the *Okhrana*. Most of the names mentioned do not otherwise figure in the annals of Russian Social Democracy; however, one participant, Mikhail Batyrev, later became a key person in the Odessa Committee. See Garvi, pp. 117 ff.

[17] Biographical information on Kok was supplied to the author by the late B. I. Nicolaevsky, who recorded it from Kok's own words.

[18] For the intelligentsia group with which Kok was probably in contact, see Polevoi, pp. 495–98, and Ermanskii, chap. 1.

guidance of the local intelligentsia, Kok and his comrades read the works of Marx and Lassalle and eagerly followed the workers' movement in Western Europe through the pages of the liberal newspaper *Russkie Vedomosti*. Inspired by these sources, he became obsessed with a desire to travel abroad and observe at first hand the life and political activities of European workers.[19]

In 1896, with the aid of his intelligentsia acquaintances, Kok was able to fulfill his ambition. Through Buchholtz in Berlin he was put in touch with the leading circles of the German Social Democratic party.[20] He was deeply impressed by his observations of the German movement, particularly by the new doctrines of Bernstein. His experiences in Russia had already firmly convinced him that the workers must exercise their own leadership in their own cause, free of tutelage by the intelligentsia. Bernstein's emphasis on the importance of the workers' day-to-day victories simply confirmed Kok's own predilections.

When the Berlin colony of Russians received the first two issues of a genuine "workers' organ," Kok was overjoyed and quickly decided to make use of his contacts in Berlin to offer technical aid to the new enterprise. Securing the address of Radchenko from Buchholtz, he set about his mission. His success exceeded his expectations. He received from the St. Petersburg group not only the unprinted manuscripts for the third issue, but also a virtual carte blanche to handle the affairs of *Rabochaia Mysl'* abroad. The St. Petersburg *praktiki* put him in touch with their comrade in Geneva, Ivanshin (who had become a co-editor of *Listok Rabotnika*), and his Berlin acquaintance, Kuskova, put him in touch with Takhtarev in Brussels. Ivanshin, Takhtarev, and Kok formed the

---

[19] Kok was not the first educated worker to be thus inspired. Viktor Obnorskii, the worker-founder of the Northern Union of Russian Workers (1878–79), had undertaken a trip to Western Europe to "see for himself" as early as 1874. See Franco Venturi, *Roots of Revolution* (New York, 1960), p. 541. Other Russian workers made such pilgrimages with similar motivations—A. Shotman, G. M. Fisher, V. N. Nogin, and V. I. Babushkin.

[20] Arranging this was no great problem, as there was a considerable colony of Russian students and émigré Social Democrats who cultivated contacts with the leaders of German Social Democracy (for example, B. Krichevskii, who was later a correspondent for *Die Neue Zeit* in Paris). O. A. Ermanskii, who had been on the fringes of the Tiflis Social Democratic circle, studied in Zurich in the mid–1890's, and there were undoubtedly many others who could have been of help to Kok.

informal editorial collegium of *Rabochaia Mysl'* abroad. Although he found the aid of such talented *literatory* indispensable, Kok had a relatively free hand in determining the basic tone of the paper by his selection of material and his authority as a genuine worker.

Under the new arrangements, the technical and conspiratorial aspects of the undertaking were brought to a high degree of virtuosity—so much so, that even though materials had to be secretly collected and shuttled in and out of Russia, *Rabochaia Mysl'* survived longer than any other illegal organ before *Iskra*. The *Okhrana* did indeed intercept a few transports and learn the identity of the émigrés engaged in editorial functions, but it was unable to establish with certainty where the issues were printed or how they were so efficiently distributed despite frequent arrests. The new format of *Rabochaia Mysl'*, unlike the usual pocket-size underground publications, was similar to that of most St. Petersburg dailies, a fact occasioning considerable pride on the part of the capital city's workers.

In spite of the contributions of the émigré *intelligenty*, Kok's influence and the voluminous correspondence regularly sent to *Rabochaia Mysl'* from almost every factory district of St. Petersburg determined its character as a "workers' newspaper." The final editing and printing was done in Berlin under Kok's direction, with the aid of the German Printers' Union, and Takhtarev and Ivanshin sent their contributions from Brussels and Geneva respectively.[21] Kok commuted regularly between St. Petersburg and Berlin on false passports to fetch manuscripts and deposit fresh issues. Sometimes the matter of smuggling in large bundles required the use of alternate routes via Warsaw or Finland, whence they were fetched by members of the St. Petersburg group. Once a young student, Sisareva, was apprehended at the Finnish border with the incriminating material bulging suspiciously inside her corset.[22] *Rabochaia Mysl'* taunted the St. Petersburg police chief

[21] The most detailed information on the editorial group abroad is given by Takhtarev in *Rabochee dvizhenie v Peterburge 1893–1901 gg.* (Leningrad, 1924), chap. 2. This work is an expanded version of his *Ocherk* of 1902. It contains much useful information not in the earlier version, which, because of the police, had to keep certain facts from publication.

[22] See Statkovskii's report, *Byloe*, No. 16, pp. 130–31. For police intelligence on *Rabochaia Mysl'* see also L. P. Menshchikov (ed.), *Russkii politicheskii sysk zagranitsei* (Paris, 1914), pp. 51–54.

Piramidov to keep his vow that he would resign if another issue of the paper got through.[23]

While Kok attempted to guide the organ on a steady course abroad, the character of the St. Petersburg group changed radically. Although still "worker-phile," the new sponsors were at the same time loyal supporters of the *Soiuz Bor'by* and made their policy decisions accordingly. Conflicts arose within the group over the desirability of merging officially with the *Soiuz*. The advocates of co-operation gained the upper hand. The *Rabochaia Mysl'* group joined forces with supporters of *Rabochee Znamia* and other independently operating groups to wrench from Stepan Radchenko, the sole survivor of the old *Soiuz Bor'by* and jealous watchdog of its traditions, an agreement providing for "democratic principles of organization" and the inclusion of worker representatives in the central group. Late in 1898, it was decided, over objections from the émigré editors and purists in both groups, to incorporate the local organizations of *Rabochaia Mysl'* and *Rabochee Znamia* into the *Soiuz Bor'by*. The St. Petersburg group *Rabochee Znamia* was liquidated by arrests before the agreement could be carried into effect; thus the partisans of *Rabochaia Mysl'* unexpectedly gained control of the *Soiuz Bor'by*.[24]

The resulting situation was fraught with ambiguities. *Rabochaia Mysl'* purported to be simply an "organ of workers' thought," upholding the principle that the "workers' cause is an affair of the workers themselves"; but now it became an organ of the *Soiuz Bor'by* as well, and therefore an official publication of the local "Committee" of the recently founded Social Democratic Party (see Chap. 6). Moreover, despite their control of the leadership, the adherents of *Rabochaia Mysl'* failed to bring worker representatives into the *Soiuz Bor'by*, in flagrant contradiction to their theoretical commitments. Neither Akimov nor Takhtarev explains this lapse, but it was probably dictated by the requirements of secrecy, which had perpetually thrown a roadblock in the path of such reforms. Ironically, the group "The Self-Liberation of La-

---

23 See *Rabochaia Mysl'*, No. 7 (July, 1899), p. 3.

24 On the conflicts in the St. Petersburg group, see Akimov, *Materialy*, pp. 49–52 and Takhtarev, *Ocherk*, pp. 76–80. Akimov is perhaps the more reliable informant as he was a participant in the controversies. Takhtarev only received distant echos abroad supplemented by the accounts of others. The character of the St. Petersburg groups of this period will be treated in more detail in chap. 7.

bor," which arose in the summer of 1899, was formed in opposition to a local committee dominated by the most articulate partisans of worker democracy.

A second source of ambiguity lay in the relationship between the St. Petersburg and the émigré centers. There had evidently been no clear agreement concerning which group exercised the definitive rights of editorship, and the difficulty of communication added to the likelihood of misunderstandings. A crisis arose over an account of a strike at the factory of Maxwell and Paul in December, 1898. The St. Petersburg adherents of *Rabochaia Mysl'* heartily endorsed the workers' violent resistance to the police and instructed Kok to append an appropriate editorial to their glowing portrait of the workers' heroism. Much to their chagrin, the ensuing issue condemned the folly of the workers in exposing themselves to needless repression. As a result, the St. Petersburg group refused to distribute the number for several months.[25] In general, the émigré contingent continued to uphold the "workers' only" ideology of the original organ, whereas their St. Petersburg counterparts prided themselves on their status as a "Committee" of the party, and thought and acted in that spirit.

In the late spring of 1899, Takhtarev, awaiting the arrival of his future wife, A. A. Iakubova, from Siberian exile, spent several weeks with Kok in Berlin, where he helped edit the seventh number, for which he composed the lead article. Together they planned a considerable expansion of the literary output of the organ.[26] The chief offspring of this collaboration was a theoretical "Supplement" (*Otdel'noe Prilozhenie*) which became scandalous to the "revolutionary" Social Democrats because of its open appeal to Bernstein and its explicit rejection of Plekhanov's views. The harmony of the émigré editorial collegium was severely jolted by the arrival of Iakubova. She excoriated Kok for his open hostility to the intelligentsia and for imparting a totally apolitical tone to *Rabochaia Mysl'*. Also, she apparently demanded his resignation in the name of the St. Petersburg group. When news arrived of

---

[25] On this incident see Takhtarev, *Ocherk*, p. 79, and *Rabochaia Mysl'*, No. 5 (January, 1899), p. 1, col. 3.

[26] Takhtarev, *Rabochee dvizhenie v Peterburge*, p. 148. J. L. H. Keep's characterization of *Rabochaia Mysl'* as Takhtarev's "private venture" is therefore considerably wide of the mark. (*The Rise of Social Democracy in Russia* [Oxford, 1963], p. 60.)

the liquidation of that group by arrests, Kok favored severing the organ's official connection with the St. Petersburg Committee of the party and re-establishing *Rabochaia Mysl'* as an independent journal of worker opinion. Takhtarev, by this time under the influence of Iakubova (now his wife), felt obliged to abide by the wishes of the St. Petersburg comrades until their organization recovered from the arrests. Kok dutifully put out the eighth number under the old arrangements (the party label included in the heading). The material for this issue had already been sent, but the fifth page carried an announcement of the resignation of "comrade Petrov" (Kok) and disclaimed responsibility for the first five pages of the issue, as well as for a particularly offensive article in the "Supplement."[27]

Takhtarev carried on as sole editor into the following year (1900), but political events in Russia and news of the ambitious project of his former St. Petersburg comrades Lenin, Martov, and Potresov brought him to the conviction that *Rabochaia Mysl'* must either drastically revamp its position or find itself completely left out of the coming decisive struggle with the autocracy. Takhtarev went so far as to offer the editorship of the paper to Plekhanov, whom he had met at the International Socialist Congress in Paris that fall. Plekhanov, taken aback but obviously tempted, suggested that Takhtarev clear the matter with Lenin in Munich in view of the obligations which he, Plekhanov, had already undertaken with respect to *Iskra*. Takhtarev journeyed hopefully to Munich, but Lenin interposed his veto. *Rabochaia Mysl'* appeared to Lenin as the very embodiment of the tendency he was sworn to discredit, and he did not wish to be deprived of his target.

When news arrived in late 1900 of the reconstitution of the *Soiuz Bor'by* under the auspices of a genuine "Workers' Committee," Takhtarev extricated himself by transfering the whole enterprise to St. Petersburg. Although no longer appearing in such an impressive format, *Rabochaia Mysl'* now represented in fact as well as in name the viewpoint of the St. Petersburg *praktiki*. An-

27 See *Rabochaia Mysl'*, No. 8 (February, 1900), p. 5. A contemporary police report took notice of these controversies and correctly represented the role of Iakubova; however, it added the surprising (and perhaps inaccurate) information that she was supported by an official representative of the *Soiuz Bor'by*, none other than Akimov! See Menshchikov, *Russkii politicheskii sysk*, pp. 52–54. Details on Takhtarev's role are given in his *Rabochee dvizhenie v Peterburge*, pp. 149 ff.

other anomaly was removed when it dropped its billing as the "organ of the St. Petersburg workers." From the eleventh number on, the paper registered faithfully the general shift in climate in 1901 toward open confrontation with the autocracy by all oppositional elements of society.

When leafing through the pages of *Rabochaia Mysl'* of the above period, one is struck by the enormous amount of correspondence directly from this or that factory describing in minute detail the numerous abuses and unhealthy working conditions. After a few columns, the endless recitation of "swindles" and "gyps" by the bosses and bullyragging by the shop stewards, interspersed with blustering expressions of indignation, becomes wearisome. Occasionally strikes or strike plans accompanied by a series of demands are recorded, but for the most part one encounters simply a running chronicle of grievances. Having awakened to the idea that protest in their "own" newspaper was possible, the workers obviously sought to get everything off their chests at once. Much of the popularity of *Rabochaia Mysl'* can be explained by the gratification the simple worker drew from seeing the familiar details about conditions in his own plant registered in print—the names of obnoxious stewards and stool pigeons, the exact location of dangerously exposed pieces of machinery, the cataloguing of known instances of death and maiming—in short, the exposure to all the world (he felt), in a newspaper not unlike the St. Petersburg dailies, of the impossible conglomeration of abuses surrounding his existence.[28] Here was a welcome outlet for his newly acquired sense of personal dignity and moral indigation.

Considerable space was also devoted to workers' contributions on whatever subjects struck their fancy. An older worker, for example, advised his younger comrades to stop chasing after girls and drinking in pubs, and to get into a *kruzhok* and read; then they would feel better and their life would have a purpose. Another complained that *Rabochaia Mysl'* used too many foreign

---

[28] A typical report by a female worker (*Rabochaia Mysl'*, No. 4 [October, 1898], pp. 2–3) described the excessive fines for innumerable petty offenses, the suffocating dust and heat which undermined the workers' health, the heavy lifting, the frequency of accidents, the miserable medical care, the bribes required to gratify supervisors. "You can't even leave your machine to answer a call of nature; a male supervisor forces himself on a young girl, threatening to fire her if she doesn't submit; a worker whose hand is crushed by a machine is given a fleeting glance by the factory medic and sent home . . ." and so it goes on.

words, and yet another that it was wrong to ridicule individual ministers and police officials, since socialism regarded them as prisoners of their class. Some workers displayed genuine talent for imaginative writing, such as the author of a piece entitled "Fathers and Sons":

> The fathers are slaves. They have been so degraded by the existing regime that they are prepared to ruin their sons for taking part in the struggle for freedom.
>
> "Are you trying to teach the Tsar what to do?" they cry in indignation. "You won't get anywhere with that."
>
> The sons reply: "You aren't getting anywhere either, so we're going to bury you, dear fellows, for good. Do you intend to live two centuries? Your time is past; you bowed and scraped, you licked their boots, you let those scoundrels have the first night with your wives. We don't want that. Our time has come. There's no use trying to teach the Tsar and all his lackeys, because they are as hard to teach as you are. So our only job is to get rid of them and replace them with others, our people, whom we will elect and remove again if they are incapable."
>
> "Socialists!" cry the enraged fathers.
>
> "Exactly, socialists. Let us explain to you that this is no swear word, but an honorable one, signifying an honest worker, not a bootlicking flatterer ready to bow to any parasite like you, but a fighter for truth, freedom and equality."
>
> "You'll get yours!"
>
> "No, we won't, because we have the faith, the strength of will, so that no threats or suffering will deter us from pursuing the pure and holy truth."[29]

Another imaginative worker recounted having seen at a circus a boa constrictor attack and crush the life of a helpless rabbit; he drew an instructive comparison with police agents stalking unsuspecting workers. An article entitled "Thoughts of a Worker" opened on the philosophical note: "Who am I? A worker or a human being?" Through a series of dialectical steps he came to the conclusion that only in becoming a socialist does a worker find self-realization.[30]

---

[29] *Rabochaia Mysl'*, No. 3 (July, 1898), pp. 3–4. The author was able to secure a photostat of this extremely rare issue from the Bibliothèque de la Documentation Internationale Contemporaine in Paris. It has never before been cited in the literature. To the author's knowledge the first two issues are no longer extant.

[30] *Ibid.*, p. 30.

There is no question but that the possibility of creative self-expression answered a deeply felt need of this awakened generation of workers for self-definition and self-assertion. Whereas heretofore the worker was obliged either to acquiesce or to allow others to speak for him, he could now speak with his own voice, vent his own spleen, define his own values. The variety of contributions meant that each worker was likely to encounter words expressing his own emotions. The attachment of the St. Petersburg workers to "their" newspaper was such that the *Soiuz Bor'by*, in spite of their quarrel with the émigré editors, did not dare to consider replacing it with an organ of their own.[31] One should not identify this striving for self-expression ipso facto with the revolt against the intelligentsia; but the blindness of most *intelligenty* to the workers' aspirations certainly did much to provoke the revolt. *Rabochaia Mysl'* gave these aspirations free rein and constituted an irrefutable monument to their existence.

In sharp contrast to the reveries of philosophical workers and the voluminous recitation of economic grievances, a few contributions expressed militant revolutionary sentiments. A speech by a Poltava worker at a secret May First celebration, for example, forecast correctly that workers would soon be marching in the streets and singing revolutionary songs.[32] A group of exiled workers also voiced confidence that the decisive struggle with the autocracy was at hand:

> Let the bonds of international solidarity be strengthened, the bonds of persistence and courage in the struggle of Russian workers for a better life, for political freedom, for the final liberation of the working class from all oppression! Away with despotism! Long live the First of May and international Social Democracy![33]

A letter from a group of workers in Ivanovo-Voznesensk, featured prominently in the eighth issue (February, 1900), advised their fellows to "abandon all hope in the government" and to reconcile themselves to the thought that "we have to fight both the government and the capitalists." Kok obviously allowed such discordant notes to appear on the pages of *Rabochaia Mysl'* because he felt

---

[31] See Takhtarev, *Ocherk,* p. 79.

[32] *Rabochaia Mysl'*, No. 4, p. 2.   [33] *Ibid.*, No. 7, p. 2.

obliged to record all genuine expressions of "workers' thought," including those with which he disagreed.

Although these contributions testified to the existence of a small contingent of workers with developed revolutionary convictions, they were drowned in the sea of reports from the factories and other routine pieces. Such workers were not likely to find the humdrum tone of *Rabochaia Mysl'* much to their taste. A well-informed observer, who asserted that *Rabochaia Mysl'* was read in the factories "by everyone including the old-timers and tipplers," also affirmed that an increasing number were dissatisfied with its failure to touch on general social and political questions. "The same old stuff . . . we knew that a long time ago . . . again nothing in the political column," he reported as being their complaints.[34] With the rising political temperature in the country at large, the center of gravity of the workers' concerns was rapidly shifting, whereas *Rabochaia Mysl'* continued to mark time till the end of 1900. By then it expressed the concerns, not of the more alert workers, but of the rank and file, the "old-timers and tipplers." An increasing number of workers looked in their own organ not for self-reflection, but for "words of scorn and ridicule for our *oprichnina*," as promised by Poliakov's editorial of the first issue.

The extensive correspondence from workers was simply reproduced on the pages of *Rabochaia Mysl'* without commentary, criticism, or interpretation (the article on the strike at Maxwell and Paul referred to above was actually an exception). The editors conspicuously confined themselves to the conventional clichés about self-reliance and comradely solidarity. For example: "Our comrades are the only ones we can count on! . . . There is no help besides self-help; there are no means of defense except self-defense, life offers no other alternative than self-liberation."[35]

---

[34] "Peterburgskoe dvizhenie i prakticheskie zadachi sotsial-demokratii," *Rabochee Delo*, No. 6 (March, 1900), p. 31. This remarkably keen contemporary observer was one of the few to predict the "shift to politics" in the workers' mood: "Even if the mass workers' movement still expresses itself in an economic struggle, one should not overlook the overtones of powerful political discontent, not yet fully conscious, but undoubtedly having its effect on the workers' mode of thought. . . . The ever-increasing number of politically mature workers indicates that *in the very near future the workers' movement will take the form of a mass struggle . . . for political and economic liberation.*" (*Ibid.*, pp. 33–34. Italics in original.) Most Social Democrats, including the leaders of *Iskra*, were taken by surprise when this indeed occurred a year later.

[35] *Rabochaia Mysl'*, No. 4, p. 1.

Nevertheless, occasional expressions of hostility to the intelligentsia continued to appear, as in a short passage in the fourth issue:

> They say that we are "against the intelligentsia." To a great extent that is true. . . . These Russian *intelligenty* by some sad (or laughable) misunderstanding regard themselves as born revolutionaries. . . . It is well to remember that today's revolutionaries are tomorrow's prosecutors, judges, engineers, factory inspectors, in a word *chinovniki* [officials] of the Russian government.
>
> We are happy to accept their services, as well as the services of all who wish us well, *intelligenty* and non-*intelligenty*. But any interference on their part in our affairs which goes further than just these services we regard as out of place. In this sense we are against the intelligentsia.[36]

Likewise in the seventh issue ridicule was briefly cast on the "revolutionary theory" which proposed "the organization by *intelligenty* of small circles of advanced workers for—the overthrow of the autocracy."[37] Such frontal attacks on the intelligentsia probably came from Kok, who wished to make it clear to his collaborators that in this undertaking intelligentsia contributors were to be the simple amanuenses of the workers, nothing more.

Although Kok limited himself to a few such outbursts, Takhtarev attempted a more comprehensive theoretical justification for the peculiar approach of *Rabochaia Mysl'*. As a literate Marxist, Takhtarev was necessarily aware that downgrading Social Democratic theory and intelligentsia leadership ran contrary to the inclinations of most Social Democrats, and more particularly to the brand of Marxism espoused by Plekhanov. Even *Ob agitatsii* had proposed economic agitation as a device to secure Social Democratic leadership over the proletariat for the forthcoming political struggle with the autocracy. *Rabochaia Mysl'*, on the other hand, tended to treat the everyday economic struggle as an end in itself, in which leaders of the intelligentsia were to have no ulterior motives.

Takhtarev developed this theme editorially in the fourth issue, asserting that self-schooling in habits of organization and discipline would eventually shape the workers into a monolithic social force which no government counterforce could withstand. He proposed that the workers begin by organizing small groups with

[36] *Ibid.*, p. 4. [37] *Ibid.*, No. 7, p. 6.

immediate, palpable aims—funds of mutual aid, co-operative enterprises, societies for self-cultivation or amusement. Later on,
these organizations could be transformed into strike committees,
and still later into more permanent syndicates or unions. All possibilities, both legal and illegal, should be exploited. Of course, such
associations would be suppressed by the government; but if the
workers persisted and expanded their activities, the government
would eventually be outnumbered and forced to channel the
movement into approved organizations under its own sponsorship.
Such organizations could be exploited by the workers, until they
acquired in practice all the freedom their ideological opponents
hoped to obtain by revolutionary means. Takhtarev's scheme of
social development was diametrically opposed to that of Plekhanov
and his followers:

> Every strike, every workers' fund, every workers' *soiuz* only be-
> comes legitimized when it becomes a matter of custom and practice—
> forbid it or approve it, it makes no difference in the actual state of af-
> fairs. Effective law is merely a description of contemporary class
> relationships. The force of the law is the force of custom. To make
> something customary means to legitimize it, to make it legal.

Takhtarev's editorial in the seventh number proved to be even
more patently apolitical. He denied that demands for political
rights (freedom of speech, press, strikes) were in the interest of the
workers and maintained that workers were justly concerned for
the time being with better pay, fewer fines, shorter hours, and no
speedups of machinery. He reiterated the view that the government and the employers made concessions, not because of laws on
the statute books, but in spite of them, since the workers represented a unified force. He claimed that the one tested weapon the
workers understood and the government respected was the strike,
which, legal or not, often gained its aims. A union was simply a
permanently organized strike; its strength lay in the degree of its
cohesiveness and determination, not its legality. According to this
view, no revolutionary intelligentsia, no workers' political party,
indeed, no "revolution" was necessary. If the workers put their
demands into practice en masse, the political structure would
automatically conform to the new conditions; a "democratic constitution" could only put on the finishing touches.

In making these pronouncements, *Rabochaia Mysl'* merited the worst accusations subsequently voiced by *Iskra* and the "revolutionary Marxists": Plekhanov's dictum was reversed to read "political transformation through the economic struggle" (in Lenin's terms "trade unionism"); worker initiative alone was to determine the direction of the movement, obviating the need for "Social Democratic leadership" (an opting for "spontaneity" in place of "consciousness"); and, finally, historical development was to follow an evolutionary rather than a revolutionary path ("Revisionism").

Although these thoughts found other scattered echoes on the pages of *Rabochaia Mysl'*, the very notion that *Rabochaia Mysl'* represented the authentic, unshackled voice of the workers militated against such thoughts' being foisted on worker readers as editorial policy. Indeed, much that was printed in *Rabochaia Mysl'* seemed to contradict them. Nevertheless, the unorthodox editorial statements inevitably provoked criticism in other organs of the émigré press. Plekhanov's collaborator, Koltsov, writing in *Rabotnik*, Nos. 5–6, defended the Social Democratic intelligentsia against the blatant attack of *Rabochaia Mysl's* first issue. A brief editorial statement in *Rabochaia Mysl's* seventh issue, probably written by Kok, contemptuously dismissed Koltsov's comments as "abusive" and unworthy of reply, but nevertheless imparted a passing thrust at the pretentious "theories" of their ideological opponents.

> We do not regard it as necessary to analyze in any serious fashion the "positive" aspects of Koltsov's article, for his "revolutionary theory"—the organization by intellectuals of small circles of leading workers for the overthrow of the autocracy—seems to us a theory which has long outlived its time, a theory abandoned by all in whom there is the least sensitivity to and understanding of reality.[38]

Such contempt for the whole tradition of Russian Social Democracy aroused even the editors of *Rabochee Delo* (who had themselves just revolted against Plekhanov by "capturing" the Union of Social Democrats Abroad) to a spirited defense of their former mentor and the views he represented. They insisted that *Rabochaia Mysl'*, not Koltsov, had been abusive, and they compared the polemical methods of *Rabochaia Mysl'* in ridiculing Russian revolutionary traditions with the reactionary author "Nezlobin"

---

[38] *Ibid.*, No. 7, p. 6.

in the *Russkii Vestnik*. They observed logically that, while *Rabochaia Mysl'* was presumably the "official organ" of the St. Petersburg *Soiuz Bor'by*, an official committee of the party, its denial of the utility of political rights was in direct contradiction to the official Manifesto of the party of 1898, to which the St. Petersburg *Soiuz Bor'by* adhered. Moreover, a May First proclamation itemizing political demands which was specifically criticised (by Takhtarev) in *Rabochaia Mysl's* seventh issue had been put out by the *Soiuz Bor'by*.[39]

The desire to clarify their views in opposition to the *Gruppa Osvobozhdenie Truda* and the "politically" oriented wing of the movement finally overcame the editors' studied indifference to "theory": in a "Supplement" (*Otdel'noe Prilozhenie*) to the seventh issue they attempted to define their ideological position for all time. Since this "Supplement" was the most complete statement of the émigré editors and attempted to give respectable theoretical justification for their undertaking, it deserves detailed consideration.

The table of contents immediately confirmed the worst suspicions of the opponents of *Rabochaia Mysl'*: one of the major contributions came from the pen of Eduard Bernstein, the apostle of Revisionism! Although his short article "Karl Marx and the Contemporary Workers' Movement" out of condescension to his Russian audience skirted sensitive issues, it contained one thought characteristic of his Revisionism: that Marx was truer to his own scientific theory when he abandoned the revolutionary élan of the *Communist Manifesto* and conceded that "a whole series of steps in historical development must precede the realization of higher forms of life."[40]

Bernstein's ideas were actually developed at greater length in a second unsigned article, "A New Current in German Social Democracy." After an otherwise fair summation of Bernstein's critique of Marx's *Zusammenbruchs-* and *Verelendungstheorie*, the author capsulized the essence of Bernstein's "evolutionary" socialism as follows:

---

[39] See "Sibiriak" (P. Teplov), "Polemicheskie krasoty redaktsii 'Rabochei Mysli,' " *Rabochee Delo*, No. 4–5 (September-October, 1899), pp. 63–73.

[40] *Otdel'noe prilozhenie k Rabochei Mysli* (St. Petersburg, 1899), p. 33. St. Petersburg was given as the place of publication simply to irritate the police.

The development of factory legislation, workers' insurance, the participation of workers in profits, the development of trade unions will gradually transform capitalist society into socialist society. Every *kopek* increase in wages, every hour less in the working day brings us nearer to the socialist structure. The Russian worker must struggle relentlessly, not relaxing for a minute, to improve his lot under the prevailing regime, and *in this very struggle* he will obtain a better future.

Not the aggravation of the poverty of the proletariat, not the aggravation of the conflict between capital and labor, not the aggravation of the internal contradictions of capitalist production will lead to socialism, but rather the growth and development of the strength and influence of the proletariat.[41]

Although the author denied that he was interpreting or approving Bernstein's views, he betrayed a concern to point up their ideological kinship to the views of *Rabochaia Mysl'*. In so doing he was obliged to overlook the fact that Bernstein's gradualism was predicated on the increasing power of Social Democracy within the structure of a constitutional order to obtain legislation favorable to the working class.[42] *Rabochaia Mysl'* had characteristically regarded the struggle for a parliamentary structure with skepticism and envisaged progress only through a series of concessions to the raw physical force of the organized proletariat, a position much closer to Syndicalism than to Bernsteinism. According to this view, formal rights signified little, the actual correlation of social forces everything.

The lead article of the "Supplement," entitled "Our Reality" (*Nasha deistvitel'nost'*), developed at length a systematic theoretical justification of the views of *Rabochaia Mysl'*.[43] The author presented, presumably as a contrast to the romantic dreams of the

---

[41] *Ibid.*, p. 36. The identity of the author is unknown.

[42] Bernstein's article had specifically stressed the importance of "democratic rights and institutions" and an "independent worker's party" which should join the leading strata of the bourgeoisie in the struggle for a democratic constitutional order. All this must have sounded uncomfortably similar to the program of the "revolutionary" Social Democrats.

[43] *Ibid.*, pp. 1–16. According to B. I. Nicolaevsky, the author of this article was P. A. Berlin, later a prominent Menshevik. At this time he was studying abroad and occasionally contributed articles with Bernsteinian overtones to Marxist journals. Apparently he had some connection with *Rabochaia Mysl'* through the Russian colony in Berlin.

"revolutionary Social Democrats," a dispassionate analysis of the composition and potential political weight of different layers of Russian society. He applied no little erudition to demonstrate that the social underpinnings of the Russian autocratic structure had shifted since the time of the Great Reforms from the landed aristocracy to the industrial and commercial bourgeoisie. The upper bourgeoisie, he argued, already enjoyed such freedom and privileges as it required to pursue its own aims under government patronage. As proof of this he adduced the industrialists' participation in legislative commissions, their frequent conferences, the advancement of their views in trade journals, and their numerous petitions to the government which seldom went unanswered. This privileged position was contrasted with the total absence of legal rights and meaningful participation in public affairs suffered by the various sectors of the Russian "petty bourgeoisie," which he defined as professional people (engineers, writers, doctors, teachers), employees of various *zemstvo* institutions and, finally, the revolutionary intelligentsia. All these groups were seeking outlets for their social aspirations, but were frustrated at every step by the implacable bureaucratic structure of absolutism. Therefore, they were natural allies of the working class in its efforts to break loose from the shackles of the autocracy and win scope for its own social and political initiative. The "revolutionary Social Democrats" were accused of reckoning on the proletariat alone for overthrowing the autocracy and of "ignoring in this respect the other social strata and their separate groups, the economic, organizational and personal forces of which are just as important in such a struggle."[44]

In light of later developments, one can credit the author of "Our Reality" with some perspicacity in assessing social forces, but his criticism of the *Gruppa Osvobozhdenie Truda* was particularly unjustified, inasmuch as Akselrod's most recent writings had advanced an almost identical analysis of the situation, employing almost identical arguments.[45] With far greater validity, the article's

---

[44] *Ibid.*, p. 15. All further quotations from "Our Reality" below are to be found on pp. 15 and 16 of the article.

[45] Pavel Akselrod had just spelled out his definitive views on party tactics in two short brochures, *Istoricheskoe polozhenie i vzaimnoe otnoshenie liberal'noi i sotsial-demokratii v Rossii* (Geneva, 1898), and *K voprosu o sovremennykh zadachakh i taktike russkikh sotsial-demokratov* (Geneva, 1898). See particularly pp. 14–17 and 27 of the latter work.

criticism (as Akselrod's was) might have been directed against the misty ideology espoused by the majority of the party *praktiki* as epitomized in *Ob agitatsii:* that the chains of both the autocracy and the employers would be broken by the intrinsic revolutionary momentum of the mass workers' movement. In their polemical exchanges *Rabochaia Mysl'* and the *Gruppa Osvobozhdenie Truda* both took each other to task for being guilty of the same oversimplification and obstinately refused to grasp the essence of each other's position. The failure of the émigré veterans to acknowledge the subtle arguments of the theoretical "Supplement" is perhaps more understandable in that they appeared on the pages of *Rabochaia Mysl'* for the first time and might be challenged as incompatible with its customary avid proletarian patriotism.

Actually the viewpoint of "Our Reality" expressed a minor trend of thought among certain theoretically versed Russian Social Democrats, whose ideas only temporarily and partially coincided with those of *Rabochaia Mysl'*. The ideology of this trend later acquired fame in the *Credo* of E. D. Kuskova against which Lenin launched a "Protest" from Siberia and a detailed attack in *Chto delat'?*[46] These ideas were first formulated by Kuskova's husband, S. N. Prokopovich, as a result of his firsthand study of the Belgian socialist movement, and introduced by him to the émigré colony in Berlin in mid-1898, precisely in the midst of the ferment over Bernstein's Revisionism. Later disavowals notwithstanding, Prokopovich for a brief moment swayed younger Social Democrats in the Berlin colony who were seeking ideological ammunition to vent their own grievances against Plekhanov.[47] Takhtarev's thinking, influenced by his own close observations of the Belgian movement, gravitated in roughly the same orbit, even though his articles in *Rabochaia Mysl'* did not fully reflect it. *Rabochaia Mysl'* apparently exercised a temporary attraction for the incipient oppo-

---

[46] See Lenin, *Sochineniia*, IV, 393, and *Rabochee Delo*, No. 4–5 (December, 1899), pp. 13–27. The story of Credo has been told many times (for example, see Keep, *The Rise of Social Democracy in Russia*, pp. 65–66) and will not be recounted here.

[47] The only direct evidence on this episode (other than later polemical exchanges) consists of letters to Akselrod from the Berlin Social Democrats which, to the latter's chagrin, Plekhanov reproduced in full in *Vademecum dlia redaktsii "Rabochego dela"* (Geneva, 1900), and of a few passages in the correspondence of Plekhanov and Akselrod (*Perepiska G. V. Plekhanova i P. B. Akselroda*, ed. B. I. Nicolaevsky et al. [Moscow and Berlin, 1925], I, 203–7; II, 5 ff).

sition to Plekhanov, which the worker patriot Kok exploited for a time to expedite his own enterprise.

However, a stable opposition to the old guard along these lines failed to materialize. The Berlin representatives of the Union of Social Democrats Abroad, Kopelzon and Peskin, became disillusioned with Prokopovich by the end of 1898, and their opposition to Plekhanov when they launched *Rabochee Delo* employed an entirely different rationale: they forswore Bernstein and returned to an ardent espousal of their own brand of Marxist Orthodoxy (in essence, that of *Ob agitatsii*). P. A. Berlin, the author of "Our Reality," entered the camp of the Russian "critics" of Marx, contributing several articles on Bernstein to *Zhizn*. By 1900, Takhtarev abandoned his former position and was anxious for reconciliation with the "political" faction. Prokopovich and Kuskova on their return to Russia forsook active participation in Social Democratic circles and, carrying out the prescriptions of *Credo* (pure "economics" for the workers' movement, but revolutionary "politics" for liberal oppositional circles), dedicated themselves to rallying the liberal *zemstvo* and professional circles to the cause of political freedom. By 1901, when *Iskra* launched its attack on Economism, there was not a trace of this dangerous heresy in the Social Democratic movement.

The balance of "Our Reality" developed thoughts roughly parallel to Takhtarev's articles in *Rabochaia Mysl*. When Akselrod and the "revolutionary Social Democrats" summoned the working class to "organize," they understood thereby a conspiratorial revolutionary workers' party led by the Social Democratic intelligentsia. The ideologist of *Rabochaia Mysl*, in addressing the same appeal, understood it quite differently. "Our most immediate task," he argued, "is the development of workers' organizations, i.e., chiefly trade unions, societies of mutual aid, consumer and cultural societies, etc." Only thus, he felt, would the workers acquire "that economic and personal (social) strength which alone enables them to struggle more successfully against the exploitation of the employers and the arbitrariness of the government." The author viewed effective power in a given historical situation as a function of the degree of internal cohesion and organization of the social group in question for pursuing specific economic needs and requirements. Without such "material" underpinnings, a revolutionary organization of the intelligentsia and advanced workers as proposed by the *Gruppa Osvobozhdenie Truda* was a phantom. Since Russian workers were as yet only aware of their immediate needs, any political tasks foisted on them from the outside could only force them into battle before they were organizationally and psychologically prepared.

The article insisted that the enlightened class will of the proletariat was the sole instrumentality of historical advance; such was the chief principle of economic materialism, and history in this regard refused to be forced. In the words of the article:

> For the workers to carry on a fully conscious and independent political struggle, it is necessary that the struggle be conducted by the workers' own organizations, that their political demands express specifically recognized current needs and interests, that they be advanced by the workers' own professional organizations, that they be worked out by consensus . . . on their own initiative, as the collective social will of their members.

The workers might understand a demand to participate in legislative commissions which did "already exist" (established by the law of June, 1897); but they were not capable of understanding the current demand of agitational leaflets for specific political rights, presupposing institutions which did not exist. The relentless self-organization of the working class with assistance from the outside by individual *intelligenty* rather than tutelage over the masses by a party of Social Democratic intellectuals—such was the formula advanced for the deliverance of the proletariat.

A corollary to this principle was the rejection of the revolutionary dogmatism of the Orthodox Marxists. Noting that the Russian intelligentsia had espoused the cause of the "liberation of labor" solely in order to escape its historical quandary formulated by Plekhanov of "whence to draw strength for the struggle with tsarism," the author challenged the sincerity of the intelligentsia's adherence to the "workers' movement" ("What workers' movement?" he mocked—"The strike campaigns? societies of mutual aid? propaganda circles?"). In sharp contrast to the classic formula of the founders of Russian Social Democracy of a two-step revolution, the theoretician of *Rabochaia Mysl'* envisaged the realization of both political freedom and socialism as a gradual process unfolding in a series of countless piecemeal victories.

> We see it [socialism] within the workers' movement itself, in the
> present and future development of social and political initiative
> [*samodeiatel'nost*]—in the development of workers' organizations . . .
> in the gradual transition of contemporary private production first to
> social control by the organized workers (trade unions), and subse-
> quently to a social authority democratized by the workers, democ-
> ratized by their active participation in the organs which supervise
> various industrial affairs—courts of arbitration, all sorts of assemblies,
> commissions, and conferences on labor legislation—further by worker
> participation in organs of local self-government and subsequently in
> the general representative institution of the country.

This passage, with its explicit redefinition of socialism as an imma-
nent quality of peaceful social processes, simply elaborated a position implicit in the very existence of *Rabochaia Mysl'* and defended
from time to time in its earlier editorial articles.

The author, however, did not stop with a Bernsteinian construction of social development. He proceeded to round out a complete
philosophy of history:

> Taking the view that *socialism, flowing out of the development of*
> the social methods of production which inevitably leads to com-
> plete socialization [*obobshchestvlenie*] . . . *is nothing else than the*
> *further, higher development of contemporary social life* [*obshches-*
> *tvennost*], we regard the essence of the historical process to consist
> in the progressive inclusion of the various classes which compose the
> population of a state into the administration of its affairs, until finally
> all enjoy uniform rights and privileges.

This placid philosophical confidence in the benevolent impetus of
historical objectivity was capped by a poetic thrust at the rational
voluntarism of the Orthodox Marxists.

> Do you presume to measure the distant future by your own customs,
> concepts, means of production [sic]? Do you indeed suppose that
> your remote progeny will be such as you?—Fear not, they shall be
> wiser than you. Tend to the affairs of your present (social) life, and
> care for the fate of posterity leave unto posterity.

One could interpret these passages as a reaffirmation of the
idealistic heritage of Marxism. A number of the great philosophers
of the early nineteenth century—Hegel, Schelling, Stirner, and
Schopenhauer, for instance—regarded the historical process as the
work of a hidden Reason (or un-Reason) beyond the ken of its

participants. Individuals, however, in following the guidance of their own particular reason, in pursuing particular aims and goals, were viewed as unwittingly fulfilling the purposes of World-Reason. The clashes of wills embodied in various historical collectivities merely elicited "dialectical contradictions" which impelled the gradual unfolding of the content of World-Reason and were eventually to be "superseded" (*aufgehoben*) in a higher synthesis. With one foot, Marxism stood in this Idealistic tradition, except that social classes, rather than culturally determined individualities served as the tools of Universal Reason. The destiny of the world process was to be worked out through the blind pursuit of "class interests" which would spontaneously drive forward the development of new forms of productive relations, eventually culminating in Socialism, the final incarnation of Reason.[48]

With the other foot, however, Marxism stood in the world of eighteenth-century rationalism and nineteenth-century Positivism. "Science" was viewed as a revelation of the secret formula of the world order, and its conscious practical application to human affairs would progressively reconstruct society on a rational basis. In the hands of the ultrarationalist, Plekhanov, this side of Marx was carried to its logical extreme. Despite the sociological objectivism of Plekhanov's theoretical constructions, he held that the vehicle for bringing about socialism would be a revolutionary workers' "party" consciously guided by Marxist scientific principles in all matters of tactics and program. Therefore, in his practical politics he insisted that the key party instances be staffed by schooled Marxists (preferably from his own group) to ensure that party policy always be enlightened by Orthodox Marxist theory.[49]

---

[48] The logic of this "dialectical" relationship of Marx to German Idealism persuaded some of the talented Russian Marxists, such as Struve, Bulgakov, and Berdyaev, to renounce materialism and launch a movement "back to Idealism" via Kant and Ferdinand Lassalle. In the Marxist theoretical works of this time (1899–1901) one can discern a series of intermediary steps, one of which is represented by the article cited. The movement reached its culminating point in the symposium edited by Nicolas Berdyaev entitled *Problemy Idealizma* (St. Petersburg, 1903). See Kindersley,chap. 4. For the relationship of Marx to Idealism see Karl Löwith, *Von Hegel zu Nietzsche* (Stuttgart, 1953), pp. 65–136 and Herbert Marcuse, *Reason and Revolution* (New York, 1954), pp. 273–322.

[49] In his theoretical writings Plekhanov hewed to a stricter construction of Marx —that the entire proletariat must develop a socialist consciousness; but in his practical endeavors in party politics he operated on exactly the same assumptions as those which Lenin spelled out theoretically in *Chto delat'?*: that the party must guide

The ideologist of *Rabochaia Mysl'*, on the other hand, drew his inspiration from the idealistic side of Marx, which, standing Hegel on his head (or perhaps setting him on his feet), envisaged the realization of socialism through the ineluctable dialectic of material forces and their reflection in the class struggle. The workers, in pursuing their immediate class interests (that is, in struggling for "everyday needs and demands"), were unconsciously fulfilling a historical mission to bring about the complete liberation of mankind. It was unnecessary for them to be guided in their actions by "Social Democratic principles" or to be subjected to the discipline of an all-wise "party." The "cunning of Reason" was at work in their simple, "spontaneous" efforts to defend their interests and better their situation. The progressive "organization" of the working class in the pursuit of these aims constituted in and of itself the process of achieving the "complete generalization of production," namely, Socialism. One could in good conscience "leave the care for the fate of posterity unto posterity," since, as Hegel observed, "the owl of Minerva flies only at dusk."

This inversion of the legitimate relationship between "spontaneity" and "consciousness" was regarded by the "revolutionary" faction as a betrayal of the historic responsibility of enlightened Social Democrats. Plekhanov graphically styled it "contemplating the behind of the proletariat," and Lenin called it, simply, *khvostism* (tailism). The philosophy of the author of "Our Reality," after all, was little more than a sophisticated version of the thought advanced in the first issue of *Rabochaia Mysl'*, that the workers should take "their own fate into their own hands" and fight "not for future generations, but for themselves and their children," knowing full well that the "political always obediently follows the economic" and that "every square inch of territory wrenched from the enemy represents one more step on the ladder to their well being."

Despite the variety of sentiments which found refuge on the pages of *Rabochaia Mysl'*, a consistent line of thought threaded its

---

the proletariat, and the Marxist theoreticians must guide the party. Proof of this was his unrelenting attempt to entrench his own leadership in the party and to eliminate that of the theoretically unversed "youngsters," against whom he directed his *Vademecum*. See Samuel Baron, *Plekhanov: The Father of Russian Marxism* (Stanford, 1963), p. 207, where precisely this point is made.

way through the successive issues and underlay the spirit of the whole enterprise. This way of thinking squarely opposed, both in letter and spirit, the mainstream of Russian Social Democracy, from the theoretical precepts of its founders to the workaday philosophy of its underground practitioners in Russia. Although *Rabochaia Mysl's* ideologists made use of Marxian concepts of economic materialism and class egoism, their enterprise itself represented the temporary combination of what proved to be incompatible social elements: simple workers seeking to articulate their chaotic emotions, experienced workers exercising leadership in their own cause, repentant *praktiki* effacing themselves in the cause of the people, and erudite Marxists confirming their theoretical constructions. The "Supplement" of the seventh issue represented the high point of this unstable alliance. Thereafter, under the new editorship, belligerent hostility to the mainstream of Social Democratic tradition was no longer in evidence.

For the next few numbers, *Rabochaia Mysl'* dutifully published routine correspondence from the factories reporting on the unbearable working conditions. Editorial comment vanished from its pages entirely. A few contributions suggested, however, that the politically articulate workers were becoming restive with the monotonous lack of belligerence of their "own" organ. A letter from an exiled worker appearing on p. 10 of the eighth issue called for "more fire! more life, and enough of dry scholasticism!" Discussions of Chernyshevsky, Bernstein, and Marx, it averred (in an apparent reference to the "Supplement"), represented intelligentsia, not workers', thought. If *Rabochaia Mysl'* would switch to a more militant line against the whole system of oppression, it would find that the worker is "not simply one who needs a crust of bread, but an honest individual who possesses the sense of duty of a citizen and the same willingness for self-sacrifice as the intelligentsia."[50] In the tenth issue (November, 1900) a worker's letter (p. 8, no editorial comment) openly disputed *Rabochaia Mysl's* position on the level of class consciousness attained by Russian workers. It categorically asserted that it was "as clear as day that the workers have already begun the struggle for rights, for legality, for the inviolability of human personality," and that the worker was

---

[50] *Rabochaia Mysl'*, No. 8 (February, 1900), p. 10.

"the sworn enemy of the tsarist government," since the fight for "legality and equality before the law" was tantamount to the "abolition of bureaucratic autocracy and the establishment of the responsibility of our ministers."

The eleventh issue (April, 1901) marked an abrupt change of course for *Rabochaia Mysl'*. An opening editorial entitled "The Vital Question" categorically stated: "The time has come for a decisive battle . . . a battle for our rights, for our very life, for freedom." In an open break with its characteristic apoliticism, *Rabochaia Mysl'* now nailed to its masthead the specific goals of "the right to strike, to assemble and form unions, freedom of personality, word and press," and, in an obvious paraphrase of the *Manifesto* of the party, claimed they were "as vital to us as air, as food, as life itself." It accompanied this sharp reversal of objectives with a new formulation of tactics, namely, "the transition from separate clashes to a general clash, to a mass encounter, from separate strikes and petty skirmishes with the police to mass strikes and political demonstrations against the whole capitalist class, against the whole governmental structure." *Iskra* could scarcely have been more militant in sounding the tocsin: "We call upon you comrades, gather your forces, prepare for the decisive battle! Do not be caught unprepared!"

This sharp change of course coincided with the general "swing of politics" of Russian society in early 1901. The St. Petersburg Workers' Organization, which was now the sponsor of *Rabochaia Mysl'*, shifted sharply to the left as the result of the March demonstration in Kazan Square and immediately infused its organ with the new spirit. Nothing was left of the elements that had given *Rabochaia Mysl'* its former stamp: the worker-patriot editor and the Revisionist ideologists were no longer at the helm; the worker intelligentsia, conscious of its isolation, was anxious not to be left out of the shaping struggle; and, finally, even the psychology of the masses underwent a precipitate change under the impact of the events of early 1901. The watershed for the latter, however, was not the intelligentsia demonstration of March 4, but the May First campaign and the ensuing Obukhov Defense. Wholesale arrests swept away nearly all the active workers in this old bastion of worker socialism, but the image of having stood their ground against mounted police and of the blood shed by their fallen comrades was indelibly stamped on the minds of even unindoctrinated workers.[51] The unrest in the capital continued through the summer, infecting one factory after the other. The new spirit was expressed in increasingly intransigent demands (the cancellation of fines, release of arrested comrades, the recognition of workers' representatives for bargaining) and in the stubbornness of worker crowds in the face of bayonets, whips, and rifle salvos.

Rabochaia Mysl' no longer yielded to *Iskra* in seeking to arouse mass indignation with the autocracy and the thirst for political liberty. *Rabochaia Mysl'* could still claim (although it no longer did so explicitly) to be the organ of the workers' thought, but that thought had now reached a new plateau. The old journal of workers' grievances and self-introspection was a thing of the past.

---

[51] For an account of the Obukhov Defense see *ibid.*, No. 12 (July, 1901), pp. 3-4. Its impact on the St. Petersburg workers can be traced in the subsequent issues.

CHAPTER 6

The Quest for a Party

In his reminiscences Martov relates that during 1892 and 1893, before his exile to Vilna, his small circle cherished the intention of constituting themselves the organizational nucleus of the future Social Democratic party. It was a thought which quite naturally and spontaneously entered the heads of these ambitious and sanguine youths, their recent conversion to Marxism notwithstanding. They were convinced that if their group cultivated the necessary cohesiveness, conspiratory skill, and political perspective, they could gradually build up a network of communication between local groups, satisfy their needs for literature and information, and thereby acquire a reputation for leadership spontaneously recognized by all. Subsequently their position was to be made official at a founding congress of the Russian Social Democratic Party, summoned by themselves.

Later, in Vilna, Martov was pleased to discover that the Vilna Social Democrats entertained similar hopes and, for that reason, kept in touch with groups in other parts of Russia. Vilna was already in a strategic position to take such an initiative in that she had already established a role as the purveyor of literature from abroad and operator of an underground railway over the border for fugitives from the police. Moreover, natives of Vilna attended many of the Russian institutions of learning and could serve as communication links with Russian Social Democratic groups.[1] Al-

---

[1] See Martov, *Zapiski sotsial-demokrata*, pp. 147–49 and 213–23.

152

though premature from the practical standpoint, such aspirations were deeply embedded in the psychology of this generation of Social Democrats. As *intelligenty* proudly identifying themselves with the revolutionary movement of the past, they dreamed of organizing as speedily as possible a disciplined underground party to coordinate the activity of all local revolutionary centers and direct the political struggle against the autocracy. This, as a basic point in the program of the *Gruppa Osvobozhdenie Truda,* was the decisive factor in attracting to Marxism the scores of young radicals who were disillusioned with the apolitical ideologies of the 1880's.

In practice, however, this article of faith came into conflict with another equally inviolable: that the revolutionary movement could succeed only if it drew the *masses* into the struggle, and specifically in the form of a *mass* Social Democratic *workers' party.* The implied elitism of the strategy of the People's Will was explicitly rejected, whereas the German Social Democratic Party, with its ever more impressive successes at the polls, served as the model to be emulated.[2] If Social Democracy at this time were to concentrate on uniting the widely scattered *kruzhki* into a single organization, it could still claim to represent only a handful of *intelligenty* and propagandized workers from the major centers. Early in 1894, the Vilna Social Democrats actually conducted a survey of the leading Social Democratic groups to ascertain the potential strength of the movement. Nowhere, they discovered to their dismay, had the movement struck firm roots in the factory districts. The disappointing results convinced the Vilna *praktiki* that the time for unification was not yet ripe, and they turned their attention to new methods of extending their influence over the masses.[3] Utopian organizational schemes, here as elsewhere, were aban-

---

[2] Martov brought out these elements in the psychology of his generation of Social Democrats in an introductory paragraph to an underground pamphlet put out by his group. Characteristically, the position was expressed as a Hegelian triad: "Populism of the seventies—thesis—social revolution through a peasant uprising bypassing a bourgeois constitution. The People's Will—antithesis—political revolution by the efforts of 'critically thinking individuals,' bypassing the people. Social Democracy—synthesis—social revolution through political transformation effected by the conscious working class." (*Ibid.,* pp. 148–49.) This was also roughly the scheme of Plekhanov's influential work *Socialism and the Political Struggle,* from which Martov perhaps borrowed his theme.

[3] *Ibid.,* pp. 221–22.

doned in favor of putting local work on a sound footing; in Vilna, this new emphasis led to discovery of the new technique of agitation.

This is not to say, however, that the dream of a united political party vanished from the mental horizon of Social Democrats—they simply awaited the auspicious moment to take appropriate steps. Even though the efforts of the following decade were sporadic and ended in failure, it would be a serious mistake to accept without challenge the claim of Soviet historiography that Lenin alone envisaged a political party "of a new type" and brought it into being through his leadership in the *Iskra* organization of 1901–3. As with the question of worker independence, the building blocks of Lenin's ideological conceptions rested upon long-established precedents and merely constituted a hypertrophied version of certain clearly discernible trends, which in previous efforts had ordinarily been balanced off by opposing trends. On the questions of the role of the future party, the strategy for bringing it into being, and the principles of its internal structure, Lenin upset the balance by throwing his entire weight to one side of the scale. Therefore an examination of early attempts to build a party provides rewarding insights into the mentality of Russian Social Democrats and into controversies which subsequently ended in a permanent schism.

Despite their preoccupation with cultivating the workers and eluding the vigilant eyes of the police, the Social Democrats of the early nineties seldom lost sight of the goal of creating a nationwide Social Democratic party. Within the limits of their capabilities and resources, they made modest efforts in that direction. Thus, personal acquaintances with Social Democrats from other localities were greatly valued. The unusual mobility of the intelligentsia— achieved by transfers to other universities, temporary exile from the capitals, the assumption of new professional positions, or vacations with relatives and friends—greatly facilitated such contacts. Quite frequently, moves were deliberately planned to promote organizational plans. For example, Martov had chosen Vilna as his place of exile to acquaint himself with that active center of Social Democratic propaganda; at the same time he kept his former circle in touch with each other, Gofman remaining in St. Petersburg, and Liakhovskii transferring to the University of Kiev. The Vilna Social Democrats also took advantage of every opportunity to broaden their acquaintance with other Social Democratic groups. Martov, of course, provided the link to St. Petersburg, and Liakhovskii to Kiev; Aaron Lure and several other natives of Vilna studied in Kharkov; Aizenshtadt had relatives in Odessa whom he frequently "visited"; Sponti of the Moscow *Rabochii Soiuz* was known to them through his term of military service in Vilna.

Nizhni Novgorod, where Skvortsov carried on his extensive indoctrination, sent forth its fledglings to all parts of Russia. These young Social Democrats were mainly products of the local gymnasium who subsequently kept in touch with each other. N. A. Silvin left to attend the University of St. Petersburg, N. A. Vigdorchik, for the University of Kiev, Mitskevich, for Moscow. Lenin, knowing Skvortsov by reputation, sought him out in Nizhni Novgorod; the Nizhni circles put him in touch with the Moscow *Rabochii Soiuz* through Mitskevich. Lenin also was tied to Moscow circles through his sister and brother-in-law, the Elisarovs. Social Democrats in both Moscow and St. Petersburg kept in touch with the *Rabochii Soiuz* in Ivanovo-Voznesensk through a lower court judge, S. P. Shesternin, who had married one of the Neustrova sisters from Nizhni Novgorod; two other Neustrova sisters taught in the factory Sunday Schools in St. Petersburg. Such examples could be multiplied ad infinitum. Exiles from major industrial centers frequently settled in minor industrial centers and served as contacts for their former comrades, even though they might be obliged to remain aloof from local work. All such personal ties were scrupulously kept up with the aim of eventually establishing more permanent, binding relations among Social Democratic groups. Each major center could boast its own set of connections: the Moscow *Rabochii Soiuz* to Vilna, St. Petersburg, Ekaterinoslav, Nizhni Novgorod, Ivanovo-Voznesensk, and Tula; Kiev to Vilna, Moscow, Ekaterinoslav, Odessa, and St. Petersburg; Vilna to St. Petersburg, Moscow, Kharkov, Odessa, Kiev, and many other cities of the West and South; Odessa to a group of southern cities, including Kremenchug and Nikolaev.

This represents only a very incomplete list of known relationships among groups in the mid-1890's. Contacts were frequently interrupted because of the arrests of key persons (although the arrested usually tried to leave reliable successors), and regular communication was dangerous due to police surveillance of the mail of suspected persons. These far-flung listening posts were thus at best very inadequate means for consolidating the movement. Nevertheless, on the basis of such tenuous personal ties, occasional attempts were made to call together representatives of various groups in the hopes of founding a party. Vilna Social Democrats were not alone in harboring such thoughts, which, by 1896, had been the subject of discussion in Moscow, Kiev, and St. Petersburg. There are a number of references in the memoirs, frequently contradicting each other, to the soundings of this or that group.

In the spring of 1895, E. I. Sponti of the Moscow *Rabochii Soiuz* set out on an odyssey which took him to Vilna, St. Petersburg, and Geneva. On behalf of his group, he intended to propose an arrangement under which the *Gruppa Osvobozhdenie Truda* would print popular propaganda literature for workers and the Vilna group would supervise its transit across the border into Russia. Upon his arrival in Vilna, his old acquaintances broached the subject of a party congress and suggested a conference with St. Petersburg Social Democrats as a preliminary step. Sponti and Timofei Kopelzon of Vilna journeyed to St. Petersburg to sound out the *stariki*. Although a meeting took place, no decisions or agreements for further negotiations resulted. The St. Petersburg comrades announced that they had already made their own plans to get in touch with the *Gruppa Osvobozhdenie Truda* and did not presently wish to enter into binding commitments with other groups.[4]

Reasons of health aside, Lenin's trip to Switzerland that summer was to carry out the plans of the St. Petersburg group. When Lenin called upon Plekhanov in Geneva, he was unexpectedly "introduced" to a comrade from Moscow with the suggestion they coordinate their efforts; both embarrassed, according to Sponti's account, they studiously avoided discussing organizational plans.[5] Later in Zurich, Lenin and Akselrod came to the understanding

---

[4] For E. I. Sponti's recollections see "Kratkaia avtobiografiia," *Na zare rabochego dvizheniia v Moskve*, pp. 41–47 and "Vstrechi s Leninym," *Zapiski Instituta Lenina*, No. 3 (1928), pp. 73–75. There is also a brief account by Timofei Kopelzon in *O Lenine: Vospominaniia*, ed. N. L. Meshcheriakov (Moscow, 1925), pp. 21–22.

[5] See Sponti, *Zapiski Instituta Lenina*, No. 3, pp. 73–75. Lenin's coolness to the overtures from other groups probably was not because of his indifference to broad organizational plans, but because of his firm intention that the St. Petersburg group should play the key role.

that the latter should edit a journal for workers to be called *Rabotnik*, for which the St. Petersburg *Soiuz Bor'by* should supply material on developments in Russia. On his part, Lenin received Akselrod's sanction to handle relations between the *Gruppa Osvobozhdenie Truda* and groups inside Russia. The arrests of Lenin and other key persons in his group in December, 1895, put an end to these arrangements, although Akselrod dutifully put out several issues of *Rabotnik*.[6]

The following year, Finn-Enotaevskii, a member of the reconstituted Moscow *Rabochii Soiuz* (Sponti and most of the former members were in prison), visited the Kiev and St. Petersburg organizations, instructed by his group to negotiate on the question of organizing a party congress.[7] According to him, these organizations agreed to the proposal and its realization was forestalled only by arrests. In a series of commentaries on Finn's recollections of the matter, B. L. Eidelman, a leading figure in the Kiev group at the time, denied the occurrence of such negotiations, while Krupskaia and Elizarova-Ulianova, who were privy to Finn's talks with the St. Petersburg *Soiuz Bor'by*, recalled only that regular communications were discussed, not a congress. Krupskaia added that Finn was treated with great caution because of the presence of a known provocateur in the Moscow group.[8]

---

[6] See *Perepiska G. V. Plekhanova i P. B. Aksel'roda*, I, 113 and 265–72. Oddly, Akselrod described in detail his impressions of Sponti and the young "Ulianov," but made no mention of the organizational agreements reached. The editor's information, not having the benefit of Sponti's recollections, is somewhat inaccurate inasmuch as he assumes that some accord had been reached at the St. Petersburg meeting, and that Lenin spoke in the name of all three local groups. See also Lenin's letters to Akselrod in the fall of 1895, *Sochineniia*, XXVIII, 17–20, which deal with the affairs of *Rabotnik*.

[7] M. Liadov also discussed the efforts of the Moscow *Rabochii Soiuz* to negotiate with other groups on the question of a party congress, but dated them to the spring of 1895. In view of the difficulties of reconciling his version with the recollections of Sponti (who attributed the initiative to Vilna), it is more likely that he had the negotiations of Finn-Enotaevskii in mind and simply erred in his dates. He himself was in prison at the time. See Liadov, II, 26–27.

[8] For these short recollections, see "K voprosu o pervom s'ezde," *Pervyi S'ezd R.S.–D.R.P.*, ed. V. A. Algazov (Kiev, 1923), pp. 183–87. In subsequent references this work will be cited as *Pervyi S'ezd* (1923). M. F. Vladimirskii, another member of the *Rabochii Soiuz*, recalled that his organization did work out some document in 1896 to be presented to a proposed congress, but otherwise his recollections are quite vague and cautious. The testimonies of Vladimirskii and Liadov confirm that the idea of forming a party was at least discussed at length by the Moscow group, even if Finn exaggerated the serious import of his negotiations.

While flatly denying Finn's assertions, Krupskaia elsewhere wrote that in the summer of 1896 she was sent by the St. Petersburg *Soiuz Bor'by* to confer with other centers about the publication of a nation-wide illegal newspaper and preparations for a party congress.[9] She told of a preliminary meeting in Poltava with Tuchapskii from Kiev and Aaron Lure from Kharkov, but offered no further details on the content or outcome of their discussions; news of the textile strikes drew her back prematurely to the capital. Tuchapskii's rather detailed memoirs record no such negotiations and Eidelman explicitly denied any knowledge of them. Perhaps this journey also was vaguer in purpose than it seemed to a chronicler in later years.

Confusing though these data may be, they do illustrate that the idea of convoking a congress and organizing a party was in the wind and could easily crop up in various places quite independently.[10] More important than the truth or error of particular recollections is the mold in which such aspirations were cast: the way the group approached its task, the means it thought to employ, the role it envisaged for its own organization. Liadov records the thoughts of the Moscow *Rabochii Soiuz* on this matter in 1894 (before the trips of Finn and Sponti):

> The Moscow organization . . . brought up in one of its sessions the question of putting out a "manifesto" to present the point of view of the organization . . . to once and for all solidify its political physiognomy. The initiators of this idea saw in the very fact of publishing such a manifesto a first step toward the creation of a unified party. The Moscow *Soiuz*, they said, could serve as a core around which to rally all who were like-minded. . . .

---

[9] See *Pervyi S'ezd R.S.–D.R.P.* (Moscow, 1958), p. 130. In subsequent references this work will be cited as *Pervyi S'ezd* (1958) in distinction to the earlier work of the same title, which will be cited as *Pervyi S'ezd* (1923).

[10] Another early instance of nationwide organizational plans was the proposal of the *Gruppa Chetvertogo Listka*, a group of former *narodovoltsy* which cooperated closely with the St. Petersburg Social Democrats. This group proposed that, if the latter convoked a congress of active Social Democratic organizations from other centers, it would put its excellently functioning secret printing press in Lahti, Finland, at their disposal. The uncovering of the press by the police in July, 1896, forestalled these plans. See Akimov, *Materialy*, pp. 45–46. Unfortunately, Akimov gives no information as to the exact time or circumstances of this offer. It is possible that it bore some connection with Krupskaia's trip to the South.

The Moscow organization would furnish other organizations with a uniform type of literature, it would collect and distribute to other organizations information about the workers' movement all over Russia and thus facilitate genuinely uniform action by all Social Democrats.[11]

Like Martov's group, the Muscovites hoped to transform their organization into a party center by rendering practical services to other groups; but they felt obliged to abandon the effort in view of the fact that they did "not yet dispose of the resources to unify all of the 'lone-wolves' operating in Moscow, let alone all of Russia." However, in proposing a definitive program to "rally the like-minded" and "solidify the political physiognomy" of the movement, they added one more motif to the ideas which made up the fabric of Social Democratic thinking on the subject in the years to come. These ideas combined the Russian Marxists' ingrained conviction that "correct theory" was essential to action with the conception of a political party inherited from the People's Will: a tightly disciplined organization whose directives commanded unwavering obedience from the membership. That these notions might conflict in practice with their concurrent commitment to a mass workers' party guided by the democratically expressed will of the masses occurred to very few Social Democrats at the time.

The cause of unifying Social Democratic groups was soon taken up again, this time by Kiev and Vilna.[12] In the winter of 1896, Alexander Kremer of Vilna took a trip to St. Petersburg to discuss the possibility of regular communication with and a joint ap-

---

11 Liadov, II, p. 26. These discussions preceded by at least a year the above mentioned journey of Moscow representatives, and thus Liadov was undoubtedly a participant in them (even allowing for possible error on his part as to the exact time of the discussions). Liadov was arrested in the fall of 1895.

12 The two most useful accounts are Akimov, "Pervyi S'ezd," *Minuvshie Gody*, II (1908), pp. 128–68 and B. Eidelman, "K istorii vozniknoveniia r.s.d.r.p.," *Proletarskaia Revoliutsiia*, No. 1 (1921), pp. 26–66. Although Akimov was not a direct participant in the events in question, he interviewed all the leading figures, the only historian of the party to use this technique systematically. However, a good deal of his information is disputed by Eidelman, who was himself a key participant. See "Po povodu stati tov. Akimova," *ibid.*, pp. 67–81. These articles and most of the other important memoirs on the events leading up to the First Congress were reprinted in *Pervyi S'ezd* (1923). Henceforth, for the sake of simplicity, references will be drawn from this work wherever possible rather than from the work in which they first appeared, and after the first reference the title of the article under discussion will be omitted.

proach to the émigré leaders, Plekhanov and Akselrod. In the capital, Kremer's friend Gorev, a native of Vilna, put him in touch with Radchenko, Potresov, and Iakubova who conducted negotiations on behalf of the St. Petersburg *Soiuz Bor'by*. According to Akimov's account, the parties agreed to seek permanent relations with the *Gruppa Osvobozhdenie Truda*. Akimov further claimed that Kremer was to continue on to Kiev to draw in the group *Rabochee Delo*. The Kievan group supposedly welcomed the proposals and authorized Kremer to treat with the *Gruppa Osvobozhdenie Truda* in their name.

There is reason to believe, however, that Akimov's version is not entirely accurate. Eidelman's account questions that such negotiations with Kremer ever took place and denies that the Kievan group knew of, much less officially approved, any proposal to negotiate with the *Gruppa Osvobozhdenie Truda*.[13] It was Eidelman's claim that the idea of organizing a party originated in Kiev, and that with such an aim in view he made the rounds of the Vilna, St. Petersburg, and Moscow organizations about the same time as Kremer. The Kievan organization, like Vilna and Moscow, aspired to become the apostolic seat of the movement and clearly distrusted the efforts of potential competitors. Their thinking, as described by Eidelman, merely embellished slightly that of the Moscow group.

> There was no more convincing method [of proving the advantages of unification] than to disseminate information on the workers' movement in all parts of Russia and to illuminate the facts of Russian life from a Social Democratic point of view through the instrumentality of a newspaper published at regular and frequent intervals, i.e., by actually taking on one important function of a central party organization. Thus, the group *Rabochaia Gazeta* [the name they

---

13 See *ibid.*, p. 70. Eidelman is undoubtedly correct about Kremer's visit to Switzerland. Kremer makes no mention in his memoirs of the Kievan mission, stating merely that in May, 1897 (i.e., at least four months after the date given by Akimov for the trip to Kiev), he traveled to Switzerland to negotiate with the *Gruppa Osvobozhdenie Truda* in the name of only the Vilna and St. Petersburg organizations. For Kremer's account see "Obosnovanie Bunda," *ibid.*, pp. 152–59. Akimov's account of the earlier negotiations with the St. Petersburg *Soiuz Bor'by* is not open to doubt, however, inasmuch as Gorev confirms that he put Kremer in touch with the *stariki*, and that they conferred at length on some question unknown to Gorev. In the context of Gorev's memoirs this encounter must have taken place early in 1897. See Gorev, p. 11. For the outcome of Kremer's mission to Switzerland, see pp. 171–73.

assumed when they became an all-Russian instead of merely a local group] intended to set up an operating center, whose functions would be expanded into actual direction of the party.[14]

The notion that specifically an underground newspaper of national circulation (rather than simply a manifesto or regular exchanges of information) should be employed to build up a spirit and a party organization rounded out the ideas which were passed on to *Iskra* as the legacy of the 1890's.[15] Constructed from the practical experiences of energetic underground workers who thought in terms of party statesmanship, these notions invariably took on a similar pragmatic form. Other instances of such thinking cropped up in the ensuing years.[16]

The Kievan organization had already put out a few mimeographed numbers of a local news sheet *Vpered* (*Forward*) and was making arrangements to set up a secret printing press in Ekaterinoslav. Hoping to establish the ascendancy of Kiev, Eidelman suggested to the organizations of other cities that his group be authorized to put out a newspaper to help create the "proper atmosphere" for a party congress. The Vilna and St. Petersburg organizations cautiously vetoed this suggestion, claiming that a preliminary conference of Social Democratic groups should be held first. Such a conference was held in the middle of March, 1897, in Kiev. Gorev from St. Petersburg and an inexperienced student from Moscow were the only delegates not from Kiev. The Vilna and Ivanovo-Voznesensk organizations failed to respond to invitations. Gorev passed on rumors about provocateurs in the

---

[14] *Pervyi S'ezd* (1923), p. 61.

[15] Lenin voiced *Iskra's* viewpoint in his article "Where to Begin" in the fourth issue of *Iskra:* "A newspaper is not only a collective propagandist and agitator but also a collective organizer. . . . In carrying out the task of a newspaper a permanent organization forms of its own accord, occupied not only with local work, but with regular nationwide work. The technical work itself—furnishing the paper with regular materials and distributing it—compels the erection of a net of local agents of a unified party, agents who are acquainted with the general state of affairs, in constant active communication with each other, accustomed to the regular execution of detailed functions on a nationwide scale, who test their powers in the organization of this or that revolutionary action." (*Sochineniia*, IV, 111–12.) Cf. also *Iskra's* official "Declaration" announcing its aims (*ibid.*, pp. 39–40).

[16] Lydia Dan in discussing this period with the author once aptly remarked that whenever a group succeeded in setting up an underground press, they automatically raised the question of organizing a party.

Moscow organization and the student, after reporting on Moscow affairs, was told the conference had been cancelled. Three representatives from Kiev, and Gorev from St. Petersburg, therefore, carried on the business on hand, arriving at the following decisions: to postpone the calling of a party congress until the following year; to establish an all-Russian group, *Rabochaia Gazeta*, which was to publish a Social Democratic organ of the same name; to entrust the arrangements for the future congress to this group; to request that local groups express their common solidarity by accepting the uniform designation of *Soiuz Bor'by za Osvobozhdenie Rabochego Klassa;* and to entrust the writing of a program for the party to Plekhanov.[17] The new group, *Rabochaia Gazeta,* of course, was made up primarily of Kievan Social Democrats. Despite the flimsy representation at the conference, the Kievans felt they had acquired a mandate to make preparations for the future party congress. In the meantime, they were free to exploit their projected newspaper to obtain a position of hegemony in the movement.

The Kievan innovators' most important task for the moment was to achieve the smooth operation of their newspaper in order to establish its reputation among Russian Social Democratic groups. Given the high caliber and long revolutionary experience of Eidelman, Poliak, Petrusevich, and Vigdorchik, the technical aspects of the undertaking were soon mastered—setting up secret quarters, securing printing paraphernalia, arranging channels of information from other localities. The chief deficiency of the group was in good writing talent by Social Democrats versed in Marxist theory. As the time for the appearance of the first number approached, the editors still did not have an article articulating the "Social Democratic physiognomy" of their organ. At the very last moment the editors hurriedly composed an article replete with all the standard clichés of ordinary agitational literature. The Social Democratic publicists faced a dilemma typical for the illegal organs of the period: whether to aim at the ordinary but receptive

---

[17] On the Kiev Conference in 1897 see Gorev, p. 13, and the accounts of Eidelman, Tuchapskii, and Akimov in *Pervyi S'ezd* (1923), pp. 48–49, 175, and 97–99 respectively. According to Akimov, the Kievan representatives were N. A. Vigdorchik, K. A. Petrusevich, and an unknown representative of the Polish group. Gorev's recollection that Tuchapskii attended the conference is doubtful, as it is not supported by the other memoirs, including those of Tuchapskii himself.

worker, or at the more sophisticated worker socialist. Eidelman maintained that he had energetically fought for the second alternative as more in keeping with the wider mission of their group, but had been overruled. By the second issue, he had won his colleagues over to his view; correspondingly its articles were written in a more militant Social Democratic spirit.[18]

The contrast between the two numbers is indeed striking. The first issue of *Rabochaia Gazeta* (August, 1897) made only one reference to the aim of a party, and even this remark was buried in a tedious recitation of strikes:

> Only by uniting into one powerful union, into one powerful workers' party, will Russian workers achieve victory over factory owners and the government. . . . And here our workers' paper will further this great cause. . . . It will attempt to explain to the worker his situation . . . and will unite all Russian workers in comradeship for the common struggle.[19]

The second issue (November, 1897) spoke out unreservedly against the "yoke of the autocracy" and on behalf of political freedom, which must embrace the legalization of strikes and unions, freedom of the press, assembly, and so on. Russian workers could achieve such goals only under the red banner of International Social Democracy. Socialism, defined as social ownership of the means of production, was set forth as the ultimate aim of the movement. Moreover, it formulated in clear terms its conception of the tasks of the immediate future.

> *The Russian workers' movement will multiply its strength tenfold if it unites into one harmonious whole, acquiring an established reputation and a well-balanced organization.* It is no longer enough that Russian workers sympathize with each other. . . . It is necessary for them to unite in fact. The time has come when separate, scattered workers' circles and organizations should be transformed into one common union, one all-embracing party.[20]

Thus, although the second issue of *Rabochaia Gazeta* was adapted to the level of the propagandized workers, it boldly advanced the

---

[18] See *Pervyi S'ezd* (1923), pp. 63–65. Most of the above information on *Rabochaia Gazeta* is supplied by Eidelman. For the text of Nos. 1 and 2 of *Rabochaia Gazeta* see *K dvadtsatipiatiletiiu pervago s'ezda partii*, pp. 176–282, and *Pervyi S'ezd* (1958), pp. 241–302.

[19] *Pervyi S'ezd* (1958), p. 244.　　　　[20] *Ibid.*, p. 273.

full program of Social Democracy. Eidelman could now take satisfaction in the conviction that his group was measuring up to the mission which it had undertaken.

The belated fulfillment of its chosen task by the group *Rabochaia Gazeta* was not without its unfortunate consequences. It seemed only natural to Russian Social Democrats at the March conference to entrust the writing of a program to Plekhanov. Yet the group *Rabochaia Gazeta* implemented this decision in a rather ambiguous fashion. Tuchapskii, a member of the group *Rabochaia Gazeta* had been sent to Switzerland in the fall of 1897 (before the appearance of the second issue) to sound out the reactions of Akselrod and Plekhanov to the first issue and to request them to contribute to future numbers. He was also to request the *Gruppa Osvobozhdenie Truda* to assume responsibility for writing and publishing of a series of propaganda brochures for Russian workers. Nothing, however, was said about the plans for a party congress or the writing of a party program.

The reception of the Kievan envoy was disappointing—Akselrod and Plekhanov had not read the first number, even though copies had been circulating in the émigré colony.[21] They rejected immediately the suggestion of writing popular literature for workers, the explanation being that they had no time or resources for such tasks. They did, however, offhandedly promise literary contributions for *Rabochaia Gazeta*. Tuchapskii left with the impression that both Plekhanov and Akselrod were far removed from Russian realities and more concerned with the debates in the legal Marxist journals than with the fate of the Social Democratic movement. He returned to Kiev to communicate the disheartening results.

Despite their coolness toward the emissary from Russia, Plekhanov and Akselrod kept their promise of literary collaboration. A month or so later a certain Tesler, who had been studying in Switzerland, arrived in Kiev with manuscripts of articles by Akselrod and Koltsov, and a "letter" from Plekhanov. The interest of the *Gruppa Osvobozhdenie Truda* in and its literary contributions to their undertaking were greeted enthusiastically by the members of *Rabochaia Gazeta*. The prestige of Plekhanov's name was essential to their efforts to create a party.

---

[21] For accounts of this mission by Eidelman, Akimov, and Tuchapskii, see *Pervyi S'ezd* (1923), pp. 69, 110–12, and 177, respectively.

Plekhanov's letter, however, aroused mixed feelings. On the one hand, he congratulated the Kievan comrades for their efforts to combat the "narrow group spirit" in local Social Democratic organizations and flatteringly offered his collaboration in the future. On the other hand, he suggested that they had not sufficiently stressed the political objectives of Social Democracy:

> A second no less important condition of the further success of the movement is the working out and dissemination through our ranks of correct views on the political tasks of our party in Russia. If I am not mistaken, our Russian comrades at present do not always keep in mind the extremely important thought of Marx that *every class struggle is a political struggle.*[22]

The implied reproach stung the Kievans in a particularly sensitive spot, as they had just engaged in a bitter dispute on this issue with a group of *narodovoltsy* and a few "worker-revolutionaries" under the influence of the unorthodox Social Democrat Moisei Lure. These groups had charged that the Kievan Social Democrats, by turning to agitation, had abandoned their revolutionary tasks. The printing of Plekhanov's letter in *Rabochaia Gazeta* could only lend credence to these accusations. Had Plekhanov seen the second number, they felt, he would certainly not have expressed this embarrassing criticism. Apparently, some consideration was given to printing only part of the letter, leaving out the reproaches, but finally it was decided to send a representative abroad to request Plekhanov himself to alter it.[23]

The collaboration of the *Gruppa Osvobozhdenie Truda* in *Rabochaia Gazeta* proved to be stillborn. The contributions of the émigré group arrived too late to be placed in the second issue, and the appearance of the third issue, scheduled immediately after

---

[22] *Pervyi S'ezd* (1958), p. 293. (Italics in original.) Nicolaevsky discovered the letter of Plekhanov in Akselrod's archive and published it with critical notes. See "Pis'mo G. V. Plekhanova v redaktsiiu 'Rabochei Gazety,'" *Letopis' Revoliutsii*, No. 1 (Berlin, 1923), pp. 138–41. It was apparently not preserved in the materials of *Rabochaia Gazeta* appropriated by the police upon the arrest of the group, most of which have been reprinted (see n. 24 below).

[23] Eidelman has denied Akimov's assertion that his group discussed these possibilities. Akimov's version is confirmed, however, by the text of a letter to Plekhanov making such a request which was found on Tesler when he was arrested. See *Krasnyi Arkhiv*, No. 29 (November–December, 1926), pp. 207–9. For the conflicting assertions of Eidelman and Akimov see *Pervyi S'ezd* (1923), pp. 144 and 112, respectively.

the First Congress, was forestalled by mass arrests. The manuscripts were seized at the time of the arrest of the editors.[24] The uneasy relationship between the young *praktiki* and the émigré veterans revealed in this encounter was symptomatic of the wide gulf in attitudes separating the two generations. Had Plekhanov and Akselrod been more fully informed, they might have reacted with a good deal more enthusiasm to the Russian undertaking, but the only evidence they had to go on was the uninspiring first number of *Rabochaia Gazeta*. Moreover, the request to write and publish propaganda brochures for workers hit upon what had long become a sore point for the émigré leaders.[25] The veterans of Marxism felt that their task was to maintain broad theoretical perspectives for the movement, and they resented the repeated efforts of younger comrades to use them as errand boys for various practical chores. Tuchapskii's representations were viewed as just one more such imposition.

The Kievan leaders, on their part, apparently entertained certain doubts about the advisability of drawing the émigrés into their secret plans. In spite of their reverence for the founding fathers of Russian Marxism, the young *praktiki* inside Russia had quite early developed a suspicion of possible interference by the

---

[24] It is curious, but perhaps accidental, that in the list of articles scheduled to appear in No. 3 of *Rabochaia Gazeta*, Akselrod's article (the first half of his brochure *K voprosu o sovremennykh zadachakh i taktike russkikh sotsial-demokratov*) and Plekhanov's letter are not listed. Of the contributions from abroad only an article by Koltsov ("Gorod i derevnia") is listed and is followed by a question mark. There is no mention in the memoir literature of displeasure with the contributions of Akselrod and Koltsov (a close collaborator of the *Gruppa Osvobozhdenie Truda*). See *Pervyi S'ezd* (1958), pp. 93–94.

[25] As early as 1892, A. Voden, a literate young Marxist from St. Petersburg, visited Plekhanov and forwarded the request of the Brusnev group for popular literature for workers rather than for the heavy theoretical journal *Sotsial-Demokrat* put out by the *Gruppa Osvobozhdenie Truda*. Plekhanov remarked caustically that obviously these young *praktiki* "lacked the desire to learn to think like Marxists," and it seemed to Voden that he spoke "with vexation accumulated over a long period of time." ("Na zare legal'nogo marksizma," *Letopis' Marksizma*, No. 3 [1927], p. 80.) The reader is already acquainted with the similar missions of Lenin and Sponti (the latter was dismissed by Akselrod as "primitive in reasoning . . . driving me to despair"—see *Perepiska*, I, 265). There were no less than six such missions before 1895, all ending in irreconcilable conflicts. Plekhanov's wife, Rosaliia Markovna, described his irritation with the "uncouthness, crudeness, and presumptuousness . . . of these various provincial Lassalles" who in his words "came to measure shoulders with us." ("Nashi vstrechi so znatnymi poteshestvennikami," *Gruppa Osvobozhdenie Truda: Sborniki*, ed. L. G. Deich [Moscow, 1926], III, 219.)

émigré leaders in the organizational affairs of the movement, of which a number of instances are recorded in the literature. Given the desire of the young Social Democrats to prove their own mettle and organizational competence, they easily formed the opinion that Plekhanov and Akselrod were "out of touch" with the real situation in Russia, or that while astute theoretically, they were incompetent in practical matters.[26] In addition, the Kievan group was preoccupied with a host of urgent practical problems—setting up their secret press, establishing communications with other local groups, making arrangements for the Congress, dealing with lingering factional disputes, completing the reorientation to agitation, and, finally, defining the relationship between the group *Rabochaia Gazeta* and the Kievan *Soiuz Bor'by*. Many of these problems had to be solved expeditiously, without discussion or thoughtful consideration; among these was the very important but neglected question of the relationship between Russian *praktiki* and their émigré leaders.

With the operation of an all-Russian newspaper functioning relatively well, the next order of business was to work out ground rules for calling the Congress. The group *Rabochaia Gazeta* framed these in a brief document entitled *Ustav Kollokviuma* (*Rules of the Colloquium*).[27] The *Ustav* proposed to invite only those Social Democratic groups that acknowledged the "timeliness" of unification. It called for two delegates from each organization—one *intelligent* and, if possible, one worker. It requested on the one hand that delegates be empowered with "the broadest possible discretion" so as not to impede the proceedings of the Congress, but, on the other, that delegates should be provided by their groups with previously worked out positions on suggested questions.[28] These questions, which were circulated among the invited groups, subsequently served as the order of business at the Congress itself.

Most of the questions concerned the function and authority of

26 The Bolshevik, Liadov, expressed such opinions, drawing on his experiences in Moscow in 1895 (see his *Istoriia*, I, 100 ff.) as did O. A. Ermanskii concerning his encounters with Plekhanov in 1893 (*Iz perezhitogo*, p. 33).

27 For the text of the *Ustav* see *Pervyi S'ezd* (1958), pp. 86–87.

28 This point was misconstrued by Akimov as stipulating "binding mandates" on all questions. See *Pervyi S'ezd* (1923), pp. 98–99.

the Central Committee. How was it to be elected? Which questions should it decide on its own authority and which, only by consulting member groups? Should it have the right to create or recognize new groups, to administer the party press, to co-opt replacements, to control finances, or to negotiate in the name of the party with other parties and groups? Another section concerned the competence of the Congress itself. Did it have the authority to elect the Central Committee, to establish a party organ, or to confirm a party program?

Although these points were presented as questions to be decided by the local groups, it is clear that the authors sought two important objectives: first, a Congress with broad powers to deliberate and decide in the name of local groups; and, second, a strong Central Committee invested with authority to direct the movement and to speak in its name. The document reflected the sentiments of one of its co-authors, Eidelman. His original draft had been even more centralistic in spirit, framed in the form, not of questions, but of propositions to be accepted or rejected. The text had been reviewed by Vigdorchik, however, who insisted that it be considerably shortened and toned down.[29] In a number of respects Eidelman's views anticipated those of Lenin in the *Iskra* period. He summarized them in this way:

> Once a central organization exists, it is possible to create immediately at all new points colony-committees. In this way one preserves the experience of old party workers. . . . In place of the parochial patriotism of particularists a party spirit [*partiinost'*] is cultivated. This precludes the formation of an "opposition."[30]

He was only partially successful in gaining acceptance of his views by his colleagues of *Rabochaia Gazeta,* to say nothing of the First Congress, but it is instructive to note that the notion of using "agents" to build up pliant local organizations had already suggested itself to energetic *praktiki.*

Representatives of *Rabochaia Gazeta* made the rounds of existing Social Democratic organizations to inform themselves on the state of local Social Democratic work and to judge which of the

---

29 For details see Eidelman's account in *ibid.,* pp. 146–48.

30 *Ibid.,* p. 74. Akimov records similar appraisals of Eidelman's views by two of his informants (probably Tuchapskii and Kremer), *ibid.,* pp. 120–21.

extant groups were sufficiently mature and well-organized to deserve representation. The criteria employed were that the group conduct propaganda and agitation among the workers in a Social Democratic spirit, and that it be thoroughly dependable in its conspiratorial practices. Thus, although the *Rabochaia Gazeta* group was familiar with young Trotsky's group in Nikolaev, they regarded it as insufficiently schooled in rules of conspiracy. Other strong provincial groups of Social Democratic intelligentsia, such as those in Samara and Tula, did not carry on activities among workers.

In one case, *Rabochaia Gazeta* actually employed Eidelman's notion of sending an "agent" to set local work in order. The group had heard rumors of factional quarrels over introducing agitation in Ekaterinoslav. Petrusevich was dispatched to the scene to win over the opposition and create a climate of sympathy for the plans of *Rabochaia Gazeta*. Aided in part by arrests which happened to cripple one of the factions, he accomplished his mission in a few months. The program of agitation was officially adopted and the warring groups combined into one Ekaterinoslav *Soiuz Bor'by*. Petrusevich's later selection as delegate from Ekaterinoslav to the Congress promised to strengthen further the hegemony of *Rabochaia Gazeta*.

The pre-Congress negotiations revealed that the *Rabochaia Gazeta* faced several rivals for leadership in the future party. Akimov recorded the reply of the Kharkov Social Democrats, who declined the invitation to the Congress:

> To unify the party, it is necessary first of all to create a group standing particularly high in moral authority over all other Social Democratic groups; only such a naturally created center of the Social Democratic movement, acting as its soul, can gather around itself all real forces.[31]

Clearly this group viewed Kharkov, and not Kiev, as the "moral" authority in question.

---

[31] *Pervyi S'ezd* (1923), p. 102. This is not a direct quotation from a document, but the description of its contents by Akimov's informants. Very little practical work was carried on by the Kharkov Social Democrats, but they represented a notably distinguished group of intelligentsia. Among them were Cherevanin (Lipkin), Avilov, and Bogdanov, all of whom later became prominent theoreticians and authors in the party. They appear to have had some connection with *Rabochee Znamia*. See p. 195.

Another potential rival was the group *Rabochee Znamia,* whose indefatigable organizer, Moisei Lure, had fanned the opposition of the group of "worker-revolutionaries" to the Kiev *Soiuz Bor'by.* Eidelman declares that *Rabochee Znamia* was not invited to the Congress because it was regarded as "not yet well-defined in its views," and "too friendly to the Kievan group of S.R.'s."[32] Shortly before the First Congress, invitations were received by the St. Petersburg and Kiev organizations to join *Rabochee Znamia's* Social Democratic party (supposedly already in existence) on the basis of its freshly printed program *Zadachi russkoi rabochei partii* (*Tasks of the Russian Workers' Party*). The invitation, of course, was ignored. Lure knew of the preparations for the First Congress, but he hoped to forestall them with his own plans.[33] Thus two independently operating Social Democratic groups were attempting to use their literary organs as the focal points for creating a Social Democratic party and were maneuvering against each other to gain the advantage. To be sure, Lure's high-handed tactics had little prospect of winning the support of local Social Democratic groups, but they temporarily unnerved the leaders of *Rabochaia Gazeta.*

A third and far more formidable rival was the Social Democratic organization in Vilna. Vilna was in many respects in a far better position to launch the party than Kiev. Its organization was by far the most effective, the most diversified, and the most imaginative in all of Russia. Practically undisturbed by arrests, it had enjoyed a continuity and security in its activities unmatched in Russia proper. Moreover, it had long performed "certain functions of a central institution of the party"—supplying literature from abroad, mounting guard at the border, and serving as a center of communications. As initiator of the whole program of agitation, Vilna enjoyed a prestige excelled only by St. Petersburg, which could lay claim to the momentous textile strike. Moreover, the Vilna Social Democrats had repeatedly sought to spur the creation of a party. Only the apparent unripeness of the Russian

---

[32] *Pervyi S'ezd* (1923), p. 78. The use of the term "S.R.'s" for a local group of *narodovoltsy* in 1897 was of course a slight anachronism.

[33] See the memoir fragment of A. Solts in *K dvadtsatipiatiletiiu pervago s'ezda partii* (*1898–1923*), pp. 74–75 and *Pervyi S'ezd* (1923), p. 78. The history of *Rabochee Znamia* is treated in the following chapter.

movement for such broad plans had persuaded them to concentrate on the Jewish workers' movement. The mushrooming of the Jewish movement did not alter fundamentally the ambitions of the Vilna veterans. When the local movement assumed mass proportions, the veteran leaders drew in representatives of the *poluintelligenty* and workers, to whom were assigned most of the day-to-day functions of local work. The Russian-educated, Russia-oriented older generation—Kremer, Kopelzon, Srednitskaia, Mutnik, and Levenson-Kossovskii—formed a special cell to concentrate on advancing the interests of the movement as a whole. (It goes without saying that the undertaking was kept secret from other members of the Vilna Committee.)[34]

What is difficult to determine is whether members of the cell were aware of the Kievan efforts, and if they were aware of them, whether they deliberately moved to outflank the Kievans in the question of leadership. The evidence is confusing and full of gaps; some information in the literature is manifestly untrustworthy, notably in the accounts of Akimov and Kremer. How much the two groups learned of each other's intentions in the overlapping trips of Eidelman and Kremer in early 1897 is uncertain, but the absence of a delegate from Vilna at the Kievan Conference in March was quite remarkable. Eidelman's flimsy excuse that the invitation did not reach Vilna in time seems to depend upon a strange oversight, in view of the frequent contacts between Vilna and Kiev during this period.[35] It is much more likely that organizational rivalry was at play. Either the Kievan Social Democrats, fearing a challenge to the role they had adopted for themselves, intentionally delayed sending the invitation, or the Vilna group, not wishing to acknowledge the legitimacy of the conference under Kiev's auspices, ignored it. Otherwise it is incomprehensible that the Vilna Social Democrats dispatched Kremer to the *Gruppa Osvobozhdenie Truda* on an important mission which left the Kievans' efforts entirely out of consideration. If members at Vilna did not know the results of the Kiev Conference early in 1897, the

---

[34] See the memoirs of D. Tsoglin (Kats) in the collection edited by Dimanshtein, *Revoliutsionnoe dvizhenie sredi evreev*, pp. 134 ff. The recollections of Kats are far superior to those of Kremer in clarity and respect for historical accuracy, even though Kats did not become a member of the inner circle until later.

[35] See *Pervyi S'ezd* (1923), p. 48.

Kievan organization was inexcusably negligent in not informing them.

So far as can be determined (discounting Akimov's version) Kremer's negotiations with St. Petersburg in early 1897 had the immediate objective, not of convoking a congress, but of arranging for the Russian movement to be represented that summer at the International Conference on Labor Legislation at Zurich. The two organizations worked out a joint report to be submitted in the name of the two local organizations only.[36] On the other hand, there is the convincing testimony of the Vilna Social Democrat David Kats that when Kremer reported to the Vilna Committee on his plans before going abroad, he was asked why all Jewish organizations were not to be represented. Kremer replied darkly that the "question of founding a general [Russian] party, not simply a Jewish one, is now being discussed and will be determined very shortly."[37] This suggests either that by this time (May, 1897) Kremer was informed of the Kievan efforts or, just as likely, that he had in mind an effort under the exclusive auspices of Vilna. In any event, he proceeded abroad in May to negotiate an agreement with the *Gruppa Osvobozhdenie Truda* on future representation of Russian groups at international congresses and did not deem it necessary to consult with Kiev.[38]

Another striking fact is that Kremer, immediately upon return-

---

[36] See Kremer's account, *ibid.*, p. 154. The text of joint report was printed in *Rabochaia Gazeta*, No. 2. See *Pervyi S'ezd* (1958), pp. 296–98.

[37] Dimanshtein, p. 136.

[38] This encounter very nearly resulted in an embarrassing rupture due to Plekhanov's intransigent attitude toward agitation to which the Russian organizations were committed body and soul. Akselrod and Zasulich managed to bridge over the controversy and bring about a formal agreement. Unfortunately, the text of the agreement has not been preserved, as it would clear up a few important points. It certainly provided that the Union of Social Democrats Abroad should regularly receive mandates to represent Russia at international congresses, but it is very doubtful that any mention was made by Kremer of his plans for founding a party. Takhtarev, who was present at the negotiations and sided with Kremer, recounted all the other details, but when he heard news of the First Congress the next year, he was taken by surprise and deplored it as premature. See his *Rabochee dvizhenie v Peterburge*, pp. 110–11 and 114. Akselrod's project was presented to the Congress, and a telegram was immediately sent designating the Union of Social Democrats Abroad as the official representative of the party. See also Akimov, *Pervyi S'ezd* (1923), pp. 94–95. His version is slightly different and attributes the near breach to Plekhanov's demand for formal leadership of the movement. His source was probably Kremer. Kremer's own account confirms the meeting and the participants, but mentions neither the unpleasantness nor the terms of the agreement.

ing from Switzerland, addressed himself vigorously to the task of unifying the Jewish Social Democratic groups into one organization. His efforts culminated in the first constituent Congress of the Bund of September, 1897.[39] This is very puzzling in view of his earlier efforts, in May, to discourage unification. Probably Kremer and his Vilna comrades, realizing that the efforts of *Rabochaia Gazeta* to call a Russian congress could no longer be thwarted, now sought to establish a firm Jewish organization to prevent incursions into their own territory by the party center, which was likely to be dominated by Kiev. The best they could now hope for was to guarantee the autonomy of a Jewish organization within the framework of an all-Russian party.[40] The delegates to the Bund Congress decided that their organization should enter the future all-Russian party only as an independent whole, and a memorandum giving arguments for such an arrangement was worked out for presentation to the future Congress. Their own position now secure through the new organization, the Jewish Social Democrats accepted the inevitability of Kievan ascendancy and henceforward co-operated closely with the group *Rabochaia Gazeta* in preparing for the First Congress.

Only five organizations were actually represented at the First Congress—the Bund, St. Petersburg, Moscow, Ekaterinoslav, and

---

[39] See Kremer's account, *ibid.*, pp. 155–56. The First Congress of the Bund anticipated in many details the First Congress of the Russian party. The major actions of the Bund Congress were: 1) to establish an official name for the party; 2) to define the functions of the Central Committee (which is resolved in a highly centralized spirit); and 3) to declare *Die Arbeiterstimme,* an already extant publication, the official organ of the party. Just as at the Russian Congress, there was no mention of a party program.

[40] It is significant that the arguments advanced in favor of autonomy for the Bund were pragmatic in character and betrayed as yet no trace of "nationalism": 1) the Jewish organizations required publications in the Yiddish language, which a Russian central organization would not be equipped to handle; and 2) a Russian organization might not attack with sufficient energy the laws that discriminated against Jews. One might detect here an as yet inarticulate nationalism, although Kats goes to great length to discount this (see Dimanshtein, pp. 137 ff.). He states that the chief reason for desiring autonomy could not be explicitly stated: that the Bundists felt the Russian Social Democrats were very poor conspirators and that direct relations of local Jewish groups with a Russian Central Committee might "infect" them with police surveillance. It is true that most Jewish Social Democrats at this time were still Russia-oriented, but in my opinion Kremer was above all anxious to forestall any interference with his group's primacy in the Western Pale. After all, the Jewish movement was already a mass movement, whereas the Russian movement was still barely on its feet.

Kiev. Attempts to invite several other groups failed because of the difficulty of making contacts or because of the fear of risking association with organizations that were inexperienced in maintaining the rules of conspiracy. Akimov's reproach that the organizers deliberately left out Ivanovo-Voznesensk in deference to Moscow's claims to represent it seems to be founded on conjecture.[41]

The notion of sending a worker delegate was given up by all the groups except the Bund, one of whose delegates, David Kats, though of petty bourgeois origin, was by trade a watchmaker.[42] The Kievan *Soiuz Bor'by* had conscientiously submitted the question to its workers, but the latter surrendered their mandate to Tuchapskii, who was the representative of the intelligentsia center in the Workers' Committee. Tuchapskii had also received the mandate of the intelligentsia center and therefore controlled two votes at the Congress. In Ekaterinoslav, only the Jewish artisan group was given the opportunity to select a delegate, but they also deferred to Petrusevich, one of the intelligentsia.[43] Radchenko of St. Petersburg would hardly have considered the sending of a worker delegate on conspiratorial grounds;[44] Viktor Vannovskii,

---

[41] An invitation to send a representative to the Kiev Conference in 1897 had been sent through Moscow to Shesternin, a lower court judge in Ivanovo. But just about that time he had been transferred to another judicial district because of his partiality toward workers whose cases he handled. Thus Kiev's contact in Ivanovo-Voznesensk was lost. Akimov evidently was not aware that the "well-functioning group" of which he speaks was plagued by arrests during the whole year 1897 and that not one active *intelligent* was left. Perazich, who had been dispatched by the Moscow *Soiuz Bor'by* to strengthen their organization, was immediately arrested. See M. Bagaev, *Za desiat' let* (Ivanovo, 1930), pp. 72 ff.

[42] Because of the peculiarities of the Jewish social milieu, the categories "worker," "*poluintelligent*," and "*intelligent*" were quite fluid. The son of an impoverished Jewish middle class family was typically a *poluintelligent*, but, given the tremendous drive such youngsters often had for a Russian education, he might eventually qualify as an *intelligent*. However, to support himself, he might be obliged to learn a trade or craft which qualified him as a "worker." Many of the skilled *praktiki* of the Pale, like Kats, were of this peculiar type.

[43] See the memoirs of I. I. Vilenskii in *Istoriia ekaterinoslavskoi*, p. 90. Vilenskii had originally been selected by the Jewish workers, but since he was involved in the underground press of *Rabochaia Gazeta* he surrendered his mandate to Petrusevich. Babushkin, it will be recalled, bitterly resented not being drawn in on the plans for the Congress. See p. 105.

[44] Akimov records the bitterness of the rank and file *praktiki* in St. Petersburg over Radchenko's claim to represent them even though he had not informed them of the forthcoming Congress. Radchenko as the sole survivor of the *stariki* still claimed to represent the "center" of the St. Petersburg organization despite the fact that all prac-

the delegate from Moscow, also represented only the intelligentsia.[45] The absence of worker delegates at the Congress was noted by Kats, the "worker" from the Bund, who expressed the opinion that at the next congress "the more workers the better." For this declaration, it is reported, he received a round of applause.[46]

In addition to the problem of accrediting the representatives of Russian Social Democratic groups, the organizers of the First Congress were obliged to define their relationship to the Social Democratic parties of Lithuania and Poland. As for the P.P.S. (the Polish Socialist Party founded in 1892), the situation was somewhat delicate. The P.P.S. was already a highly centralized party with local groups operating among the Polish minority in Kiev, Vilna, Odessa, and other centers where Russian and Jewish Social Democrats also carried on work. For a long time, relations between the nationality groups had been friendly, and they had willingly rendered each other mutual services. However, these friendly relations ended abruptly after the Fourth Congress of the P.P.S. in the winter of 1897–98, which laid down two conditions for future co-operation with Russian groups: that the Russian party include in its program the territorial separation of Poland from Russia, and that it enter into no organizational arrangements with other parties operating on Polish soil without the consent of the P.P.S. This would have precluded any relations with the Jewish Bund or the Lithuanian Social Democratic Party. (Lithuania was regarded by the P.P.S. as an integral part of Poland.) These nationalistic pretensions put any further negotiations with the Polish party out of the question.

The existence of a Lithuanian Social Democratic Party, although it had existed since 1895, was not known to *Rabochaia Gazeta* until shortly before the First Congress. Through the Bund, an invitation was sent, but arrests had temporarily crippled the Lithuanian party, and it was unable to send a delegate. The Lithuanians were inclined to co-operate with the Russian movement, since they, too, resented the pretensions of the P.P.S. Fur-

---

tical work and all contacts with the workers had been taken over by several groups of "youngsters." See Akimov, *Materialy*, pp. 47–49.

[45] See his recollections, "Pervyi S'ezd R.S.D.R.P.," *Sotsialisticheskii Vestnik* (February 20, 1950), pp. 22–23.

[46] *Ibid.*, p. 23.

thermore, they advanced no nationalistic claims of their own.[47]

In spite of the small number of delegates, the First Congress was about as representative as could be expected at this early stage of the movement. Even the organizations in the major centers were still not on a firm footing. The Bund took upon itself the physical arrangements, and the date for the proposed congress was set for March 1, 1898, in Minsk. There were nine delegates in all—one each from St. Petersburg, Moscow, Kiev, and Ekaterinoslav, two from *Rabochaia Gazeta*, and three from the Bund.[48] The proceedings were singularly uneventful. Whatever may have been the potential points of discord (such as the hegemony of Kiev and the separatism of the Bund), they were lost in the elevated atmosphere of comradeship and of participation in a great historical event.

Few formalities were observed. Eidelman assumed the chairmanship; questions of procedure were resolved automatically; the order of business outlined in the *Ustav Kollokviuma* was accepted without dispute; and a record was kept of official decisions but not of the discussions. Most points of substance resolved themselves quite naturally without rancorous debate, even where differences of opinion were noticeable. In contrast to the Second Congress of 1903, it was obvious that the delegates had not yet developed strong views or factional temperaments on particular questions of party organization. Theoretical and tactical problems of Social Democracy were scarcely touched upon, and the delegates seem not to have been disturbed by these omissions.

Questions were taken up as they appeared in the *Ustav Kollokviuma*. The party name was agreed upon very quickly: all concurred that it should be identified as "Social Democratic," and that local groups should be called "committees" of the party. There was some discussion of which prefix, *Russkaia* or *Rossiiskaia*, should be used. The latter word was chosen on the suggestion of the Bund delegates to emphasize the fact that the party represented, not simply Russian workers, but workers of all nationalities

---

[47] Information on relations with the P.P.S. and the Lithuanian Social Democratic Party is supplied by Eidelman and Akimov, *Pervyi S'ezd* (1923), pp. 78 and 105.

[48] The names were, respectively: S. I. Radchenko, Viktor Vannovskii, P. L. Tuchapskii, K. A. Petrusevich, B. L. Eidelman, N. A. Vigdorchik, Alexander Kremer, Mutnikovich (Gleb), and David Kats.

in the territory of Russia.[49] It was debated whether to include the word *rabochaia* (workers) as well. The suggestion was rejected by one vote on the grounds that workers were not as yet adequately represented in the organization. Nevertheless, the modifier *rabochaia* was subsequently inserted by Peter Struve into the Manifesto of the party.[50] Struve's arbitrary action was never challenged (the party's existence became known through the Manifesto), and the party entered history as the Russian Social Democratic Workers' Party.

The Congress concentrated most of its attention on the question of party structure. Almost all of the points worked out by the group *Rabochaia Gazeta* were accepted without objection. There were no long discourses on the ideal form of party organization, and the delegates did not act as if any vital Social Democratic principles were at stake. The few disputed points that did arise were resolved with what seemed to be obvious compromises. Apparently nobody was inclined to pursue issues to the extent of evoking bitter feelings. Yet, certain opposing attitudes did reveal themselves in the course of the discussions, the results being decisions that were often based on conflicting assumptions. For example, it has been pointed out that Eidelman's own views were highly centralistic. From their work in the Kiev organization, Eidelman's colleagues of *Rabochaia Gazeta* had long been aware of his inclinations and had been obliged at times to curb his impatient authoritarianism. Eidelman apparently realized that most of the delegates were anxious to preserve local prerogatives, and, unlike Lenin five years later, he was prepared to make concessions for the sake of unanimity. In any event, he did not press for the adoption of his views at the Congress.

The Congress made two major concessions to localist sentiments. First, accepting the Bund's demand without objection, the Congress acknowledged the right of the Bund "to enter into the party as an autonomous organization, independent only in ques-

---

[49] The word *"russkii"* is exclusively ethnical in meaning, as in *"russkii iazyk"*; *"Rossiiskii"* is a political and territorial term, as in *"Rossiiskaia Imperiia."*

[50] See Akimov's remarks in *Pervyi S'ezd* (1923), p. 127. Struve insisted on the inclusion of the term even after he was informed by Kremer of the decision of the Congress.

tions that especially concern the Jewish proletariat."[51] The arrangement seemed natural in view of the comparative maturity of the Jewish organization and its historical services to the movement. It must be noted, however, that the decision allowed autonomy solely in questions of "special concern to the Jewish proletariat." Where relations with outside groups and general decisions of the party were concerned, the Bund was theoretically bound by the same obligations as any other local group. Thus, the Bund's autonomy was closely circumscribed.

Second, Petrusevich announced that he had been instructed by the Ekaterinoslav *Soiuz Bor'by* to demand the right for local groups to refuse to execute directives of the Central Committee, provided that they submit detailed statements of their grounds for so doing. This seeming affront to the predilections of the organizers was also accepted without dispute. Although the memoir accounts record Petrusevich's request in the above form, the actual resolution recorded in the "Decisions" of the Congress, went a step further: the local committees were entitled to execute directives "in that form which they find most appropriate under local conditions" and, in all matters not explicitly covered by directives, they could act "completely independently, guided only by the program of the party." Thus, local groups were not bound in any way to await instructions from the party center and were to enjoy considerable latitude in interpreting them. An explanation was apparently obligatory only in the event of a flat refusal to carry them out. This represented a serious limitation on the authority of the Central Committee and reflected the prevailing concern of the local groups with preserving their freedom of action.

On the other hand, the Central Committee was invested with many specific functions which suggested a centralistic conception of the party. It was authorized to initiate common undertakings (May celebrations, proclamations on special events of national significance); to disburse party funds and allocate resources; to administer and edit party literature including the party organ; and to handle all negotiations with other revolutionary parties and

---

[51] The official "Decisions" of the Congress are reprinted in full in *Pervyi S'ezd* (1958), pp. 82–85, from which this and all passages cited below are taken.

groups, both in Russia and abroad, as well as all relations between local Social Democratic committees. Thus, all technical and organizational matters above the local level were to be the exclusive domain of the Central Committee. So that there should be no misunderstanding of the Central Committee's prerogatives in this regard, an explanatory footnote was added to the point on contacts with other revolutionary groups: "Local committees may enter into relations with such organizations only with the knowledge and according to the directives of the Central Committee." Finally, the Central Committee was allowed to perpetuate itself by cooptation in case of unexpected arrests.

The authority of the Central Committee, however, was carefully bound to that of the party Congress. The Congress, composed of local representatives, was defined as the "highest organ of the party." Each Congress was to set the date of the following Congress; extraordinary Congresses could be summoned by the Central Committee or upon the request of two-thirds of the local groups. One article stipulated that the activities of the Central Committee were to be guided by the decisions of party congresses; another, that questions admitting of delay must be deferred to the next Congress, while only the most urgent questions were to be resolved by the Central Committee on its own authority. Even the latter procedure required a unanimous vote of its membership, and such decisions had to be reported to the next Congress. The authority of the Central Committee was clearly construed as a derivative authority, carefully hedged in with certain guarantees in an obvious attempt to prevent its abuse.

A comparison of the "Decisions" of the Congress with the *Ustav Kollokviuma* establishes that the latter suggested most of the technical and organizational functions of the Central Committee adopted at the Congress (the party press, intergroup relations, all-Russian undertakings), whereas the provisions subordinating the authority of the Central Committee to party congresses were drawn from other sources. The Kiev and St. Petersburg organizations had worked out draft plans of party organization in response to the questions outlined by the *Ustav Kollokviuma*. The plans agreed with the *Ustav* in defining the practical duties of the Central Committee, but also dealt explicitly with the source of its authority, upon which certain limits were set.[52] The St. Petersburg draft defined the Central Committee as a "representative institution," whose functions werer "initiatory" and "executory" (*ispolnitel'nyi*); that is, the Committee could initiate measures and was obliged to carry out party directives, but the measures themselves had to be ratified by the local party groups. (The draft did not specify ratification by a Congress.) The Kievan plan also stipulated that the Central Committee must "execute the instructions of the congresses," and in particular stressed that "the definition of relations with groups of other tendencies, except purely routine matters, must be left to the Congress." It is clear from these points that pressure from local groups, including those closest to *Rabochaia Gazeta*, led to the measures taken by the Congress to circumscribe the authority of the Central Committee.

The decisions adopted by the Congress on organizational matters failed to carry through consistently either of the two basic motivating ideas of its participants. The model of party organization in its original outlines—the omnicompetent Central Committee, with the local committees as so many organs of its will—was obviously a reflection of the profound respect the participants held for the revolutionary predecessor of the new party, the People's Will. Yet, as if fearing the monster it was about to create, the Congress hedged the authority of the center with numerous exceptions, immunities, and controls. Obviously at work here was not only localist pride in the accomplishments of particular groups, but also the uneasiness of conscience which affected revolutionary idealists whose creed, in part at least, was demo-

---

[52] See *Pervyi S'ezd* (1923), p. 113 and the "Kievskii Ustav" and "Piterskii Ustav" in *Pervyi S'ezd* (1958), pp. 88–92. The history of the *Piterskii Ustav* is very puzzling. It was first printed by Takhtarev in his *Ocherk peterburgskago rabochego dvizheniia* (1902). It is entitled "Materialy dlia istorii pervago s'ezda (vesnoi 1898) R.S.D.R.P." and provided with the notation "from the archive of *Rabochaia Mysl*." A number of documents from the archives of the *Soiuz Bor'by* were taken abroad by Takhtarev following the large wave of arrests at the end of 1898. It will be recalled that late in 1898 the group *Rabochaia Mysl'* took over the leadership of the *Soiuz Bor'by* from the few remaining *stariki*. Radchenko may have surrendered documents in his possession to the new leadership out of fear that they would fall into the hands of the police. In any event, the *Piterskii Ustav*, by virtue of its contents, cannot belong to the group *Rabochaia Mysl'*, and we know of no other historical circumstances than the First Congress under which it could have been written. The background of the document remains a mystery, which, if it should be cleared up, would shed interesting new light on the history of the First Congress. Considering his role at the First Congress, it is unlikely that Radchenko himself composed the document.

cratic. After the turn of the century, the rising tide of revolutionary enthusiasm was to engulf these democratic sentiments, and, under the leadership of *Iskra,* the principle of organizational centralism was carried through with ruthless consistency. This temporary ascendancy of the traditions of the People's Will turned out, of course, to be ephemeral. At the Second Congress in 1903, the same issues emerged with a virulence completely absent at the First Congress. Unexpectedly, democratic reservations cropped up in the *Iskra* camp itself, inflicting a schism on the movement which proved to be permanent. Bolsheviks and Mensheviks came to champion two opposing conceptions of the character of the Social Democratic party which their predecessors of the 1890's were unable to bring into meaningful harmony.

With the question of the organizational structure settled, the major business of the Congress had been disposed of. *Rabochaia Gazeta* was declared the official party organ and the Union of Social Democrats Abroad (*Soiuz Russkikh Sotsial-Demokratov Zagranitsei*) was established as a branch of the party and its official representative abroad. Somehow a resolution was inserted declaring "the right of every nationality to self-determination." It was apparently designed to dispel fears of Great Russian nationalism, but at the same time to reject the claims of the P.P.S. to represent other nationalities "operating on Polish soil." Eidelman refers to it as "the only programatic decision of the Congress."[53] With this, the work of the Congress was substantially complete.

It is a striking fact that neither during the preparations nor at the Congress itself were meaningful steps taken to draw up a party program.[54] Every good Social Democrat was aware, of course, that a Social Democratic party must have a program, and the Kiev Conference of March, 1897, it will be recalled, had resolved to commission Plekhanov for this task. The *Ustav Kollokviuma* likewise had recommended that the Congress consider a draft program written by Plekhanov "if it should be presented."

---

[53] See *Pervyi S'ezd* (1923), p. 81.

[54] Eidelman claimed that it was the intention of the Central Committee to call a second party congress in six months to consider a party program. However, none of the other memoirists mentions this fact, and the "Decisions" did not register it, even though they specified that each Congress was obliged to set the time for the following Congress. See *Pervyi S'ezd* (1923), p. 82.

At a session of the group *Rabochaia Gazeta,* various programatic questions were assigned to different individuals for study and formulation, but nothing came of it. Eidelman offers the explanation that "there was neither enough time nor forces to write a program."[55] Tuchapskii seems to have been the one most concerned with the problem. He drafted a "Manifesto" embodying the major minimum and maximum demands of Social Democracy and presented it to the Kiev *Soiuz Bor'by* for consideration.[56] His draft having been rejected on the pretext that it took no position on the agrarian question, Tuchapskii suggested once more that the task be assigned to Plekhanov. This suggestion was incorporated into the Kievan draft plan.[57] Thus, Plekhanov's name was repeatedly mentioned in connection with the writing of a program, although the initiators of the Congress, Tuchapskii in particular, failed to carry out this resolution, for reasons unknown, even when the opportunity presented itself.

The draft plan of St. Petersburg, by contrast, declared that the Congress should regard the program as its basic task. Pointing to the Erfurt Program as a model, it recommended taking positions on the agrarian question, *kustar* and *artel* industry (cottage and craft production), interclass relations, relations with other parties, the political versus the economic struggle, the class character of the autocracy, criticism of Populism, questions of tactics, as well as "the theoretical foundations of Russian Social Democracy." It announced the intention of the St. Petersburg *Soiuz Bor'by* to present the draft of such a program to the Congress. Yet no such

---

[55] *Ibid.,* p. 72.

[56] The document has survived. It spoke in broad terms of the development of capitalism in Russia, of the irreconcilable struggle between the proletariat and its enemies, the bourgeoisie and the government, and of the urgent need to form a Russian Social Democratic workers' party. As its minimum demands it listed: 1) freedom of speech, press, unions, and assembly; 2) universal, secret, direct, and equal suffrage; and 3) the eight-hour working day and various protective legislation for the workers. It declared its ultimate goal to be a socialist order, defined as the ownership of the means of production by the "whole people." Thus, though very brief, it did advance the most typical programatic demands of Social Democrats of the period. See *Pervyi S'ezd* (1958), pp. 84–85, first printed in *Proletarskaia Revoliutsiia,* No. 1 (1921).

[57] At this same session the *Kievskii Ustav* was drafted and Tuchapskii was selected as the delegate from Kiev, i.e., shortly before the Congress. See *Pervyi S'ezd* (1923), p. 113. The resolution stated that "if the program is not to be written by Plekhanov, then it must at least be given to Plekhanov for perusal." (*Pervyi S'ezd* [1958], p. 89.)

draft was submitted by the St. Petersburg delegate, Radchenko; nor are there any specific references to this document in the literature.

Toward the end of the Congress deliberations, Tuchapskii on behalf of Kiev suggested once more that the writing of a program be entrusted to Plekhanov. Kremer and Radchenko objected that carrying on negotiations abroad would lead to unnecessary risks and delays, and revealed that a fully trustworthy, competent Social Democratic theoretician from St. Petersburg had already consented to execute this task. Caught off guard, Tuchapskii acquiesced, although he complained in his memoirs he would not have done so had he known that the result would be only a "Manifesto" and not a program.[58] No objection was made to this arrangement, since all present understood that the requirements of conspiracy militated against any curiosity as to the identity of the proposed author. The Central Committee was made responsible for the content of the document.

The theoretician whom Radchenko and Kremer had in mind was Peter Struve. Akimov, who alone has preserved a few details on the ensuing negotiations, stated that Struve was given a completely free hand in drawing up the Manifesto, except for a stipulation of the Congress that it should in some way acknowledge the indebtedness of Russian Social Democracy to the People's Will.[59] Since Eidelman was arrested soon after the Congress, Kremer and Radchenko handled the arrangements with Struve. Radchenko seems to have been very enthusiastic about the results. Kremer, however, complained that Struve's text pleased him "neither in spirit, nor in tone."[60] After discussing it with his comrades in the Bund, he returned to St. Petersburg and pleaded with Struve to revise the text. Struve declined, stating that he had conscientiously performed his task, and that his draft had to be accepted or rejected. After the arrest of Eidelman and the group *Rabochaia Gazeta*, responsibility for printing the Manifesto devolved upon the Bund. In view of the devastating arrests affecting nearly every local organization, Kremer and his comrades in the Bund unhesitatingly set aside their qualms and printed the docu-

[58] *Pervyi S'ezd* (1923), p. 180.

[59] *Ibid.*, p. 77.   [60] *Ibid.*, p. 158.

ment; its appearance had become a point of honor for the movement, since the existence of the party had to be proved.

The working ideology of the Russian Social Democrats of the nineties was excellently summed up in the Manifesto; in this respect Struve executed his task well. After briefly outlining the Marxist scheme of historical development and supporting its applicability to Russia, the document advanced the usual demands for political freedom and political rights, supported by the well-worn arguments of the period:

> He [the Russian worker] is deprived of those advantages which are freely and peacefully enjoyed by his comrades abroad: participation in government administration, freedom of the printed and verbal word, freedom of assembly and association—in a word, all those instruments and means by which the proletariat of Western Europe and America improve their situation and . . . struggle . . . for socialism. Political freedom is as necessary to the Russian proletariat as pure air is necessary for healthy respiration. It is the precondition of his free development and successful struggle for both immediate improvements and final liberation.[61]

The Manifesto set forth the urgency of overthrowing the autocracy, a task the Russian proletariat must take on its "own strong shoulders" in view of the "cowardice" and "weakness" of the Russian bourgeoisie. The crushing of the autocracy was to be the "first step toward the realization of the historical mission of the proletariat—the creation of a social structure in which there is no place for the exploitation of man by man." In short, in a few succinct phrases the Manifesto perfectly expressed the ardent proletarian patriotism and concern with political freedom of the Russian *praktiki* of the period.

Conversely, on a number of points, Struve's handiwork departed from the theoretical propositions of the *Gruppa Osvobozhdenie Truda*. The problem of securing "allies" in the struggle for political freedom was not touched upon; nor was any attempt made to outline the "mutual relations of other classes" to be exploited by the proletariat to its own advantage. Both these points had been stressed in Plekhanov and Akselrod's writings. The Manifesto, on the contrary, enjoined the proletariat to rely exclusively on

---

[61] *Pervyi S'ezd* (1958), p. 80. All other quotations, pp. 80–81.

its own resources. "The political freedom which it requires," the document triumphantly declares, "can be won only by the proletariat itself." This was far closer in its pathos and formulation to the views prevalent among Social Democratic *praktiki* than to those of the émigré leaders.

The Manifesto concluded with the declaration that the movement had now entered the stage of "conscious class struggle," and that for this purpose all Social Democratic groups had united into one mighty Social Democratic Workers' Party. In keeping with the request of the First Congress, it acknowledged that Social Democrats were continuing the struggle with the autocracy begun by "the glorious figures of the 'People's Will.'"

If the Manifesto embodied a typical expression of the outlook of the *praktiki* of the period, it is strange that it should arouse objections from the Bundists, who in most respects were the prophets of the movement. Akimov confessed that his informants (among whom were most of the persons concerned) gave him no satisfactory answer. He plausibly refuted the later charge that the Bundists were ardent "Economists" and that possibly the sharply political tone of the Manifesto offended them. The Bundists were the first to advance the slogan "Away with the autocracy!" and their literature was replete with the political slogans found in the Manifesto. Akimov himself hazarded no explanation of the Bund's dissatisfaction, and neither Kremer nor Kats shed any further light on the question.

There is one respect, however, in which the Manifesto could not but have displeased the Bund. It consistently employed the qualifier *russkii* (*russkii proletariat, russkaia sotsialdemokratiia, russkie rabochie*), instead of *rossiiskii*. This was by no means a small point, since the Polish and Jewish workers could not have been expected to respond to appeals to the *Russian* proletariat. For this reason, the Bund had gone to great pains to insist on the term *rossiiskaia* in the party label. Although this point might help to explain the attitude of the Bund, it must be admitted that the conjecture is not supported by concrete evidence. Other considerations, of which no traces have remained in the literature, may have entered in as well. On this, as on many other important problems of the period, the sources supply no definitive answer.

The First Congress was not destined to play a decisive role in the history of the party. Zubatov, chief of the Moscow section of the *Okhrana*, had long since been planning a decisive blow against the Social Democratic organizations. The leaders of the major centers had been under observation and their movements followed to uncover as many organizational threads as possible before drawing in the net. Although some of the delegates had been traced to Minsk, Zubatov had no notion of the forthcoming Congress, and he discovered its significance only upon subsequent investigation. He had been interested chiefly in uncovering the location of the underground press of the group *Rabochaia Gazeta*. After the Congress, Eidelman and Petrusevich were followed to the press's location in Ekaterinoslav, and Zubatov rightly surmised that the appropriate moment had arrived. On his orders, simultaneous arrests were carried out in all major centers. A clean sweep was made of the Moscow, Kiev, and Ekaterinoslav organizations, and of the entire group *Rabochaia Gazeta* (with the accidental exception of Vigdorchik). The arch-conspirator, Radchenko, successfully eluded observation, and in St. Petersburg the arrests affected only the periphery. The Bundists were temporarily spared, through Zubatov's forebearance. That summer, however, they too suffered the inevitable blow, which removed both their leaders and their secret presses.[62]

The Central Committee succeeded in carrying out only one

---

[62] For details on the activities of *Okhrana* in pursuit of Social Democratic leaders in 1898, see L. P. Menshchikov, *Okhrana i revoliutsiia* (Moscow, 1928), Vol. II, part 1, 9–34, 70–82, and 107–14. See also Kats's account in Dimanshtein, pp. 160 ff. Although it covered all parts of Russia, the investigation was conducted by the Moscow section of the *Okhrana*, headed by Zubatov. Its success in rounding up the Social Democratic leaders was due almost entirely to the system of "external observation" (*naruzhnoe nabliudenie*) of their movements by "tails" (*filery*). So adept were Zubatov's agents in concealing their observation that even so skillful a conspirator as Eidelman was convinced that he had successfully eluded them before his departure to Minsk. Eidelman, Vigdorchik, and Tuchapskii were followed separately to Minsk, much to the surprise of the three *filery*, who immediately telegraphed to Zubatov for further instructions (see *ibid.*, p. 33). After the Congress, as Zubatov had hoped, Eidelman and Petrusevich led their pursuers to the typography in Ekaterinoslav, and, at the same time, to members of the Ekaterinoslav *Soiuz Bor'by*, thereby causing its collapse. Kremer and Mutnik, picked up by Zubatov's agents in Minsk, were held under observation several months longer to uncover the organizational network of the Bund (*ibid.*, pp. 109 ff.). Despite the simplicity and effectiveness of this method in this case, it is interesting that Zubatov was able to form only the vaguest conception of the nature of the Minsk conference, the existence of which he discovered only by accident. Later he perfected another even more effective method—*vnutrennaia agentura*, i.e., the use of informers.

decision of the Congress—to print the Manifesto proclaiming the existence of the party. Although Eidelman had already been arrested, Kremer and Radchenko conferred twice in St. Petersburg concerning the Manifesto. After this, Kremer complained, Radchenko made himself scarce.[63] In July, shortly after issuing the Manifesto, Kremer himself was arrested, leaving no successors. The members of the Central Committee had not even attempted to exercise their right to co-optation to guarantee the continued existence of a party center.

This was the heaviest single blow the movement had ever suffered. Besides aborting the all-Russian party center, the police rounded up over five hundred of the most active Social Democrats, both workers and *intelligenty*, from all the major centers of the movement. The surprise move, preventing Social Democratic groups from adequately preparing successors, temporarily paralyzed local work. The shock nullified the hoped-for effect of announcing the creation of the Russian Social Democratic Party and merely intensified the isolation and helplessness of local organizations.

Promulgated in a vacuum, the Manifesto was greeted with little initial enthusiasm; it circulated very slowly, some groups not receiving a copy for several months or more. Once they recovered from the initial shock, however, surviving Social Democrats slowly regained their self-confidence and repaired their shattered organizations. As they did so, they began to give serious attention to the Manifesto and to its significance for the movement. Few data have survived on this obscure moment in the history of the party, but the following report on the Ivanovo-Voznesensk movement gives some suggestion of what was happening.

At first it [the Manifesto] did not produce a strong impression on the comrades, it did not inspire courage and energy; but already in the fall of 1898 a lively discussion of it began, and at the same time our *Rabochii Soiuz* became "The Ivanovo-Voznesensk Committee of the R.S.-D.R.P."[64]

Babushkin affirms that as soon as the Workers' Committee in Ekaterinoslav received the Manifesto, it assumed the appellation

---

[63] *Pervyi S'ezd* (1923), p. 158.

[64] *Rabochee dvizhenie v Ivanovo-Voznesenskom raione* (Geneva, 1900), p. 27.

"Ekaterinoslav Committee of the R.S.-D.R.P." Exactly when this took place is not clear—probably in the summer of 1898.[65] Apparently the Kiev organization also quickly adopted the designation "Committee of the R.S.-D.R.P."[66] Throughout the year 1898, however, very few documents bore the party identification. Two minor leaflets in Kiev and Odessa, of June and November, respectively, bore the incorrect title of the party, one omitting the term "Workers," the other the term "Social Democratic." The only local committee to release a special leaflet announcing the founding of the party in 1898 was the hitherto unheralded Don Committee (Rostov) of the R.S.-D.R.P.[67]

From the beginning of 1899 on, the party designation rapidly came into use. Ekaterinoslav issued a special proclamation in January, 1899, affirming its adherence to the R.S.-D.R.P. and explaining the significance of the event for the movement.[68] The January issues of the local organs *Rabochaia Mysl'* and *Vpered* bore, respectively, the subheadings "St. Petersburg" and "Kiev" Committees of the R.S.-D.R.P. In February, three leaflets appearing in Kiev employed an official Committee seal. In accordance with the decision of the Congress, the Union of Social Democrats Abroad announced in the first issue of its organ *Rabochee Delo* (March, 1899) that it was the official representative of the R.S.-D.R.P. outside Russia and thereafter placed the party name at the head of its publications. Henceforward, all Social Democratic groups made use of the party label. Although no party apparatus actually came into being, emotional identification with an all-Russian enterprise was now irrevocably established, and Social Democrats everywhere regarded the resurrection of a party center

---

[65] See Babushkin, pp. 102–3.

[66] See P. N. Moshinskii, *Na putiakh k pervomu s'ezdu R.S.D.R.P.* (Moscow, 1928), p. 65.

[67] See *Rabochee dvizhenie v Rossii*, Vol. IV, part 2, 153, 221, and 230. Obviously only the Don Committee was directly inspired by the Manifesto. It is interesting that even the May proclamations of 1898 in St. Petersburg, to which Akimov refers as "all-party proclamations," bear only the seal of the St. Petersburg *Soiuz Bor'by*. Perhaps this was because the Manifesto was not yet widely distributed and it was regarded as inopportune to use the party name until its existence became broadly known through its Manifesto. Also proclamations from Kiev and Ekaterinoslav of the fall of 1898 still do not use the party designation. See *Rabochee Delo*, No. 1 (April, 1899), pp. 97–98.

[68] See *Pervyi S'ezd* (1958), pp. 106–7 and *Rabochee Delo*, No. 1, pp. 90–100.

as a question of time. For the next few years the energies of the party *praktiki* were absorbed in reconstructing local organizations or in mere survival, but the need for unity, for a disciplined, effective nationwide party, for an authoritative party organ, and an official party program continued to be acutely felt. That the dream of party unity was very much alive is indicated by the repeated efforts to achieve it until, under the banner of *Iskra*, it was brought to the threshold of realization only to be snatched away again.[69] In the meantime, the fiction of the clandestine existence of a Social Democratic Workers' Party was scrupulously maintained.

Aside from its moral significance in engendering a spirit of party unity among Social Democrats, the First Congress left few permanent traces. All vestiges of the work of the Congress were thoroughly effaced by the efficient measures of the *Okhrana* and the police. The Manifesto and the "Decisions" of the Congress remained only symbols of the faith, not binding principles of common action; the compromise arrangements on party organization and the rudiments of a nationality policy passed unnoticed. For subsequent generations, the significance of the First Congress consists primarily in what it revealed concerning the aspirations and quandaries of Russian Social Democrats in this innocent era before factional lines were drawn. Thereafter a certain polarization of incompatible elements in the prevailing ideological amalgam becomes noticeable. One could say that one motif of the Congress—the concern for democratic controls over the leadership, the pious wish to draw more workers into this "workers'" party, the predilection in favor of vigorous, self-reliant local organizations—developed into the trend represented by *Rabochaia Mysl'*. The other, increasingly dominant motif, stressing a strong Central Committee, an authoritative party organ, and the speedy settling of accounts with the autocracy, found expression in such politically-oriented groups as *Rabochee Znamia, Iuzhnyi Rabochii,* and subsequently Lenin's *Iskra. Rabochaia Mysl'* was willing to sacrifice the goal of forging a political party for the sake of entrenching the roots of the movement in the masses. The politically-oriented groups, true to their intelligentsia essence, were willing to sacri-

---

[69] See pp. 223–24.

fice their roots in the masses for the sake of creating a solid core
of irreproachably Orthodox Marxist revolutionaries to combat the
autocracy.

The far-reaching impact of this polarization did not impress itself on the minds of the leaders of the movement until it was laid
bare in the rancorous debates over party organization during and
after the Second Congress. Bolshevism carried its banner high for
the pure tradition of blatant elitism; Menshevism became a refuge
for all those who could not reconcile themselves to all of the ruthless implications which elitism incorporated. But in the course of
time the Menshevik leaders, Akselrod, Martov, and Dan, worked
their way back to an espousal of consistent organizational democracy and workers' initiative, which betrayed their unmistakable
ideological kinship to the formerly despised "Economists." Our
attention having been devoted thus far primarily to the one trend,
it is now time to examine the other.

CHAPTER 7

The Banner of Revolution

Although there were a number of potential sources of discord in the Social Democratic movement during the 1890's—the "worker question," the elective as opposed to the selective principle, economic as opposed to political agitation, and even the structure of the party itself—factional groupings were the exception rather than the rule. In this era of untroubled faith in the revolutionary potential of the masses, the majority of *praktiki* obediently followed the precepts of *Ob agitatsii* and deplored the sectarian notes of organs like *Rabochaia Mysl'* and *Rabochee Znamia*. The very emphasis in *Rabochaia Mysl'* on the workers' bread-and-butter interests, however, was bound to arouse a protesting voice urging that the revolutionary tenets of Social Democracy be espoused openly and proudly. Such a voice of protest was *Rabochee Znamia*. Although the scope of its labors was more limited than that of its rival, its role was significant primarily in what it augured for the future: it anticipated *Iskra* by calling to its banner all the intransigent partisans of revolutionary action for a decisive battle with the autocracy. Such bold crusaders were few in the mid-nineties, but their number swelled dramatically with the approach of the new century. By the time *Iskra* appeared on the scene in 1901 they had become an unmanageable host. The task of absorbing, organizing, and guiding this host was well beyond the resources of *Rabochee Znamia* and, indeed, proved to be beyond the resources of the talented leaders of *Iskra* as well. The

same ground swell brought about a revival of terrorism and revolutionary Populism and a marked shift to the left of all disaffected
elements of Russian society. *Rabochee Znamia* was the political
barometer which registered these storms in advance; as a group,
it was compounded of the very stuff which later erupted into a
nationwide movement.

Rabochee Znamia was actually not one, but several successive
and overlapping groups and sub-groups (as well as sundry individuals), all inspired by the militant revolutionary tone of the
first issue of the underground journal which made its unheralded
appearance under that name in the summer of 1898. There would
have been very little continuity to or interconnection among these
groups had it not been for the limitless energy and virtuosity of
the originator and self-appointed custodian of the enterprise,
Moisei Lure. A self-educated typesetter of impoverished Jewish
origin from the small White Russian community of Velikomir,
Lure had acquired in the Social Democratic circles of the early
nineties a smattering of Russian culture, which he scrupulously
passed on to his adherents (he insisted that they read the poetry
of Uspenskii aloud). Nevertheless, he spoke Russian with a heavy
accent and moved very uneasily in the circles of the more fully
assimilated Social Democratic intelligentsia in the Jewish movement. Lure was the perfect embodiment of a revolutionary conspirator—uncommunicative, swift and unexpected in his movements, demanding of himself and others, and totally indifferent to
the amenities of life. His mannerisms and appearance were so
crudely proletarian that it sometimes embarrassed even the workers with whom he had to deal. Such a worker reports that once
when Lure showed up unexpectedly on one of his mysterious jour-
neys, his comrades refused to let him out on the street until they
could procure a decent set of clothes for him.[1]

By contrast, his brother, Mikhail, also self-educated and a
skilled jeweler, presented a clean-cut appearance and had acquired the poise, the pure speech, and the sophistication of a
genuine *intelligent*. Moisei Lure's imperfect assimilation into the
Russian movement was partly the result of his early associations

---

[1] For the above information see the excellent biographical sketch by his co-worker
S. Gelman, "Pamiati romanovtsa M. V. Lure," *Katorga i Ssylka*, No. 56 (July, 1929),
pp. 152–64.

with Polish Social Democrats, with whom he worked for a while smuggling illicit publications over the border and whom he vastly admired for their daring and conspiratorial skills. Throughout his career he kept in touch with the P.P.S., helping it to organize Jewish affiliates and unswervingly supporting its nationalist pretensions against the Russian movement.[2]

As a typesetter, Lure was afforded a certain mobility. He roamed through the western and southern provinces winning adherents, training lieutenants, smuggling out type from his places of employment, and making contacts that might be useful for his plans. The center of his operations was Belostok, whither he summoned a few of his faithful followers, including his brother, Mikhail, to staff a secret press. By the end of 1897, he had extended his activities to Kharkov, Kiev, Gomel, Minsk, and other towns of the Western Pale. In each locality he formed closely-knit cells of "worker revolutionaries," frequently proselytizing them through existing Social Democratic organizations—the example of Kiev has been mentioned in the previous chapter.

Despite his ability to command unrestricted admiration and devotion from individual workers, however, the groups he established proved to be rather ephemeral. The network of organizations in the provinces, of which he occasionally boasted, never consisted of more than a handful of dedicated followers whom he could move from place to place at will. The typesetter D. Gershanovich was one of Lure's typical worker devotees. "I became strongly attached to Moisei," he wrote in his brief memoirs, "all the more so in that, as my revolutionary ambitions developed, they became more and more closely tied up with the personality of Moisei, whose authority in my eyes knew no bounds."[3] Characteristically, Gershanovich was never initiated into the nature of Lure's revolutionary plans, but simply carried out his instructions with blind devotion—collecting type and printing equipment, moving to this or that locality, waiting patiently for further instructions.

---

[2] This point, made by Gelman, is confirmed in a report on Lure's activities by the chief of the Russian secret police abroad, Rachkovskii. See L. P. Menshchikov, *Russkii politicheskii sysk zagranitsei* (Paris, 1914), pp. 31 ff.

[3] "O Moisee Vladimiroviche Lure" in *K dvadtsatipiatiletiiu pervago s'ezda partii*, pp. 166–67.

Lure's association with the Social Democratic movement was dictated far more by convenience than by thoughtful convictions. His guiding precept was that both systematic study and economic agitation were a waste of effort, and that the chief purpose of Social Democratic organizations should be to prepare for immediate revolutionary action to abolish the autocracy. Gershanovich stated that Lure was a convinced terrorist and often gave him publications of the *narodovoltsy* to read. In Kiev in 1897, Lure made common cause with a group of worker *narodovoltsy* to prevent the Kiev *Soiuz Bor'by* from introducing agitation. In the process, he won over several members of the regular Workers' Committee. Eidelman complained with good reason that Lure was no Social Democrat, but an "anarchist" who "jammed sticks in our wheel spokes."[4] Throughout his career, Lure sought the collaboration of revolutionary Populists in his various projects, and in 1905 he did indeed succumb to the anarchistic doctrine of Makhaiskii. This was a final confirmation of Lure's unstable views and of the essentially emotional character of his revolutionary commitment.

The immediate aim of Lure's far-flung exertions was to acquire a solid reputation among Social Democratic circles for his printing enterprise in order to use it as a springboard for more ambitious operations. Somehow he acquired a report on the International Socialist Congress of 1896 in London and a secret circular of the Minister of the Interior Goremykin to factory inspectors. These and a translation of a Polish pamphlet, *The Spy*, were his first publishing achievements in mid-1897. These pieces were duly distributed to the various contacts he had amassed in the course of his travels. To a trusted subordinate, S. Gelman, he frankly confided that these ventures were "strictly for advertising."[5] Lure now controlled the means to fulfill the natural ambition of successful *praktiki*: a revolutionary organ through which to become the authoritative voice for party unification.

However, with Lure this urge was curiously intertwined with a marked distrust of the intelligentsia. Gelman recorded Lure's opinion that "the majority of the intelligentsia joined the workers' movement solely to pull its own chestnuts out of the fire and had

[4] *Ibid.*, p. 36. Eidelman wrote the introduction to this collection.

[5] Gelman, p. 155.

little concern for the workers' interests; hence, one should always keep an extra stone in one's sling, the best stone being in his opinion a printing press."[6] One sees here both a parallel and an interesting contrast with the attitude of Kok, the organizer of *Rabochaia Mysl'*: whereas Kok regarded his undertaking primarily as a means to liberate the workers from the revolutionary dogmas of the intelligentsia in favor of more tangible gains, Lure saw his printing venture as a means of keeping the intelligentsia harnessed to the interests of a genuine proletarian revolution and of preventing them from selling the workers short with an amputated "bourgeois" revolution.

Lure was soon to become a legendary conspirator, but neither he nor his proletarian disciples could boast literary or theoretical talent. He clearly understood that connections with some group of intelligentsia were indispensable, and for this reason he cultivated good relations with the gifted Kharkov Social Democrats, who enjoyed a reputation for both erudition and heterodoxy. Two of these, Aaron Lure (no relation to Moisei) and I. M. Romm, had moved to St. Petersburg to continue their studies in 1897 and served as Moisei's contacts in the capital. With their collaboration, he was able to put out in late 1897 a program brochure, *Zadachi russkoi rabochei partii* (*The Tasks of the Russian Workers' Party*), under the imprint "The Group of Worker Revolutionaries."

Lure's clumsy attempt to outflank the Kievan Social Democrats by acting as if a party were already in existence deceived his own followers more than it did the sponsors of the First Congress, who knew him only too well. When Aaron Lure received word of the First Congress in St. Petersburg, he assumed this was the fruit of Moisei's efforts and was dismayed when informed otherwise by Moisei's brother, Mikhail. Mikhail assured Aaron Lure that the *Rossiiskaia* party had already been liquidated by the police and that their own *Russkaia* party could now effortlessly step in to fill the breach. It was important to soothe Aaron Lure's troubled conscience, notes a close colleague, since for him "questions of conscience were primary and the party needed him as our best theoretician and writer."[7]

---

[6] *Ibid.*

[7] A. Solts, "Moia priznatel 'nost,' " *K dvadtsatipiatiletiiu*, p. 175.

In May, 1898, the first issue of the new party organ *Rabochee Znamia* came out and was circulated in competition with the Manifesto of the rival party. Hope of supplanting the stillborn *Rossiiskaia* party was crushed that summer by arrests which wiped out the Belostok press and nearly all of Moisei Lure's helpers. He himself escaped thanks to his extreme caution as a conspirator. Deprived of subordinates except for the faithful Gershanovich, Moisei decided to flee abroad to see if his printing enterprise could be put on sounder foundations beyond the clutches of the tsarist police. With the help of his Polish acquaintances, he finally landed in Christchurch, England, where he became a typesetter for Chertkov, the publisher of Tolstoy's forbidden works, a position he hoped to exploit to repair his revolutionary fortunes.

Although Lure's organization in Russia was now virtually defunct, the literature of *Rabochee Znamia* acted as a magnet on the militants in the movement. Above all, the opening article of the journal's first issue, entitled "The Battle Cry of the Working Class," set the impulses of susceptible Social Democrats in motion. It began ominously: "Fifty years ago, a mighty, commanding appeal resounded throughout the world, frightening some, quickening the hearts of others. . . ." The article unrolled in vivid colors the worldwide panorama of the proletarian movement which the Russian worker was called upon to join—an international army without uniforms, without a fatherland, with nothing to lose but its chains. Although the ultimate aim was to forge the bonds of international solidarity for the destruction of world capitalism, the immediate aim should be to "employ all means of propaganda and agitation to develop class consciousness in Russian workers and to train them into an organized revolutionary force to overthrow the autocracy."[8]

This combination of international perspective and vibrant revolutionary élan also distinguished the program statement, *Zadachi*. The first half of this piece was borrowed directly from *Le Programme du parti ouvrier* (Paris, 1897), a popular exposition of Marxism by the militant French socialists Paul Lafargue and Jules Guesde. It explained how the capitalist order, in enlisting workers

---

[8] *Rabochee Znamia*, No. 1 (April, 1898), pp. 1 ff.

in the national army, "teaches them to handle weapons, gives them the possibility to practice mass operations, molds them into skilled, disciplined soldiers for the future workers' revolution." "Revolution is inevitable," it asserted flatly. "A voluntary surrender by the exploiters of their political and economic dominion over the proletariat is unthinkable."[9] The feature of "The Battle Cry" and *Zadachi* which attracted a certain segment of the Russian *praktiki* was not any theoretical argument against "pure economics," but rather their unapologetic, romantic revolutionary pathos.

When it came to concrete practical matters, the literature of *Rabochee Znamia* offered little in the way of imaginative suggestions and by no means matched the sustained and ultimately quite sophisticated line of *Rabochaia Mysl'*. Indeed, some of the items in the official program *Zadachi* sounded like echos of *Rabochaia Mysl'*: "In its initial phases the workers' movement must concentrate its energies on the task of internal consolidation . . . the building of local associations by profession, funds of mutual aid during strikes." Like the Manifesto of the R.S.-D.R.P. and much of the ordinary underground literature, *Zadachi* deplored the "complete lack of rights" of Russian workers and regarded their achievement an essential requirement for further struggle; similarly it explained the defeat of the heroes of the People's Will by their failure to draw the masses into the struggle, asserting that "only a party standing at the head of the workers' movement will possess sufficient resources to combat the autocracy, to cast off this despicable yoke from the shoulders of the Russian people."[10] Finally, its position on economic agitation appears to have been borrowed directly from *Ob agitatsii*, except perhaps for a somewhat more optimistic view concerning the possibility of exploiting economic discontent for immediate political agitation. Thus the official program statement of *Rabochee Znamia* reflected very little of Moisei Lure's bias against the prevailing practices of the Russian movement; even more than Kok, Lure was obliged to come to terms

---

[9] *Zadachi*, 2d ed. (London, 1900), p. 16.

[10] *Itogi revoliutsionnago dvizheniia v Rossii*, ed. G. A. Kuklin (London, 1903), Section III-5, p. 8 (no continuous pagination). Since an abbreviated version of *Zadachi* is reprinted in this more accessible collection of documents, it will be referred to hereafter, and cited as *Itogi*.

with the fact that most of his co-workers were not schismatic by temperament and identified much more closely than himself with the normative traditions of the movement.

On the strength of these two documents, and practically on their strength alone, *Rabochee Znamia* was adopted as the banner of those romantic revolutionaries whose impulses did not find enough satisfaction in the conventional modes of Social Democratic activity. The Belostok press had put out a thousand copies of each and several thousand separate flyers of "The Battle Cry." Lure printed 1,800 more copies in London which he distributed on a trip to Russia in the fall of 1899. Early in 1900, a third edition of *Zadachi* was requested by St. Petersburg adherents. A second and a third number of *Rabochee Znamia* were put out by Lure in late 1900 and early 1901; they added little, however, in terms of defining or developing the ideological position of *Rabochee Znamia* and are scarcely mentioned in the literature.[11]

Since most of the groups which rallied to the new banner were indigenous to the capital, further attention should be given to St. Petersburg's underground milieu after the disappearance of the original *Soiuz Bor'by*.[12] Like *Rabochaia Mysl'*, the groups adhering to *Rabochee Znamia* arose as a result of the fragmentation of the St. Petersburg organization after the large-scale arrests of late 1896 and early 1897, which swept away all but one or two veterans of the movement. It frequently happened in the wake of such setbacks that the periphery was restored to working order long before the center. In St. Petersburg, several unconnected groups cropped up, each fostering its own particular ties with workers in given factory districts, but seldom communicating with other groups or with the "center." Often the members of such groups belonged to the same educational institution or professional group. For a while, most of the supporters of *Rabochaia Mysl'* were medi-

---

[11] The author located and made extracts from the second number in the Bibliothèque de la Documentation Internationale in Paris, but has seen no evidence that the third number is extant. Data on the printing ventures is to be found in Gelman, p. 152 and Menshchikov, *Russkii politicheskii sysk*, pp. 33–35.

[12] Data on the St. Petersburg organizations of this period are provided chiefly by Akimov, *Materialy*, pp. 46–56 and Takhtarev, *Ocherk*, pp. 73–80. Indispensable information and insights were afforded the author through his interviews with Lydia Dan, who personally participated during this period in the group under discussion. Most of these interviews were recorded on tape, transcripts of which are deposited in the files of the Project on the History of the Menshevik Movement.

cal students and (later) forestry students. Two other groups consisted primarily of mechanical engineers and of mining engineers, respectively. Although each group was cohesive within itself and avoided outside associations, all of them regarded themselves as members of the *Soiuz Bor'by* and usually issued their leaflets in its name. By mid-1897, the "center" consisted of a few holdovers from the old organization (still called the *stariki*), who monopolized certain important functions: communication links with outside groups, fund-raising and disbursement, and the procurement and delivery of literature. Out of touch with activities in the factory districts, the *stariki* were reduced for the most part to performing certain services for the younger groups, the *molodye*. The *stariki* could exert influence over the ambitious "youngsters" only by rendering aid on a selective basis; against the resultant pressure, the latter quite naturally revolted. They particularly resented Radchenko's claim to have "represented" St. Petersburg at the First Congress when in fact he had neither consulted with nor informed any of the groups active in the capital ahead of time.[13]

Thus, by 1898 the *Soiuz Bor'by* had become a loose conglomeration of groups, each one consisting for the most part of impulsive, inexperienced students bound to each other by close ties of comradeship and mutual trust. The authority of the *stariki*, in both a formal and a moral sense, was no longer effective, and initiative proceeded from the periphery rather than from the center. Given this insulation of groups one from another, particularities in outlook and habits could easily develop. Lenin and *Iskra* were later to denounce this indifference to discipline and party spirit as *kustarnichestvo*, a twin evil of Economism. However, the reason for this mode of operation was not simply the small-mindedness and "opportunism" of its practitioners, but the unceasing pressure of the police. Ambitious organizational undertakings were extremely vulnerable and short-lived, even when guided by skilled conspirators, whereas a small circle of intimate acquaintances en-

---

13 See note 44, p. 174. As the member of the *Soiuz Bor'by* responsible for maintaining conspiratorial contacts and restoring them after arrests, he had always remained somewhat aloof from practical work, seldom even attending sessions of the "center" when he was formally a member. On Radchenko's role in the *Soiuz Bor'by*, see I. I. Radchenko, "Stephan Ivanovich Radchenko," *Staryi Bol'shevik*, No. 5 (March-April, 1933), pp. 170–75. With all practical work now in the hands of younger comrades, his role had become particularly anomalous.

gaging in a limited sphere of activity had the best chance of survival. There were many such groups, both large and small, operating in St. Petersburg in the years 1897–1901. (This is to say nothing of the numerous "lone wolves" who conducted propaganda on
their own.) Some of the splinter groups, such as those that supported *Rabochaia Mysl'* and the *Gruppa Samoosvobozhdenie Truda*, cut themselves off permanently when they adopted the workers' cause. A fair number, however, saw no need to burn bridges.
They conceived of the workers' cause as an integral part of the
general protest of "society" against the political order and felt that
their immediate task should be, not the relatively insignificant improvement of the workers' situation, but the enlistment of the
workers in the over-all battle for freedom.

This goal was not so consciously espoused by the first splinter
groups, but took shape in their minds over a period of time. Already in 1897 specific differences with the *Soiuz Bor'by* had arisen
over whether or not groups were to participate in student demonstrations. Both the *stariki* and the majority of the rank-and-file
praktiki felt that participation in the student movement was a
waste of time—students were no real social force—and an invitation
to observation by the police. But some of the more fervent young
Social Democrats could not see why they should stand idly by
while the leadership of the spirit of protest fell into the hands of
Populist-oriented students. The temptation to intervene was
strengthened by the fact that the Social Democrats had at their
disposal the facilities to print and distribute leaflets, which the
students sorely needed.

One such occasion was the Vetrovskaia demonstration of
March, 1897.[14] Vetrovskaia was a young student *narodovolka* imprisoned in the fortress of Peter and Paul who had reportedly been
raped by some government official. In despair, she had soaked her
clothes in kerosene from her cell lamp, ignited herself, and died in
great agony. Seizing upon the occasion, several thousand students
and sympathizers gathered in the square around the Kazan cathe-

---

[14] For an account of this incident see V. O. Levitskii, *Za chetvert' veka*, 2 vols.
(Moscow, 1926), I, 67–71. Levitskii, another member of the Tsederbaum family,
recounts that his sister Lydia was one of the chief organizers and inspirers of this
demonstration. Although the author conversed at length with her about this incident
she modestly neglected to mention her own role.

dral, only to be quickly dispersed by the police. Against the explicit instructions of the *Soiuz Bor'by*, several student Social Democrats helped plan the affair and supplied leaflets. Among the organizers were Lydia Tsederbaum-Dan and other later adherents of *Rabochee Znamia*. Such irrepressible students formed the backbone of the groups in the capital which subsequently leaned toward *Rabochee Znamia*; henceforward, they, rather than Moisei Lure and his "worker revolutionaries," put their stamp on the anti-Economist tendency. All of Lure's efforts to reassert his authority through his organizing talents and control over the printing press gave way before the irascible self-assurance of these exuberant young revolutionaries.

The first such group to rally to the standard of *Rabochee Znamia* constituted itself in the autumn of 1898 because of a quarrel with Stepan Radchenko, the lone survivor of the *stariki*, who adamantly refused to surrender the official engraved seal of the *Soiuz Bor'by*. (By custom, the seal was required to authenticate every piece of literature coming out in the name of the *Soiuz*.) Plans had already been made for an ambitious strike campaign which several co-operating groups were to carry out in their respective factory bailiwicks. Frustrated in their plans to unify their efforts in the name of the *Soiuz Bor'by*, the respective groups concentrated on their individual efforts. Some individuals, such as N. N. Lokhov and N. V. Berenstam, gravitated toward the remnants of the *Rabochaia Mysl'* group. Their friend, Sergei Andropov, established his own group with two comrades closer to himself in temperament, Mikhail Smirnov and Olga Zvezdochetova; later they were joined by two Tsederbaum siblings, Sergei and Lydia. (Martov was the eldest of this large tribe.)

Andropov's group surrounded their common labor with a moral earnestness and personal intensity unique in Social Democratic circles. The atmosphere is well described in the memoirs of V. O. Levitskii (another Tsederbaum), who, although he was then only sixteen years of age, carried messages and performed other routine chores for the group.

> There was something in them that radically set them apart . . . from the majority of party Social Democrats with which I have had to do, some sort of remarkable human sensibility [*dushevnost'*] and a considerable store of idealism, which in the case of Zvezdochetova

mounted to rapture. In their practical relations with people they were able to introduce great sincerity and warmth. A spirit of Christian love and apostolicity wafted from all three.[15]

Andropov had been a Tolstoyan, whose stern asceticism and moralism carried over into his Social Democratic phase; Zvezdochetova was one of those gifted teachers in the factory Sunday Schools whose patient ability to communicate knowledge earned her the boundless admiration of her pupils; and Smirnov, a somber, no-nonsense theoretician, was very much concerned with the defense of Marxist orthodoxy against Populist and, later, Revisionist detractors. Their cult of friendship pulsated with the pure romanticism of Herzen's generation. (Zvezdochetova's husband, Davydov, was apparently outside this intimate circle, whereas the admiring young Levitskii was included.) Such intensity of feeling was much more likely to respond to the revolutionary dithyramb of *Rabochee Znamia* than to the humdrum factory reports of *Rabochaia Mysl'*; upon acquainting themselves with its literature they declared themselves forthwith the St. Petersburg group of *Rabochee Znamia*.

However, they also endorsed the Manifesto of the First Congress and considered themselves members of the *Rossiiskaia*, rather than of Lure's hypothetical *Russkaia* party. They regarded as temporary their quarrel with the local "Committee" of the party, the *Soiuz Bor'by*; indeed, they soon entered into unification negotiations which included *Rabochaia Mysl'* and other dissident groups.[16] Both groups were to be constituent parts of the *Soiuz Bor'by*, *Rabochaia Mysl'* serving the needs of average workers and *Rabochee Znamia* of more sophisticated worker socialists.

The arrest of the *Rabochee Znamia* group in late December, however, forestalled the realization of the plan. The arrest of *Rabochee Znamia* was brought on by a strike that their agitational leaflets had stirred up at the Maxwell and Paul textile mills which culminated in a pitched battle between workers and police in the factory barracks.[17] Andropov's group had been aided in this enterprise by a very talented master dyer, Viktor Nogin, who developed

---

[15] Levitskii, I, p. 104. Lydia Dan relates that many student Social Democrats enjoyed playing pranks designed to embarrass their Populist rivals and readily made moral compromises in the interest of the cause. Andropov found this impossible.

[16] See p. 130.   [17] See p. 131.

a lasting friendship with Sergei Tsederbaum and Andropov. Those arrested all received comparatively light sentences: Smirnov and Zvezdochetova were simply placed on probation in the capital pending the selection of a place of residence in the provinces; Sergei Tsederbaum and Nogin were exiled for three years to Poltava; Lydia Tsederbaum-Kantzel (she had married in the meantime) was given a like term to Yalta. Andropov, the only one of the group slated for a heavier sentence, decided to flee abroad rather than serve out his term.[18]

For over a year, Moisei Lure was out of touch with groups inside Russia. He spent his time in England reprinting large stocks of his former publications on Chertkov's press, and preparing for a journey to Russia to deliver them and revive his old organization. While in England, he had gravitated entirely into non–Social Democratic circles—Tolstoyans, Polish socialists, Stepniak's Free Russian Press group, and Socialist Revolutionaries such as Burtsev and Shishko. Probably to finance his own journey, he agreed to deliver their publications along with his own.

From October, 1899, to January, 1900, he made the rounds of Kiev, Kharkov, Odessa, St. Petersburg and the western provinces to deposit literature, and then returned to England. He also collected material for a second issue of his organ, but, his later claims notwithstanding, probably had little success in conjuring up new local organizations. His visit to St. Petersburg is recorded by no source on that side. It is known, however, that he deputized an agent Nikolai Tatarov, one of his Polish acquaintances, to search out the St. Petersburg group and request funds and support in the name of *Rabochee Znamia*.[19]

By the fall of 1899, friends of Adropov and Smirnov, principally a certain Martha Furman, had indeed revived the St. Petersburg group, reestablished broken ties with the workers, and lined up a staff of propagandists with sizable reserves against possible depletion through arrests. They quickly built up a thriving propaganda establishment, but forswore strike agitation, because, as Martha Furman later declared in her deposition to the police, "we re-

---

[18] See Levitskii, I, p. 111.

[19] The best source for Lure's activities during this period is Rachkovskii's report in Menshchikov, *Russkii politicheskii sysk*, cited above.

garded it as our primary task to raise the level of political consciousness of the workers . . . and denied the significance of
strikes in this political struggle."[20] For this reason, they refused to
co-operate with "The Group of Twenty," another otherwise anonymous splinter group, sympathetic to *Rabochee Znamia* but in
favor of strikes. Through Abram Lure, Aaron's brother, Tatarov
was able to communicate with the Furman group and propose
official collaboration. He urgently requested funds for the printing
of the second issue of the journal, and the group, having excellent
connections in "society," turned over to him 800 rubles. He helped
Andropov arrange his flight over the border, and the latter hastened to England to join Lure.

Instead of the desired fruitful collaboration, however, the encounter ended in bitter mutual recriminations. Tatarov had returned to the capital in a short time without the promised literature, claiming that the amount collected had not been enough.
The St. Petersburg group, suspecting skulduggery or police provo-
cation, sent word to Adropov to look into the matter and confirm
whether Lure had indeed received the money and whether it was
being applied to publications requested. Lure met Adropov's stern
representations coolly, feigning suspicion of Adropov's credentials
and professing ignorance concerning the 800 rubles. Actually
Lure's behavior was governed by widely practiced rules of conspiracy which stipulated that familiarity with organizational matters should not be betrayed to unknown persons until they had
been vouched for. (Lure had never seen Andropov face to face
before.) Nevertheless, Andropov took deep offense and threatened
Lure with the prospect of a comrades' court. Soon Andropov was
able to flourish an official letter from the St. Petersburg group naming him editor of *Rabochee Znamia* in place of Lure and directing
Lure to hand over the funds and the press. Crestfallen, Lure submitted.[21]

This incident would scarcely be worth mentioning, had it not
revealed the deep gulf created by differences in values between

---

[20] "Peterburgskaia gruppa 'Rabochego Znameni,'" ed. S. N. Valk, in *Istoriko-revoliutsionnyi sbornik*, ed. V. I. Nevskii (Leningrad, 1924), I, 128.

[21] The affair of the 800 rubles may be traced in the correspondence of the *gruppa* with Andropov, reprinted in *ibid.*, pp. 130 ff., and in Rachkovskii's report in Men-shchikov, *Russkii politicheskii sysk*, pp. 56–59.

the two social elements which made up *Rabochee Znamia*. The fiercely idealistic student Social Democrats were the pampered darlings of radical "society" in St. Petersburg: Smirnov held forth against Struve and Tugan-Baranovskii in debates at the Free Economic Society; the husband of Martha Furman was secretary to Vladimir Posse, the editor of *Zhizn'*; the students knew personally many famous editors, authors, and professors, attended their "open houses," and invited them to speak at student *vecherinki*. Even more important, students could easily raise large sums of money for their clandestine purposes. Lure, on the other hand, smarted under the stigma of being an outcast: eternally in need for money and all too familiar with hunger and privation, he had acquired his modicum of Russian culture through heroic efforts of self-education. He found it utterly impossible to do anything about the personal habits and accent which betrayed his lower-class Jewish origin, and knew no other way of life than that of a rootless nomadic conspirator. His ventures in the service of the Social Democratic movement were merely a passing outlet for his deep-seated antipathy to the entire hierarchy of values surrounding him; his periodic infatuation with more drastic creeds of revolutionary action—terrorism, Makhaiskii's anarchism—were perhaps more genuine expressions of his inner orientation than Social Democracy was. Although dependent on the radical student intelligentsia for the success of his enterprise, he resented them as a product of the social order he despised.

Conversely, Andropov's assessment of Lure betrayed the prejudices of his own milieu, combining typical intelligentsia condescension with a moral code not of this world. Dismissing Lure as "very low in intellectual and moral stature," he lamented that "some sort of dirty, half-literate person, vouched for by no one and totally uneducated, should hold in his hands our precious cause and declare himself a representative of *Rabochee Znamia*."[22] His low estimate of Lure's morals was influenced less by the controversial 800 rubles than by an affair in Lure's private life. The Chertkov's chambermaid had been left in an embarrassing condition by some unidentified scoundrel, and Lure, to rescue her reputation from bourgeois England's rigorous code in such matters, had offered to

---

[22] Letter of March 2, 1900, in *Istoriko-revoliutsionnyi sbornik*, I, 132.

marry her. Andropov understood well the expedience of fictitious marriages for party purposes (say, to give a cover address to a secret press), but could not understand such a gesture of chivalry toward a girl with no political convictions, who, moreover, was "known to go around with everybody."[23]

Andropov soon found out that his aspirations for *Rabochee Znamia* were also running counter to the purposes of his St. Petersburg comrades. In his letters from London, he passionately implored them to "sound the alarm," to summon the workers to political struggle, and to undertake a campaign in print against *Rabochaia Mysl'* and its notorious "Supplement." "A journal at the present time must serve just one immediate practical purpose," he declared, "namely, the establishment of strong organizations that will draw the workers into the political struggle."[24] A few days later he wrote that he had received from Plekhanov himself a copy of *Vademecum dlia redakstii "Rabochago Dela,"* the latter's scathing attack on the supposed Bernsteinian tendencies of his rivals in the émigré organization.

> My dreams have come true. Kamenskii [Plekhanov] has made a strong, cutting attack on the "economic tendency" and warns of the danger for Russian Social Democracy in such phenomena as *Rabochaia Mysl'* and the Bernsteinism of Struve and others. . . .[25]

Andropov requested permission from his comrades in Russia to officially approach Plekhanov, with whom he had been corresponding, and to offer to put the resources of *Rabochee Znamia* at the disposal of the émigré leader's campaign for orthodox purity and revolutionary commitment. Above all, Andropov argued, *Rabochee Znamia* must be expanded into an all-Russian organ.[26] Much to his disgust, his comrades replied that their resources for such

---

[23] This same affair is recounted from an entirely different standpoint by Gershanovich. See *K dvadtsatipiatiletiiu*, pp. 167–68.

[24] *Istoriko-revoliutsionnyi sbornik*, I, 132.

[25] *Ibid.*, p. 133.

[26] Andropov had actually conducted preliminary negotiations with Plekhanov by correspondence, hoping soon to receive an official mandate from his group. Plekhanov's reply to Andropov was very sympathetic and invited him to come to Geneva for more extensive plans. For the text of Plekhanov's two letters to Andropov see "G. V. Plekhanov i peterburgskaia gruppa 'Rabochego Znameni,'" *Proletarskaia Revoliutsiia*, No. 31–32 (August-September, 1924), pp. 323–24.

imposing tasks were too small, and that for the time being they had to be content with a popular local journal for workers to combat the influence of *Rabochaia Mysl'*. They applauded Plekhanov's efforts to combat Bernsteinism abroad, but advised Andropov that Plekhanov "is not an issue here." "They are *teoretiki* and we are *praktiki*—thus it is possible to define our relations," they concluded with finality. Andropov was also disquieted by rumors that the St. Petersburg group was participating in plans to unify all local groups in preparation for a party congress. "First of all," he argued, "it is necessary to set one's own house in order, to define *one's own physiognomy, to establish one's own program, to manifest oneself with something substantial*—and only subsequently to arrange congresses."[27]

Andropov's thinking on how to combat the lack of ideological firmness and political concern in the movement was strikingly parallel to the program being simultaneously worked out by Lenin and Martov, although Andropov had no knowledge of it. Both plans envisaged a compact group of politically mature Social Democrats which was to set itself apart from the prevailing forms of thought to practice and align itself resolutely with the ideological bastion of Russian Social Democracy, the *Gruppa Osvobozhdenie Truda*. Together, the groups should spearhead a crusade to educate the party public to political awareness and firm Social Democratic principles, using as their chief weapon a Russia-wide underground newspaper of outstanding technical and literary quality. Finally, once it became apparent that they had won over broad support (and only then), they should proceed to organize a tightly-disciplined party adhering to the program of the crusading group.

Andropov had cast such a role for *Rabochee Znamia*, but his hopes foundered on the indifference of his comrades. By May, the Furman group was apparently liquidated, since its correspondence with Andropov ceased. Only the police seem to have been aware of its existence; neither Akimov, Levitskii nor any other informants on this period refer to it.

Andropov had also written about his plans to his old comrades, Viktor Nogin and Sergei Tsederbaum, then serving their term of exile in Poltava. Nogin replied that he and Sergei strongly ap-

---

[27] Letter of March 19, 1900, in *Istoriko-revoliutsionnyi sbornik*, p. 138. (Italics in original.)

proved of Andropov's plan for a political journal to draw the workers into a more direct and decisive struggle with the autocracy. Nogin outlined his own ideas on revolutionary tactics, touching upon such problems as the advisability of terror and the revolutionary possibilities of the "middle peasantry." Revolutionary operations, he felt, must be directed by a "special committee" with its "own organ." The workers, he was sure, would be ready to embark on a revolutionary path in the very near future, beginning with street demonstrations and ending with open armed struggle. However, Nogin, a sober worker socialist, did not succumb to the vague, romantic flights of his young intelligentsia friends, and forecast the prospects of a revolutionary upheaval with fair accuracy.

> If you consider the technical advances of the military in the past century, then it is clear that no armed uprising of the masses will produce any results, and it's hard to imagine that any sudden outburst could come to a successful conclusion. Most probably, the government will be forced to grant some sort of lousy constitution after a series of workers' demonstrations and strikes of a political character accompanied by vague opposition from other classes.[28]

Andropov must have expressed to Nogin his disenchantment with the St. Petersburg group, for in May the latter wrote to him again: "Don't despair, be of good spirit; soon we will let you know about some new developments which I think will result in the fulfillment of your plans."[29] In the meantime Sergei Tsederbaum's brother, Martov, had arrived in Poltava and had undoubtedly initiated him and Nogin into the project for *Iskra*. It is no accident that *Rabochee Znamia*'s most ambitious trio, Andropov, Sergei Tsederbaum, and Nogin, soon linked their careers with *Iskra* and became its first agents inside Russia.[30]

In the capital, a new social and political atmosphere had been in the making for over a year. From the autumn of 1899 onward, leaflet agitation and strikes had declined sharply as the result of the deepening economic crisis and the consequent threat of unem-

---

28 "Pis'ma V. P. Nogina k S. V. Andropovu," *Proletarskaia Revoliutsiia*, No. 31–32, pp. 331–32. Andropov wrote a brief introduction to this correspondence which adds a few biographical details not mentioned in other sources.

29 *Ibid.*, p. 335.   30 See pp. 231–32.

ployment. Apparently unaware of the existence of the Furman group, Eva Broido expressed the characteristic view that "the workers' voice, in St. Petersburg at least, was barely audible at this time," and that "ties with the workers were cut off by the vigilance of the police as quickly as they were established."[31] Boris Savinkov, a survivor of "The Group of Twenty," informed her that there had been no active group in the capital for almost a year (from the autumn of 1899 to the autumn of 1900). Doubtless a number of "lone wolves" and splinter groups sponsoring one or two *kruzhki* existed in addition to the Furman group, but it was easy for even a close observer like Broido to be misled because the emphasis in practical work had shifted back to unobtrusive propaganda centering on the basic social and the political goals of the movement. Social Democrats of all shades had become more sensitive to the swelling revolutionary temper of other sectors of society than the workers, particularly of the students. Marxists and Populists still carried on impassioned theoretical debates in the Free Economic Society and at the "open houses" of prominent literary intelligentsia, but illegal gatherings were becoming more and more frequent, and the partisans of all revolutionary factions thrilled to the same veiled eulogies of political freedom and to revolutionary songs sung *sotto voce*. All oppositional groups gave sympathetic attention to the students' heroic resistance to the new repressive measures of the government and became infected with their increasingly bold denunciations of the regime.

In this heightened revolutionary atmosphere, ideological lines often became somewhat blurred. The image of the worker's position at the forefront of the revolutionary movement began to fade into the background and in its place emerged the heroic radical intelligentsia, the repository of the highest ideals of the nation and courageous champion of human dignity against police truncheons, the drafting of protesting students and other humiliating abuses. To be sure, the workers were still viewed as the raw physical force which, under the enlightened leadership of the intelligentsia, would assure victory over the autocracy; but many Social Democrats unwittingly gave ground to the revived spirit of Populist

---

[31] E. Broido, "Gruppa 'Sotsialist'; 'Rabochaia Biblioteka,'" *Letopis' Revoliutsii*, No. 1 (Berlin, 1923), p. 129. This historical journal must not be confused with the Kharkov journal of the same name. Both are extremely rare.

revolutionary romanticism, which was soon to give birth to the Socialist Revolutionary Party.[32]

Itself the harbinger of this new atmosphere, *Rabochee Znamia* embodied a tendency that began to make serious inroads upon the normative patterns of Russian Social Democracy. During the autumn and winter, a new group built up an extensive network of propaganda circles and connections to "society." Its main purpose was to counteract the influence of *Rabochaia Mysl'* with consistent propaganda on the theme of the urgency of the political struggle— propaganda directed, not only at workers, but also at the intelligentsia and students. The group called itself simply *Sotsialist*, so as not to preclude collaboration with revolutionary Populists in promoting the cause of political protest. It is significant that two of its members, Boris Savinkov and P. M. Rutenberg, urged the adoption of terror as a part of its program; both later acquired fame in the terrorist organizations of the S. R. Party. Eva Broido, another of the founders, thus characterized the group:

> We agreed on a compromise which then seemed perfectly simple and natural: since we all are striving for the same goal, Socialism, but disagree over the appropriate methods of struggle for its realization, we will call ourselves simple "socialists" and form the group *Sotsialist*. The group will conduct oral and literary propaganda on the idea of socialism among the working masses and the students, and put agitation for struggle against the autocracy as the first order of business.[33]

Simultaneously, a separate group, the *Sotsial-Demokraticheskaia Rabochaia Biblioteka*, was organized to handle the writing and printing of brochures on political themes, which *Sotsialist* was to distribute and make use of in its propaganda work. Through Eva Broido's husband, Mark Broido, arrangements were made with a dissident Bundist group in Vilna to set up a secret printing press. Unconcerned about ideological credentials, the organizers of the enterprise secured the cooperation of such prominent authors as the ex-Marxists, Struve and Tugan-Baranovskii, and the

---

[32] For memoirs depicting this atmosphere, see V. Posse, *Moi zhiznennyi put'* (Moscow and Leningrad, 1929), chap. 16, *passim;* and L. Kleinbort, "M. I. Gurovich —'Kharkovtsev,'" *Byloe*, No. 16 (1921), pp. 86–107. Also Broido, *passim* and Levitskii, I, chaps. 7 and 8.

[33] Broido, p. 130.

liberal historians, Semevskii and Paul Miliukov. They succeeded in producing four or five propaganda brochures on "political" themes which received wide distribution. An editorial statement in the first work in this series argued that "the working class can attain its aims only if it is organized as a *political* party which seeks to prepare the masses for the assumption of political power."[34] The group had the misfortune, however, of making use of the willing services of the famous editor-provocateur, Gurovich, whom Struve had unwittingly recommended to them. As a result, it was liquidated in January, 1901.

Sotsialist, having survived the arrests, flowered into an influential and smoothly working organization with extensive ties among workers, students, and "society." Aware of its affinity with *Rabochee Znamia,* the group entered into negotiations with Lure's newest representative in the capital, Aaron Solts, and in a short time reconstituted itself as the local organization of *Rabochee Znamia.* In the fall of 1900, Moisei Lure had once more returned secretly to Russia with a large stock of his publications, including the second issue of *Rabochee Znamia.* He set about rebuilding his own organizations and wooing the politically oriented circles in St. Petersburg. With the help of Tatarov and Gershanovich, Lure succeeded in setting up a printing press in Kiev, which put out a third issue of *Rabochee Znamia* in February, 1901. The merger with the group *Sotsialist* once again promised the imminent realization of his long cherished organizational blueprint.

Barely had this step toward organizational consolidation been taken when the St. Petersburg group was approached by a representative of *Iskra,* which was just now beginning to advance its claims as the authoritative voice of Russian Social Democracy. Most of the former members of *Sotsialist* strongly sympathized with *Iskra's* plans and arranged for mutual cooperation and association, despite Lure's desperate attempts to dissuade them. The combined forces of *Sotsialist, Rabochee Znamia,* and *Iskra* participated in preparations for the famous demonstration of March 4, 1901, on Kazan Square. Their attempts to call out the workers over the opposition of the *Soiuz Bor'by* failed to achieve any noticeable results. During the next few months, the new coalition worked

---

[34] Cited in Akimov, *Materialy,* p. 66.

feverishly on broad plans to exploit the new revolutionary atmosphere. Their capstone was to be the organization of a grandiose workers' demonstration for May First in cooperation with the *Soiuz Bor'by,* which by now had executed a *volte face* and was totally committed to the idea of political demonstrations. All these preparations having been relayed to the *Okhrana* by Gurovich, the groups were liquidated on the eve of the grand event.[35]

With these arrests, *Rabochee Znamia* as a separate organization ceased to exist, the survivors being absorbed partly by *Iskra,* partly by the party of Socialist Revolutionaries. The roving conspirators, Lure, Tatarov, and Gershanovich, were arrested in the South on separate occasions between March and May. Thus the last remnants of Lure's perennially resurrected apparatus of professional revolutionaries disappeared. As late as early 1902, one still heard of partisans of *Rabochee Znamia* in Kiev and Odessa, who cooperated with *Iskra* agents in fomenting a politically oriented schism from the regular Social Democratic Committees. However, for all intents and purposes, the history of *Rabochee Znamia* as the standard-bearer of militant Social Democracy ends with March 4, 1901, and the history of *Iskra* begins. Lure's pioneer enterprise was swamped in the surge of political tendencies which followed in the wake of the demonstration in front of the Kazan cathedral.

---

[35] These complex interrelations were admirably dissected in a detailed report on *Rabochee Znamia* by a police official, L. A. Rataev. See S. N. Valk (ed.), "K dokumental'noi istorii 'Rabochego Znameni,' " *Krasnaia Letopis',* No. 2–3 (February-March, 1922), pp. 333–46.

CHAPTER 8

The Hollow Victory (1901–3)

Justifiably, *Iskra* has lent its name to the period in the history of Russian Social Democracy from the turn of the century to the Second Party Congress. This was conceded even by the anti-*Iskra*-ite Akimov (the lone voice of the defeated "Economists" at the Second Congress) in 1905, when he attempted to establish an alternative scheme of party history to that of *Chto delat'?*[1] From the appearance of the very first number (December, 1900), *Iskra* was widely hailed as the authentic voice of militant Social Democracy; *praktiki*, returned exiles, *teoretiki* of several hues, and even workers vied with each other in proclaiming their support of *Iskra's* "political line." In the emigration, the "official" organ of the party, *Rabochee Delo*, was soon overshadowed, despite its desperate efforts to keep up with the leftward surge of popular sentiment in Russia.

The manifest ascendancy of *Iskra* as a symbol of revolutionary aspirations should not be confused, however, with the image conveyed by Soviet historiography in which Lenin appears as a solitary hero who, despite the "opportunism" of his *Iskra* colleagues, singlehandedly routed the firmly entrenched Economists.[2]

---

[1] See Akimov, *Materialy*, pp. 5 and 93 ff.

[2] Typical of the panegyrics on Lenin in current Soviet writings is the following commentary on the Economist issue: "Thanks to Lenin, to his unbending will and tremendous energy, Russian Social Democracy succeeded in withstanding the onset

To a large extent *Iskra* was fighting an enemy which had already fled the field of battle and found it necessary to direct its sallies against "covert Economists" to justify its crusading posture. *Iskra* won in popularity precisely because the party public was already persuaded of the imminence of revolutionary events and sought authoritative guidance for the uncertainties ahead. It is true that later on, around the autumn of 1902, *Iskra* agents with instructions from Lenin were able to penetrate and control local committees in Russia, a practice which implied a basic reorientation in the structure of the movement. But until mid-1902 one could say that the movement was still impelled along primarily by its own inner momentum and that *Iskra* was simply one of the manifestations, rather than the cause, of the new spirit of revolutionary intransigence. Therefore, a more accurate picture of *Iskra*'s significance will be gained if the spontaneous shifts in the structure and character of the movement due to general political conditions are considered first. Only then can the story of *Iskra*'s dramatic victory at the Second Congress and the irony of the party split be properly understood.

The street demonstrations of March, 1901, in the major cities of Russia marked the advent of yet another phase in the long conflict of radical society with the prevailing order. The heroism and initiative of the students in combating the "provisional regulations" of 1899 gave the revolutionary intelligentsia and their liberal fringe a new focal point for their political hopes and helped free them from the spell of the working masses. With the defection of such leading theoreticians as Struve, Tugan-Baranovskii, and Bulgakov, the intellectual pre-eminence of Marxism had rapidly dwindled. The once captive authors and scholars, the impressionable ex-Populists and liberals, the worker-phile students, lawyers, and zemstvo employees now responded to new strategies and theoretical justifications for their mounting aspirations for change. In exposing themselves to the blows of Cossack whips, to the dangers of arrest and loss of social position, they developed a new sense of their own dignity and social import which Marxism had denied them.

---

of opportunism and emerging from the crisis with honor." (Pospelov, *Istoriia*, p. 339.) Every major step in the progress of the movement is credited solely to Lenin, including phases with which he had little to do, such as the founding of the party.

To be sure, they still regarded the working class and their Social Democratic champions as important "allies" in the shaping struggle, but other social factors now entered their political computations. The overly simple view, so popular a few years before, that the momentum of the workers' movement would of itself burst the shackles of the autocracy, gave place to the feeling that "all live forces" should now join in the battle for political liberty. The assassination of the reactionary Minister of Education, Bogolepov, the merciless beating of the demonstrators on Kazan Square, the arrest and exile of prominent authors and scholars (among them Struve, Annenskii, Mikhailovskii, Posse, and Gorky), the closing of journals and learned societies which had been havens of oppositional sentiment—here were concrete evidences of the capacity of educated social groups for political action and self-sacrifice, which released them from emotional dependence on the working-class buffer and brought them into direct confrontation with the bastions of political order.

In response to these events, which momentarily put the workers' movement in the shadow, Russian Social Democracy rapidly completed its shift from "economics" to "politics." Where the ruling *komitetchiki* reacted too slowly, as in St. Petersburg, Kiev, Kharkov, and Odessa, the more volatile elements of the "periphery," chiefly students, formed splinter groups thoroughly imbued with the new spirit. The group *Rabochaia Volia* in Kiev and the *Iuzhnaia Gruppa Revoliutsionnykh Sotsial-Demokratov* in Odessa had been loosely related to *Rabochee Znamia* and soon became flaming partisans of *Iskra*. The fact that the regular committees shifted far to the left after the March days and yielded to the popular clamor for street demonstrations denouncing the autocracy did not always serve to heal the breach. In Odessa, for example, the conflict seemed to revolve around a rather pedantic quarrel over the true nature of the autocracy: whether it was a mere reflection of the current balance of social forces (an impeccably orthodox Marxist viewpoint) or a self-sufficient bureaucratic structure with intrinsic interests of self-preservation, weighing equally heavily on all social classes, including the bourgeoisie. Even though both parties agreed on most questions of current goals and strategy, the former group held to inherited notions of the hegemony of the proletariat and the class essence of the struggle, whereas the latter, like its prototype *Rabochee Znamia*, reflected the newly acquired thirst of the democratic intelligentsia for the rights of man and citizen. Only in February, 1902, when both groups were hit by arrests on the eve of a jointly planned street demonstration, was the issue finally laid to rest (*Iskra* headquarters instructed the loyal *Iuzhnaia Gruppa* to dissolve itself).[3]

From March, 1901 to roughly mid-1902, local Social Democratic committees concerned themselves almost exclusively with street demonstrations and unalloyed political agitation. In part, this program simply carried forward the political trends inherent in the May First campaigns of which those of Kharkov and the Western border regions in 1900 had been the harbingers. By now, however, the context was different. Whereas the May First demonstrations had gloried in the monolithic strength of the working class and advanced purely working class goals, the new species of demonstration owed its impetus and inspiration to the students and professional intelligentsia. Caught unawares by the March events, the Social Democrats sought to recoup their impaired position of leadership by sponsoring the new mode of protest and in the process were obliged to adapt themselves to its spirit. Crude expressions of proletarian chauvinism now seemed out of place, inasmuch as political agitation now had to be addressed to all potential partners in the struggle—students, soldiers, peasants, and above all, "society." Not May First alone, but all suitable occasions were exploited for denouncing the autocracy: political events, incidents of police brutality, important anniversaries (the Emancipation of the serfs, the assassination of Alexander II, the Decembrist uprising), and even a strike of a local character, the suppression of which was cited as yet another example of political tyranny.[4]

Every Social Democratic Committee made at least one major effort during this period to bring the workers and sympathizing public out en masse. The plans envisaged imposing processions along the main avenues, the proud display of red flags and plac-

---

[3] See Garvi, pp. 135 ff., for an extended discussion of this ideological conflict. For an opponent's view, see D. Novomirskii, "Iz istorii odesskogo podpol'ia," *Proletarskaia Revoliutsiia*, No. 63 (April, 1927), pp. 181–202.

[4] For a fair sampling of the agitational leaflets of this period see *Listovki revoliutsionnykh s.-d. organizatsii Ukrainy, 1896–1904* (Kiev, 1963).

ards emblazoned with slogans, the throb of revolutionary songs and chants of "Away with the autocracy! Long live political freedom!" Some committees, particularly in the South (Kharkov, Ekaterinoslav), made repeated attempts, always hoping that they could be escalated into a major revolutionary event. With rare exceptions, however, the results fell far below such anticipations. The authorities were almost always informed in advance and took effective precautionary measures; all known trouble makers were rounded up ahead of time while troops and Cossacks secured the streets. Forced to change their plans at the last minute, the organizers seldom found it possible to gather large enough crowds in one place to give themselves protective cover. Typically a few hundred intellectuals and workers closest to the organization collected on one of the main boulevards and tried to lure timid bystanders from the sidewalk into the street. As soon as the demonstrators exposed themselves by unfurling banners or shouting slogans, Cossacks would dash out from hiding places in nearby courtyards, handily apprehend the hard core demonstrators, and subject the rest of the participants to a merciless beating.[5]

The demonstration movement petered out in the course of 1902 because the repressions were taking a heavy toll, and the worker and intelligentsia supporters were becoming less and less willing to assume risks at the order of secret committees over which they exercised no control. Furthermore, the revival of terror and the waves of agrarian unrest in the course of 1902 suggested alternative strategies and occasioned not a few defections to the newly formed Socialist-Revolutionary Party. The liberals now had their own sounding board in Struve's journal *Osvobozhdenie,* an undertaking which attracted a number of the ex-Marxist authors, zemstvo liberals, and members of the educated professions. Whereas a few months before the Social Democrats could count on financial and moral support from broad circles of the liberal and radical public (outside help was particularly essential for money, sleeping quarters, hiding places for literature and printing para-

---

[5] For descriptions of these demonstrations see Garvi, pp. 162–63 and 197–98, and Levitskii, II, 70–73. One informed but embittered observer described them as "demonstrations of weakness rather than strength." ("Rabochii" [B. M. Knuniants], *Rabochie i intelligenty v nashykh organizatsiiakh* [Geneva, 1904], p. 24.)

phernalia, and cover addresses for communications), they were now left largely to their own resources. Social Democracy had apparently played out its self-appointed historical role of arraying the working masses at the forefront of the battle against the autocracy, and prospects were dim for any recovery in the near future. The manifest failure of the program of political demonstrations, the increasing consciousness of isolation, and the heavy toll by arrests combined to spread panic and uncertainty over local committees in the latter half of 1902. This state of demoralization, as will be seen shortly, greatly favored Lenin's effort to penetrate local committees with his agents and secure their formal adherence to *Iskra's* views.

The program of political demonstrations substantially altered the character of local organizations and greatly aggravated the unresolved conflict between intelligentsia and worker groups. First of all, those techniques which had brought intellectuals and workers into intimate contact and required solidly organized worker groups for their success were rapidly falling into disuse. Strike agitation, which had called into being the *kassy*, the agitators' assemblies, and the workers' committees, abated considerably following the recession of 1899 and received little further encouragement from the intelligentsia. Although there seems to have been a brief revival of workers' study circles around 1900 to prepare members for their forthcoming revolutionary mission, the heady events of early 1901 left little time for systematic indoctrination, and this form of confrontation between workers and intelligentsia also suffered from neglect. The staging of political demonstrations, on the other hand, required only a modicum of direct contact with the workers. The arrangements for time, place and occasion were almost always worked out by a small handful of committeemen (often not even the full Committee), who consulted neither the workers nor any outside persons for fear that the "plan" would fall into the hands of the police. The new technique demanded little more than printing facilities to turn out piles of leaflets on a moment's notice, and a small staff of writers skilled in coining popular slogans and accompanying them with appropriate commentary on the events of the hour. By this time nearly every local committee had at its disposal a secret press and, if it were seized by the police, the technique of restoring it to order had long become a matter of routine.[6]

From the workers the intelligentsia nucleus required only dependable contact men whom it could inform of the appropriate time and place, and entrust with distribution of the copiously supplied leaflets. More than ever, this meant consigning the workers to the status of errand boys for the intelligentsia-dominated committee: the worker subordinates were expected to be ready at all times to deliver literature they hadn't read or approved, and to drum up enthusiasm for demonstrations, the appropriateness of which they often did not find convincing. The committee might seek these services from already organized worker groups, but frequently, to avoid unpleasantness, it turned to hand-picked, younger workers more amenable to intelligentsia guidance. Above all it was important to dampen the workers' incurable relish for discussing the issues, and to inculcate immediate, unquestioning obedience to "party" directives. In short, all those carefully built up sub-structures and techniques which had cultivated the workers' own resourcefulness—the rich harvest of the periods of *kruzhkovshchina* and agitation—now became superfluous, the very instinct for them, seditious.[7]

Even though most committeemen had lost their taste for encouraging the workers' "independent activity" (*samodeiatel'nost*), it was impossible simply to wish out of existence the sizable groups of organized workers who viewed themselves as full-fledged members of local party organizations. Such groups could by and large boast of an experienced leadership, an established tradition of elective representation, and a considerable following at the factory and district level. The Workers' Committee in Ekaterinoslav found it necessary to interpose district committees

---

[6] Mark Khinoi of New York, who as a young lad in his late teens operated no less than eight underground presses in succession in Ekaterinoslav, Kharkov, and Rostov, gives a fascinating account of his underground experiences in V podpol'nykh tipografiiakh tsarskoi Rossii. (Inter-university Project on the History of the Menshevik Movement; New York, 1960.)

[7] There was some, although not overmuch, informed discussion of the organizational question in the underground press at the time. The lead article in *Iuzhnyi Rabochii*, No. 10 (December, 1902) acknowledged the problem of worker alienation and correctly linked it to the two-story structure, but felt that the overriding demands of the era of political struggle necessitated the existing arrangements.

(*iadry*) between themselves and the countless factory cells. Even the district meetings held in outlying woods or fields attracted a hundred or so workers. Similarly complex worker organizations existed by 1901 in Kiev, St. Petersburg, Odessa, and Kharkov; invariably they adhered to the principle of *elective* representation.

Revolts against Committee leadership continued to be endemic, although the workers' object was no longer so much "self-liberation" as the recognition of their rightful place in the party. For the most part, the dissident workers could no longer be accused of "trade unionism," as they had been profoundly influenced by the new revolutionary atmosphere and more often than not looked to *Iskra* rather than to *Rabochee Delo* or *Rabochaia Mysl'* to orient themselves in events. N. Drokhanov, the leader of a workers' revolt against the Ekaterinoslav Committee in the winter of 1901–2, claimed that his followers were actually prompted to their action by *Iskra* because the intelligentsia Committee had proven itself too sluggish in initiating the political struggle.[8] The Ekaterinoslav workers were convinced that they were being deliberately isolated from the higher spheres of party leadership, as the Committee had the vexing habit of always claiming to speak in the name of the party when requesting the workers to carry out instructions. After assuring themselves of firm grass roots support, the worker leaders audaciously declared themselves Ekaterinoslav's official party Committee and magnanimously offered to co-opt the perplexed intelligentsia of the old Committee. Somehow the workers had been able to appropriate the official Committee stamp, the "symbol of authority" as Drokhanov put it (since it was affixed to all leaflets put out by the Committee). The intelligentsia meekly submitted, knowing that the workers could probably find the outside support to carry on essential functions. The "elective principle" was formally adopted and the "selective principle" formally abolished. The bicameral system was replaced by a unitary committee of both workers and intelligentsia. For over a year these arrangements were kept in good faith by both sides until a new crisis (to be discussed later) was provoked by *Iskra*.

---

[8] See his short recollections in *Istoriia ekaterinoslavskoi*, pp. 245 ff. Other points on the Ekaterinoslav organization may be confirmed by consulting the recollections of E. Adamovich, A. Krasnoshchekov, A. Beliavskii, and I. Polonskii in the same work. Police reports and other documentation are also included.

In St. Petersburg, Kiev, Rostov, Kremenchug, Batum, and in all probability elsewhere there continued to be much pulling and hauling over the same issues.[9] In general, it appears that when the workers and their intelligentsia supporters made a concerted effort to extract concessions from the regular committees, they were able to do so, but when tensions subsided the old system reasserted itself by degrees because it was convenient for current purposes and conformed to the inflexible habits of the intelligentsia committeemen. Arrests, the discovery of informers, the inertia of factory groups, and the uncertainty of the worker leaders themselves as to their legitimate function (*kassy* and strike leadership were no longer in demand) all tended to favor the intelligentsia's mode of operation. And only the intelligentsia enjoyed the leisure time and connections with "society" which could assure the successful operation of committee work. Finally, by mid-1902 *Iskra* lent the full weight of its authority to the system selection and co-optation, a question which will be treated in due course.

For all its unresolved problems, Russian Social Democracy in the years 1901-3 continued to spread its activities to ever wider areas and to build up an ever thicker network of organizations.[10] After 1900 the return flow of exiles from Siberia and the provinces was added to the influx of recruits from the normal sources of supply (students, Jewish *poluintelligenty*, younger workers). In the Northern and Central provinces this did not necessarily mean stronger organizations, but more of them. Kostroma and Samara now had "Committees" which underwent the same phases of development as those experienced earlier by other groups; Tula, Iaroslavl, and a few West Siberian towns (Ufa, Tomsk) now boasted functioning organizations, staffed chiefly by political exiles

---

9 Unfortunately, most of these situations are imperfectly illuminated by the sources, in some cases only by a fleeting reference in a single source; but in their totality they paint roughly the same picture as the excellent documents on Ekaterinoslav. The respective sources for the localities mentioned above are: *Rabochie i intelligenty* (Geneva, 1902) (a partisan version by the unorthodox Social Democrat E. O. Zelenskii ["Nadezhdin"]); "Doklad kievskogo komiteta," *Vtoroi S'ezd R.S.–D.R.P. Protokoly*, pp. 643–44; A. Stanchinskii, "K dvadtsatiletnemu iubeleiu demonstratsii v Rostove n/D," *Proletarskaia Revoliutsiia*, No. 13 (February, 1923), p. 199; Levitskii, II, 56–59; and *Iskra*, No. 23 (August 1, 1902), p. 6.

10 The proliferation of Social Democratic organizations in Russia can be most readily surveyed in *Iskra*'s regular column "Iz partiinoi zhizni" which regularly announced the formation of new groups.

and surrounded by a large periphery of gymnasium students and zemstvo employees. Iaroslavl, Ivanovo-Voznesensk, and Kostroma were soon loosely united into a "Northern Workers' Union." The number of genuine "workers" connected with these organizations was often insignificant.

In the major administrative centers—Moscow, St. Petersburg, and Kiev—the incessant incursions of the police (especially of Zubatov in Moscow), along with the inexperience and superficial indoctrination of the newcomers, brought about an even greater degree of splintering and turnover than ever before. The student periphery was certainly larger and more combative, but by the same token more unstable and unreliable (defections to the S.R.'s were frequent). The returned exiles tended to shy away from such inexperienced groups and preferred to make their services available as "agents" for *Iskra*.

The major advances in solid local organizations continued to be made in the Southern and border regions, particularly in the Caucasus. In the latter, the Social Democratic movement shifted away from the Russian ethnic element (always substantial in the railroad and major industries) to the non-Russian (Georgians, Armenians, etc.), stimulating in the process the awakening of national movements. In spite of the lingering industrial crisis, the Southern committees strengthened themselves, enlarged the scope of their activities, and spawned numerous provincial organizations (Kremenchug, Poltava, Zhitomir, Elizavetgrad, Kherson). An unusually successful undertaking was the mobilization of the scattered miners of the Don basin by the *Soiuz Gornozavodskikh Sotsial-demokraticheskikh Rabochikh* (Union of Social Democratic Mining Workers), whose headquarters nested in the offices of the largest newspaper in Rostov, *Donskaia Rech*, unknown equally to the police, the owners of the paper and the local committee of the party (the *Donskoi Komitet*).[11]

By far the outstanding achievement of the talented Southern *praktiki* was the regional underground paper, *Iuzhnyi Rabochii* (*Southern Worker*), founded early in 1900. The organizers, A. M.

11 See recollections of I. N. Moshinskii (Konarskii) in "Iz epokhi 2-go s'ezda (1900–1904 gg.)," *Katorga i Ssylka*, Nos. 45 and 46 (August, September, 1928) and "K voprosy o s.d. (Donetskom) soiuze gornozavodskikh rabochikh," *Proletarskaia Revoliutsiia*, No. 63 (April, 1927), pp. 229–37; see also A. Shestakov, "Na zare rabochego dvizheniia v Donbase," *Proletarskaia Revoliutsiia*, No. 1 (1921), pp. 156–63.

Ginzburg, Avram Vilenskii, and Moisei Dushkan, and later V. N. Rozanov and I. A. Levin, were Jewish Social Democrats who had received their practical schooling in the Bund and were masters at the technical side of the undertaking. (Vilenskii had been the typesetter for *Rabochaia Gazeta,* and Dushkan had initiated the first Yiddish underground paper *Arbeiterstimme* in 1896–97). Although Ekaterinoslav was the original center of their operations, they sought from the outset to establish a "regional organ" for the industrial South. For writing talent they turned to S. K. Kharchenko in Poltava and I. A. Levin and O. A. Ermanskii in Kharkov. To throw the police off the track, their press was located successively in Poltava, Kremenchug, Ekaterinoslav, Kishinev, and Baku. The paper was well informed on developments throughout the South and presented them in vigorous style, never failing to stress revolutionary goals. Its literary and technical excellence was a source of enormous pride to the Southern *praktiki,* who while supporting *Iskra's* political line, stubbornly refused to obey *Iskra's* demand that they surrender their "parochial" enterprise.[12]

Contrary to *Iskra's* insinuations, *Iuzhnyi Rabochii* was from the outset strongly party-oriented. The very project had originated in conjunction with Ginzburg's suggestion to the Ekaterinoslav Social Democrats that they sponsor a new party "Congress," which was set for March in Smolensk. Like *Rabochaia Gazeta* before it, *Iuzhnyi Rabochii* was to act as the chief organizer and propagator of the enterprise. I. Kh. Lalaiants was sent to Moscow to get in touch with his old friend Ulianov (Lenin), who had just returned from exile. He was to persuade Lenin's recently formed literary group (Lenin, Martov, and Potresov) to become the editors of the new party journal. The project collapsed because of arrests and the indifference of key party committees (Kiev, St. Petersburg, Kharkov).[13] Moreover, the attitude of Lenin's group was less than cooperative as they had already worked out their own plans for a political journal. Ginzburg and Vilenskii decided to concentrate

---

[12] The reminiscences of Ginzburg and Vilenskii and other materials on *Iuzhnyi Rabochii* are included in *Istoriia ekaterinoslavskoi;* see also Ermanskii, *Iz perezhitogo,* and V. N. Rozanov, "Iz partiinago proshlago," *Nasha Zaraia,* Nos. 6 and 7–8, 1913, pp. 31–38 and 37–43 respectively.

[13] See *Istoriia ekaterinoslavskoi,* pp. 156 ff. (Ginzburg's version), and I. Kh. Lalaiants, *U istokov bol'shevizma* (Moscow, 1934), pp. 75–79. The reasons for the hostility of Lenin and Martov are discussed below.

for the time being on building up a firm organization in the South, a task they executed with notable success.

In December, 1901, *Iuzhnyi Rabochii,* now under the leadership of O. A. Ermanskii (the founders had all been arrested), brought the major committees of the South together for a regional conference. The conference constituted itself as a permanent regional party organization, declared *Iuzhnyi Rabochii* its official organ, elected a Central Committee and passed a series of resolutions on theoretical and organizational matters, including one instructing the Central Committee to bend every effort to call a Second Congress of the R.S.-D.R.P.[14] A few months later, in March, 1902, Ermanskii represented the Southern Region at a hastily called "party congress" at Belostok, sponsored by the Bund and *Rabochee Delo* in the hope of heading off the growing influence of *Iskra.* An *Iskra* representative (Fedor Dan) arrived uninvited to demand that the gathering be declared an unofficial preparatory conference to a Second Congress, a demand that had already been met by those assembled, since among the major committees only St. Petersburg had sent a delegate.[15] During its entire existence (1900–1903) *Iuzhnyi Rabochii* was in the forefront of all attempts to revive the party including, as will be seen below, the actual calling of the Second Congress.

Founded before *Iskra* and outshining it for a time in popularity in the South, *Iuzhnyi Rabochii* was long a thorn in *Iskra*'s side. It was all the more irritating that the organ could not justifiably be reproached with "Economism" or lack of party spirit. From the very first, *Iuzhnyi Rabochii* hewed to an unequivocal "political" line. Its coverage of events dealt chiefly with direct clashes between the workers and representatives of the autocracy—May First processions in Vilna and Warsaw, the general strike in Riga, the shooting of workers in Mariupol. "The government has declared open war on the workers' movement," the first issue affirmed with solemnity, calling for "a decisive struggle for politi-

---

[14] A very detailed account of this conference is given by Garvi (pp. 153–83) who represented Odessa. According to him the discussions were conducted at a very high level of theoretical competence, and the participants were convinced they had taken a "great stride toward unification of the party."

[15] See "K istorii belostokskoi konferentsii 1902 g." *Proletarskaia Revoliutsiia,* No. 101 (June, 1930), pp. 139–40. The article reprints an account written by Dan immediately afterward for the benefit of the *Iskra* editors.

cal rights and the overthrow of the autocracy."[16] By the third issue (late 1900) *Iuzhnyi Rabochii* was pressing its readers to "get ready for battle and organize general strikes, mass meetings and open, resounding celebrations of May First."[17]

This political orientation owed less to the stimulus of the student and intelligentsia demonstrations or to the doctrinaire views of Plekhanov than to the inherent forward momentum of the workers' movement in the South under the impact of unceasing Social Democratic agitation. In this respect it was perhaps closer in spirit to *Rabochee Delo* than to *Iskra*. The rapid build-up of the labor force in giant new enterprises, along with the crude methods of the non-Russian employers and provincial authorities in handling this unwieldy influx (for example, the use as factory police of half-savage Cheremissian tribesmen, whose brutal acts were frequently reciprocated by the workers), provided fertile soil for giving agitation a revolutionary turn. Except in Kiev and Kharkov, the student and "part-time" intelligentsia contingent in the Southern Committees was relatively small, whereas that of the profoundly alienated Jewish *poluintelligenty* and newly arrived workers from the Western Pale was disproportionately large. *Iuzhnyi Rabochii*, a product of this milieu, epitomized the uninterrupted development of Social Democracy into a mass political movement in the South. Already suffused with revolutionary spirit, the industrial South reacted to the intelligentsia demonstrations of March, 1901 far less dramatically than the university centers. The general strikes of 1903 were the logical culmination.

If *Iuzhnyi Rabochii* maintained a certain continuity of tradition in the new era of politics, *Iskra* introduced a radically new spirit and ultimately succeeded in altering the social and structural character of the movement. These changes were not entirely the ones contemplated by the innovators, but nevertheless they were the inevitable consequences of carrying out the "idea" projected by Lenin in Siberia and enthusiastically seconded by Martov and Potresov. The two preceding chapters have shown that this "idea"

---

16 *Iuzhnyi Rabochii*, No. 1 (January, 1900), p. 33. The author was able to obtain Nos. 1, 3, and 10 from the Bibliothèque de la Documentation Internationale Contemporaine. To his knowledge these are the only issues preserved. No. 1 was reprinted in *Istoriia ekaterinoslavskii* and has been reprinted several times since.

17 *Iuzhnyi Rabochii*, No. 3 (November, 1900), p. 4.

was not without precedents, but conditions were now more favorable for its acceptance and it had found a fanatical partisan in Lenin, who ignored all obstacles, brooked no compromise, and dragooned friend and foe alike in the pursuit of his goal. Neither he nor his *Iskra* collaborators anticipated the profound convulsions which their policies were to elicit, and only the Mensheviks, in their more candid moments, were ever to acknowledge retrospectively a degree of culpability on *Iskra*'s part for the unwelcome results. In support of the above, it will not be necessary to recount the full story of *Iskra,* which is readily available in other works, but only to cover the less well-known aspects of it, more specifically, the efforts to translate the idea into practice.

As Lenin from his remote Siberian exile strove to keep abreast of developments in the Social Democratic movement, he was disturbed by the fact that since the First Congress there had been no news of efforts to revive the party or to combat seriously the centrifugal tendencies of the movement. On the contrary, the evidence pointed only to further atomization of effort, smug satisfaction with local agitational techniques, and ever-increasing ideological instability. He merely heard unsettling reports of the rift between Plekhanov and the young Social Democrats Abroad, of the reflection of Bernstein's ideas in the works of Russian "critics" of Marx, and of the popularity of the "worker's organ," *Rabochaia Mysl'*. The appearance of Kuskova's *Credo* and the theoretical "Supplement" to the seventh issue of *Rabochaia Mysl'* removed all doubt from his mind: the new trends threatened to reduce the Social Democratic movement to a mere appendage of the liberal and radical democratic oppositional groups, and only the coordinated efforts of the most mature Social Democrats and Plekhanov's Liberation of Labor Group could bring the movement back on its true revolutionary course. To Lenin, as to his predecessors, the obvious means to accomplish this was a nation-wide underground newspaper, which would attract to its banner the fumbling local groups in the name of revolutionary Social Democracy.

The broad outlines of Lenin's "draft plan" for *Iskra* had been settled in correspondence with the other members of the "triple alliance," Martov and Potresov, in the final months of their exile in early 1900. Anticipating his need for reliable subordinates, Lenin had carefully tested and prepared promising underground workers in and around his village of exile, Shushenskoe. This had been his chief purpose in summoning seventeen of his most trusted comrades to sign a "Protest" against Kuskova's "economist" *Credo.* Nearly half of the seventeen eventually served as *Iskra* agents (among them G. M. Krzhizhanovskii, M. A. Silvin, F. V. Lengnik, P. N. Lepeshinskii, N. N. Panin) and others rendered important services to the cause.[18] After their return from exile, the triumvirs made it a point to seek new recruits in provincial localities where there were numerous former exiles and "undependable" elements banned from the capitals. A decade of unremitting arrests had served to give successive generations of *praktiki* their baptism of fire, their "university" training (in prison), and the opportunity to share their experiences with fellow exiles. Having gone through a complete cycle in their revolutionary career, they were eager for some new step and were intrigued by the prospect of participating in an ambitious new venture. Lepeshinskii, a political exile in Pskov, declared that Lenin's visit there in the spring of 1900 succeeded in "performing a total revolution in the minds of the peacefully situated radical intelligentsia." He names A. M. Stopani and P. A. Krasikov as two important converts.[19] An exceptionally fruitful mission was the year Martov spent in Poltava, which he had chosen for his quarantine period of police supervision (he had received favorable reports from his brother Sergei). In spite of police prohibition, he traveled freely to points throughout the South to agitate for *Iskra,* amassing countless promises of support and lining up *Iskra* agents (L. N. and I. I. Radchenko, his own brother Sergei, K. I. Zakharova, and the worker Nogin).[20]

Thus, before going abroad, Lenin and Martov succeeded in building up a considerable reservoir of revolutionary activists sharply distinct from the typical Social Democratic *praktiki* of the past. Supposedly liberated from "local patriotism" and "econo-

---

[18] See M. A. Silvin, *Lenin v period zarozhdeniia partii,* pp. 168 ff., and P. N. Lepeshinskii, *Na povorote (ot kontsa 80-kh godov k 1905 g.)* (Leningrad, 1925), chap. 5.

[19] *Ibid.,* p. 104.

[20] Many memoirists of this period from the South mention Martov's visits. See, for example, Ts. Zelikson-Bobrovskaia, *Zapiski riadovogo podpol'shchika* (Moscow, 1922), pp. 25–26; L. I. Goldman, *Organizatsiia i tipografiia "Iskry" v Rossii* (Moscow, 1928), p. 10; and memoir fragments of Polonskii, Ginzburg, and others in *Istoriia ekaterinoslavskoi.*

mist" leanings, they were prepared to accept assignments and fight *Iskra's* battles in every corner of Russia. If they entered local committees, it was as representatives of *Iskra* with the intention of winning them over to the latter's cause. Unlike the underground workers of the previous generation, who lived legally and continued to exercise a profession or to attend the university, *Iskra* men lived on false passports, subsisted on "party" funds, and changed quarters frequently. The periphery of liberal and radical well-wishers supplied them with financial contributions, postal addresses, meeting and sleeping quarters, and numerous other minor necessities. Certain agents specialized in procuring false passports, others in raising funds, organizing border transit, or traveling back and forth for communications. Most of them were obliged to endure extreme hardships such as perpetually empty stomachs, nights spent on the street or in railroad station toilets, and long periods without a change of clothes or a bath. When Lenin outlined his conception of "revolutionaries by profession" in *Chto delat'?*, he was consciously tracing *Iskra's* lineage to the epic figures of the 1870's, those who in Bakunin's words had "broken every tie with the civil order" and were "doomed men . . . without personal interests or feelings, without even names of their own."[21]

It also became evident before their departure from Russia that Lenin and his group already enjoyed a reputation among wide circles of both the party and non-party public, who looked to them for leadership in the shaping political struggle. Not only did the ex-Marxist "liberals" Struve and Tugan-Baranovskii offer to provide money and materials for their enterprise, but the regular Social Democratic organizations (supposedly dominated by Economists) were anxious to collaborate. When the Ekaterinoslav Committee, through Lalaiants, invited the *troika* to take over the new party organ, Lenin politely refused, claiming that in view of the prevailing wavering and opportunism it was necessary to prepare the party public ideologically before undertaking so serious a step.[22]

---

[21] "Katekhizis revoliutsionera," *Bor'ba Klassov*, No. 1–2, 1924, p. 268. From the *Catechism of a Revolutionary* written jointly by Bakunin and Nechaev.

[22] See *supra*, n. 13. For Martov's account see "Iz neopublikovannykh vospominanii," *Leninskii Sbornik* (33 vols.; Moscow, 1924–40), IV, 49 ff. Martov suspected Machiavellian designs on the part of the "Economists" to split the "Orthodox" camp and thus compromise the new literary group.

Once abroad, the *Iskra* collegium continued to be approached by other groups seeking cooperation. One unknown correspondent, acting as an intermediary between *Rabochee Delo* and *Iskra*, advised Lenin that "the eyes of the *Soiuz* [i.e., *Rabochee Delo*] are on you" and that if *Iskra* would enter into "official relations" with the latter, it could help immeasurably in healing the rift with the Liberation of Labor Group.[23] Even more surprising was Takhtarev's offer to the new group of the editorship of *Rabochaia Mysl'*. To the latter Lenin insisted on a preliminary acknowledgment of an about-face in views and defended his stand in reply to Iakubova's objections:

> You say "fight us, if you are not ashamed." It is not at all shameful to fight over basic questions. . . . A fight perhaps injures the feelings of a few individuals, but it clears the air, it defines relations directly and exactly—defines who are prepared in earnest to go a separate way, as true party comrades.[24]

Lenin obviously intended to abide by the words of *Iskra*'s recently published official "Declaration" that "in order to unite, it is necessary first to air our differences." This policy of calculated schism to enable the disciplined, fully "conscious" minority to gain direct control over the movement was to distinguish Lenin's intra-party politics throughout his career. It was a ruthlessly consistent, unequivocal affirmation of that minority trend in Russian Social Democracy which valued homogeneity of views and centrally directed action over mass participation and democratic initiative, the trend which was ultimately to emerge as Bolshevism.

In spite of the unrivaled prestige and wide connections of the new literary group, the early months of *Iskra*'s existence were by no means smooth. First of all came the shock that the rumors concerning Plekhanov's dictatorial propensities were not unfounded. Tortuous diplomatic maneuverings and unpleasant scenes were required before the *troika* was able to achieve a certain freedom from his interference. Second, owing to the breakdown of negotiations, the promised aid from Struve and his liberal backers was not forthcoming, and *Iskra* was immediately placed in severe financial straits. Many of the addresses so carefully collected were

---

[23] Lenin, *Sochineniia*, XXVIII, 57–60.

[24] Letter of October 26, 1900, *ibid.*, pp. 64–65.

either illegible or outdated. Ciphered letters could not be read owing to illegibility or lack of the proper key. (They were usually written with milk or lemon juice between the lines of a harmless legal journal.) Key agents failed to correspond for months at a time, and for unknown reasons did not carry out assignments. Finally, in spite of an enormous expenditure of effort (via Persia, Egypt, Marseilles, Stockholm, Rumania) the problem of transporting *Iskra* literature into Russia stubbornly defied solution. (The use of double-bottomed suitcases proved very inadequate and unreliable.) Huge stores of *Iskra* gathered mildew at various points en route, while scattered numbers circulated irregularly from hand to hand. In spite of such obstacles, *Iskra* enjoyed relative success from the very start. Even though Russia was not saturated with *Iskra* literature, as Lenin had envisaged, that which did get through circulated widely, and swayed the minds of students, *praktiki,* and even workers. Appearing regularly (every two weeks) and reporting on a whole range of issues (instead of merely recounting strikes), *Iskra* breathed a highly professional style and militant tone which corresponded to the mood of its readers. Other illegal organs, except for *Iuzhnyi Rabochii,* paled by comparison.

Other board members might be gratified that they had produced a Social Democratic organ worthy of its high calling, but not so Lenin. Ideological ascendancy in his view had to be transposed into firm organizational control, or it lost its purpose. Nothing should be left to accident or outside initiative. The technical apparatus of *Iskra* (for gathering information and funds, for corresponding with the editorial staff, for transporting and distributing the completed issues) was to be the transmission belt for directing Social Democratic activity and the framework upon which to build the future party. Consequently, it should be a model of flexibility, coordination, and efficient operation. To Lenin the cause of revolution was no matter of petty production, but rather a complicated, large-scale enterprise requiring specialization of function, strict lines of authority, and unceasing control over constituent operations. Why should each locality at great risk and expense of energy put out an amateurish publication twice or three times a year, when by cooperating in an all-Russian effort it could enjoy a technically perfect, professionally written, biweekly newspaper covering events from every corner of Russia? Why should local committees be recruited indiscriminately from green students and lame-duck radical intelligentsia who devote to the revolution only a "free hour or evening," when a small group of carefully selected "professional revolutionaries" would be more mobile, more skilled in the art of conspiracy, less vulnerable to arrest, and less inhibited by "local patriotism" from placing party tasks first? The panacea for the besetting ills of the movement was to be a tight organization of exceptionally talented conspirators, agents of a central group which would coordinate their activities, effect a rational distribution of resources, and carry on party work on a grand scale. In Lenin's eyes the besetting sin of the movement, "Economism," was rooted in the prevalence of a provincial outlook, amateurish techniques, absorption in local needs and demands, in his terminology *kustarnichestvo* (*kustar* = handicraft worker).[25]

Measured by these standards the first generation of *Iskra* agents by no means fulfilled his expectations. The first emissaries sent by *Iskra* from abroad, the former leaders of *Rabochee Znamia*, V. P. Nogin and S. V. Andropov, were equipped with specific instructions to settle respectively in St. Petersburg and Odessa, where they were to recruit supporters and build the technical apparatus for supplying and distributing *Iskra*. Instead, they contacted their former comrade from *Rabochee Znamia*, Sergei Tsederbaum, who had been assigned the border watch in Vilna, and worked out plans for a regional organization centered in St. Petersburg with its own popular organ for workers on the model of *Iuzhnyi Rabochii*. Such a lapse from his most promising converts vexed Lenin immeasurably. He wrote them:

> What an absurdity! After a full year of agonized effort, we succeed in barely beginning to muster a staff of leaders and organizers in Russia for this gigantic and most essential task, . . . suddenly to scatter our efforts again and return to the old *kustarnichestvo!* A more suicidal tactic for *Iskra* I can't imagine![26]

---

[25] The best single expression of the above thoughts in Lenin's writings is his article "S chego nachat'?" in the fourth issue of *Iskra* (*Sochineniia*, IV, 110–12). Since it is readily available, even in English, quotations are omitted here. See *supra*, note 15, p. 161.

[26] Letter of July, 1901, *ibid.*, XXVIII, 121. For Ezhov's version, see K. I. Zakharova-Tsederbaum and S. O. Tsederbaum, *Iz epokhi "Iskry" (1900–1905)* (Moscow, 1926), p. 63 ff.

He demanded that they give up their plans and set about their assigned tasks immediately or return to Munich headquarters for further consultation. Ezhov argued weakly that a regional paper written for average workers instead of a party elite would help bring them over to *Iskra*'s cause. Lenin, however, regarded any such thoughts as an unforgivable betrayal of their commitment to *Iskra* and the nation-wide tasks of the movement.

The most effective work for *Iskra* in the early period was accomplished by an energetic group of supporters in the South contacted by Martov and Lenin during their stay in Russia.[27] The pride of the "Southerners" was the perfectly operating secret press in Kishinev. The initiator of this enterprise, L. I. Goldman, had impressed upon Lenin that it would be much easier to reprint *Iskra* in Russia than to run the risk of smuggling large quantities across the border. Lenin reluctantly assented, but insisted that the editorship remain abroad to guarantee the safety and continuity of leadership. According to Goldman, Lenin feared that his own organization might suddenly "emancipate" itself from the editors and in the name of *Iskra* propagate "some sort of heresy or its own flights of fancy."[28]

Lenin's fears were soon substantiated. When the Kiev Committee was hit particularly hard by arrests and temporarily lost its secret press, Goldman extended it a courtesy which appeared to him natural among comrades in the underground—he printed the current issue of its local organ *Vpered*. Lenin professed his disbelief that "people collecting hundreds and thousands of rubles in *Iskra*'s name for an *Iskra* printing press, would secretly desert us for another undertaking at a critical moment," and demanded an immediate conference to "straighten out this unbelievable perversity."[29] Shortly thereafter another *Iskra* press in the Caucasus printed no less than three numbers of *Iuzhnyi Rabochii* provoking

---

[27] The best single account of the activities of this group is that of Goldman, *Organizatsiia i tipografiia "Iskry"* (see n. 20). For the Caucasus group loosely associated with them see A. Enukhidze, "Istoriia organizatsii i raboty nelegal'nykh tipografii R.S.–D.R.P. na Kavkaze," *Proletarskaia Revoliutsiia*, No. 14 (March, 1923), pp. 108–67.

[28] Goldman, p. 22.

[29] Letter of December 18, 1901, *Sochineniia*, XXXVIII, 129.

Lenin's wrath again.[30] To Lenin, all regional and local organs were dangerous competitors and obstacles to Iskra's plans to co-ordinate the activities of all Social Democrats.

Lenin's meticulous demand for loyalty served to intensify already simmering tensions between the Munich center and the Russian praktiki. Lenin had proposed that the Southerners constitute themselves as a Russia-wide organization, devoted exclusively to the interests, "not of this or that region, but of the party as a whole." Members were to divide among themselves the duties of collecting money, arranging correspondence to Iskra, transportation, and so forth.[31]

The plan contained one ambiguity which could not but lead to misunderstandings. Although ostensibly the primary responsibility in organizational matters was to rest on the Russian organization, the individual agent was obliged to keep in direct touch with the editors and send regular reports of his activities, a practice which could easily be exploited to circumvent the Russian organization.

Goldman, obviously hoping to retain control of affairs by his comrades, invited the Iskra editors to send an emissary to attend a secret conference of Iskra-praktiki in Kiev. Over the pleas of Lenin's "papal nuncio" (a third rank agent, I. G. Smidovich), the conference appointed itself the "central core for all technical matters inside Russia" and resolved that, while acknowledging the leadership of Iskra and its editors in questions of ideology and tactics, they found "impossible and harmful" its intention to direct everything from abroad. Goldman later commented that this was a protest against the "increasing tendency to dispatch comrades with special instructions, commissions, and organizational tasks, which conflicted with the activities of Iskra praktiki inside Russia."[32]

---

[30] This dispute was detailed in Iskra's report to the Second Congress of 1903 (see Vtoroi S'ezd, p. 567). Lenin overlooked the fact that in equipping both printing presses Iskra benefitted from the generosity of non-Iskra organizations. Iskra had even refused to take over the debts left by the Caucasus group that surrendered to Iskra its secret press. See Goldman, p. 38.

[31] See the letter to Goldman and Ezhov-Tsederbaum of August, 1901, Leninskii Sbornik, VIII, 196. See also the letter to Krokhmal a few months later (ibid., pp. 203–4), from which it is clear that the Southerners protested over interference by the editors. Lenin replied that although "details" were left to the Russian organization, the editors insisted on the right to "over-all leadership," in keeping with their special mission.

[32] Goldman, pp. 37–38.

Thus by the end of 1901 the reins of authority threatened to slip from Lenin's hands, and he had obviously failed to infuse *Iskra*'s representatives with the spirit of his organizational plans. The task of forming dependable cadres of *Iskra* subordinates through whom to acquire control over the movement was yet to be realized.

Lenin was soon able to make a fresh start. In mid-January, 1902, he received word from Samara that Silvin and Krzhizhanovskii, comrades from St. Petersburg days and fellow signatories of the Siberian "Protest," had brought together a band of devoted *Iskra* supporters from the local colony of "politicals." Although this group had not hitherto been active in *Iskra* affairs, Lenin decided to make it a new nation-wide center to circumvent the less tractable Southerners. Its chief declared aim other than executing commissions for *Iskra* was to penetrate local committees and win them over, or, failing that, to form rival pro-*Iskra* committees. The group explicitly condemned local and regional underground papers and summoned all sympathizing *praktiki* to concentrate their efforts exclusively on *Iskra*. Several of their number were to be sent to strategic points, while Krzhizhanovskii was to head a permanent "bureau" for communications in Samara (through the local zemstvo board by whom he was employed). Silvin was instructed by Lenin to get in touch with I. I. Radchenko (a loyal *Iskra*ite who had defected from the Southerners) by whom he would be fully informed on affairs in other centers and on all *Iskra* contacts. Radchenko and Silvin were then to serve as roving agents and troubleshooters enjoying the special confidence of the editors.[33]

To instruct this new generation of *Iskra praktiki* and immunize them against the apostasy of their predecessors, Lenin in early 1902 brought out his definitive pronouncement on all theoretical and practical questions, the booklet *Chto delat'?* He devoted sixty pages of this new work to hammering away at the evils of *kustarnichestvo* and expounding his views on organizational centralism. Its effect on the partisans of *Iskra* was overwhelming. Fedor Dan, who smuggled the first copies into Russia when he attended the Belostok Conference in March, affirmed that the work provided

---

[33] See Silvin, pp. 241–42; *Leninskii Sbornik*, VIII, 223; and *Vtoroi S'ezd*, p. 578.

him with the arguments and slogans with which he confounded his "economist" opponents in the conference debates.[34] Krzhizhanovskii wrote Lenin immediately that it was "brilliantly written and in a truly excellent tone."[35] Lepeshinskii in Pskov flatly declared that "*Iskra* prevailed in St. Petersburg, in Moscow, and in other centers of the revolutionary movement only because the *Iskra* agitators had in their hands *Chto delat'?*"[36] The new *Iskra* *praktiki* quickly acquired the vocabulary, the intransigent tone, and the habit of thought of their mentor; from partisans of *Iskra* they came to be disciples of Lenin. Indeed, many disciples so fully assimilated the spirit of *Chto delat'?* that they outdid their master in zeal for the cause, contempt for opponents, and fondness for manipulations. Lenin could now hope to be spared the inconvenient errors of the earlier supporters of *Iskra*.

The ticklish problem of bringing the Southern group to heel was resolved by arrests which made a clean sweep of *Iskra* agents in the South. (Unfortunately these arrests also eliminated the two secret presses and the existing transport routes.) The Northern group of Nogin and Ezhov had already been arrested the previous fall. When Silvin and Radchenko met in Pskov at the end of February, they found themselves completely stripped of dependable *Iskra* representatives in key spots. The next few months were spent mainly in picking up and distributing the stores of literature that had been left behind by their predecessors and in sounding out their sparse contacts for new sources of support. Although they were constantly on the move and expended great efforts, they could do little more than keep a few lines of communication open and hope for a better turn of events. Soon Silvin himself was arrested.

Thus the new *Iskra* center was far from achieving its purpose. Silvin had been the chief driving force, but his brief career simply

---

[34] See "K istorii belostokskoi konferentsii," *Proletarskaia Revoliutsiia*, No. 101, pp. 139–40. See also *supra*, p. 224.

[35] Letter of May 25, 1902, "Iz perepiski 'Iskry' s mestnymi organizatsiami," *Proletarskaia Revoliutsiia*, No. 77–78 (June-July, 1928), p. 149.

[36] Lepeshinskii, pp. 123–24. See also Silvin, p. 257, and Levitskii, II, 122. Not all *praktiki* were entranced by *Chto delat'?*; Mark Khinoi recalls a debate over *Chto delat'?* among his fellow prisoners in the autumn of 1903. Viktor Vannovskii (delegate to the First Congress) subjected it to a thoroughgoing critique. See *U istokov menshevizma* (Inter-University Project, 1960), pp. 19–25.

revealed the inherent shortcomings of Lenin's hypercentralism. By insisting on regular communications and the concentration of all responsibility in a few hands, Lenin vastly simplified the task of the police: the interception of a few messages, a short period of observation and pursuit, and nearly the entire *Iskra* organization fell into their hands.[37]

Lenin, never one to become unnerved by an adverse tide of events, began to look elsewhere for the chosen instrument of his will. Dan, as special emissary of *Iskra* at the Belostok Conference in March, had successfully frustrated the attempt of *Rabochee Delo* to outflank *Iskra* in reviving the party and carried out his instructions to secure the appointment of an "organizing committee" for a party congress five months hence. The eclipse of nearly the entire Organizing Committee including Dan through the recent arrests would seem to have put an end to this project. However, when the Bund representative unexpectedly arrived abroad and inquired whether *Iskra* had any news of survivors of the conference, Lenin perceived that his opportunity had arrived. Lenin blandly informed the Bundist that successors had been appointed by the other members of the Organizing Committee before their arrest, and instructed him to contact Radchenko in Russia. To Radchenko he wrote:

> Act as if the whole affair were fully in your hands, and let the Bund for now limit itself to its own bailiwick. . . . The make-up of the Organizing Committee must be as favorable as possible for us (perhaps you could say that the committee is already organized and that you would be happy to have the Bund take part). . . . In short, make yourself the master of this undertaking.[38]

Although it met with delays and reverses, this was the strategy which Lenin doggedly pursued in the coming months and in the end brought to a successful conclusion. Henceforward, the Organ-

---

[37] See the correspondence of *Iskra* with the Samara bureau for March-May, 1902, in *Proletarskaia Revoliutsiia*, No. 77–78, pp. 14–50. For proof that intercepted correspondence was responsible for the mass arrests see O. A. Varentsova, "*Severnyi Rabochii Soiuz*" *i Severnyi Komitet R.S.–D.R.P.* (Ivanovo, 1948), pp. 50–51 and 121 ff.

[38] Letter of June 22, 1903, Lenin, *Sochineniia*, XXVIII, 140.

izing Committee (hereafter "O.C.") was in the hands of dependable *Iskra*ites.[39]

To shore up this still mythical Russia-based O.C., at least a few points of support in local committees were needed from which it could claim "mandates." Although there was wide-spread sympathy for *Iskra* in local organizations based on the militant spirit of its columns, rigid adherence to Lenin's organizational schemes was still largely confined to the small handful of *Iskra* agents. Up to this time *Iskra* could count on the loyalty only of Samara, whose authority as a local "committee" was doubtful, and of the Northern Union, which had irreproachable credentials, but had not yet proved its "firmness." He sent word to the Samara Bureau to "slip our people into as many committees as possible, and save yourself and our people as the apple of your eye until the Congress."[40] Concrete results were not long in coming. He received news from Radchenko of a successful "revolution" in the St. Petersburg Committee, which was now willing to declare openly its loyalty to *Iskra*. Word also came from *Iuzhnyi Rabochii* that the reputed "arch-intriguer" and partisan of *Rabochee Delo,* O. A. Ermanskii, had been conveniently removed by arrest and that the "firm" *Iskra*ites Levin and Rozanov had taken over. The victories were timely, since these were precisely organizations represented at the Belostok Conference, and their sponsorship would lend the required semblance of legitimacy to the operation. Samara reported that the "conquest" of Nizhni Novgorod was imminent and that prospects were bright for organizing a loyal committee in Moscow (for five years no lasting Social Democratic organization had been able to function there because of Zubatov's refined police techniques).

Thus encouraged, Lenin proceeded with the delicate task of forming a reliable O.C. under his firm control. He made a first abortive effort in August, 1902 by summoning to London repre-

<hr/>

[39] Until this time *Iskra* had deliberately dragged out negotiations with *Rabochee Delo* to arrange for a Second Congress; the Belostok Conference had instructed them to do this in case efforts inside Russia should be crippled by arrests. The *Iskra*ites were stalling to see if a pro-*Iskra* organizing committee inside Russia could be arranged. See letter of Martov to Akselrod, August 2, 1902, in *Pis'ma P. B. Aksel'roda i Iu. O. Martova,* ed. F. Dan, B. N. Nicolaevsky, and L. O. Tsederbaum-Dan (Berlin, 1924), pp. 69–71.

[40] Letter of May 23, 1902, *Sochineniia,* XXVIII, 138.

sentatives of three Social Democratic organizations who happened to be abroad (P. A. Krasikov representing the Russian organization of *Iskra,* V. A. Noskov from the Northern Workers' Union, and P. A. Krasnukh from St. Petersburg). Together they laid plans for *Iskra's* hegemony at the future Congress and constituted themselves the provisional O.C.[41] The plan suffered shipwreck when Noskov quarreled with Krasikov and resigned from the committee, and the St. Petersburg Committee held up on its public declaration of loyalty. Nevertheless, the over-all trend continued to favor *Iskra.* By October formal declarations of loyalty began to appear in the columns of *Iskra*—first, from the St. Petersburg and Moscow Committees, then from *Iuzhnyi Rabochii,* then from Kharkov. Lenin had given Radchenko specific instructions on the form in which these declarations were to appear, and for the most part these instructions were followed to the letter. They stipulated a specific renunciation of the errors of the past ("economism," *kustarnichestvo,* "ideological and organizational chaos"), an official acknowledgment of *Iskra* as the "leading organ of the party," the acceptance not only of *Iskra's* theoretical and tactical views but also of her *organizational* views as spelled out in *Chto delat'?*[42]

The *Iskra*ites in Russia soon took up the task of getting the O.C. into working order. A conference was summoned in Pskov in early November composed officially of representatives of St. Petersburg (Krasnukh), the Russian organization of *Iskra* (Radchenko), and *Iuzhnyi Rabochii* (Levin); Krasikov and Lepeshinskii attended unofficially. Lepeshinskii noted that the invited Bund delegate "somehow didn't appear," but "therefore, it was all the easier to make certain decisions and co-opt our own people [i.e., into the O.C.]." It was decided that negotiations with the Bund should

---

[41] See letters of August 12 and 16, *Leninskii Sbornik,* VIII, 271. For Lenin this was a victory over his fellow *Iskra* editors, who were trying to arrange their own conference of *Iskra praktiki* in Zurich. Noskov of the Northern Union was to be the key person, but Lenin lured him to London with a flattering letter (*Sochineniia,* XXXVIII, 98–101). This was a time of great tension within the editorial board of *Iskra,* precipitated by Lenin's critique of Plekhanov's "Program" and the removal of the editorial headquarters to London. Only Martov remained a supporter of Lenin.

[42] See letter to Radchenko of July 16, 1902, *ibid.,* 136–39, and *Iskra,* Nos. 26, 27, and 28 (October 15, November 1 and 15, 1902), pp. 7, 8, and 6, respectively.

bear a "scrupulously polite character" in order to "deprive the esteemed oppositionists of unnecessary excuses for obstruction."[43]

Iskra now enjoyed the firm tactical position Lenin had been seeking since the early summer. By maintaining correct posture in its formal actions, the O.C. enjoyed a more or less free hand to use its authority and resources to strengthen *Iskra*'s position at the forthcoming Congress. In March, 1903, Lenin advised the O.C. not to consult local committees on the agenda, inasmuch as the exclusive initiative of the O.C. in such matters had already been recognized, and unnecessary consultations could only lead to "dilatoriness and dissatisfaction."[44] Furthermore, the O.C. could heavily influence the composition of local committees or establish new ones by shifting firm *Iskra*ites to points where they were needed. The frequency of arrests made it quite simple for *Iskra*ites to enter committees wherever they chose, while they were advised repeatedly by Lenin to guard themselves against arrest at all costs until the Congress.

The continuity of the O.C. was guaranteed against fortuitous events by its inclusion of all the most active *Iskra* agents and the naming of others in reserve. Even the arrests of several key people (Lepeshinskii, Radchenko, and Krasnukh) soon after the Pskov Conference caused only temporary difficulties. By March a new "plenary session" was called in Orel to work out detailed preparations for the Congress. The delegates of *Iuzhnyi Rabochii*, Rozanov and Levin, were somewhat taken aback by the number of hard-core *Iskra*ites who turned up, although Rozanov conceded that they included "the best *praktiki* available."[45] In addition to Krasikov, Krzhizhanovskii and Stopani, who had been co-opted at Pskov, B. I. Gorev and V. M. Alexandrova had been deputized from *Iskra* headquarters in London to take responsibility for the two capitals and Kiev, respectively. (They arrived with detailed

[43] Lepeshinskii, p. 128.

[44] Letter of March 5–6, 1902, *Sochineniia*, XXVIII, 175. As early as December, 1902, Lenin had decided to force the issue with the Bund over the nationality question by having it placed on the agenda first. The strategy was to "give battle at once . . . on a basic question" in order to decide "whether to break on a serious question." (*Ibid.*, pp. 152–54.) The first open polemic against the Bund did not occur until the 33rd issue of *Iskra* (February 1, 1903).

[45] *Nasha Zaria*, No. 6, 1913, p. 38.

instructions.) Perhaps to quiet their suspicions, the Southerners were given responsibility for the vast territory of the Ukraine and the Caucasus. On the one policy question discussed, whether the regulations for the Congress worked out by the O.C. should first be submitted to local committees for approval, the Southerners were able to win their point because of the failure of one of the *Iskra* agents to follow Lenin's instructions.

Since the O.C. was under the unlimited control of hard core *Iskra*ites, it could now deputize "agents" wherever it wished, demand their admittance into local committees, and dictate pro-*Iskra* policies in the name of a "provisional party center" which traced its lineage to the Belostok Conference. Thus the O.C. had no difficulty in carrying on its program of "conquering" local committees. The loyalty declarations appearing on the pages of *Iskra* in the winter and spring told the story: in December, 1902, the Nizhni Novgorod Committee; in January, 1903, the Saratov Committee; in February, the Northern Workers' Union; in March, the Don Committee (Rostov), the Siberian Workers' Union, the Kazan and Ufa Committees; in April, the Tula, Odessa, and Irkutsk Committees; and in May, the Mine Workers' Union of South Russia and the Ekaterinoslav Committee. Although the majority of these mechanically repeated the formula of the earlier declarations—approval of the theoretical, tactical, and *organizational* views of *Iskra*, and the recognition of *Iskra* as the party (or directing) organ—a few (Saratov, *Iuzhnyi Rabochii,* the Northern Union, the Mine Workers' Union of South Russia) expressed reservations on the organizational question, albeit without specifying their nature. In all probability, they concerned the advisability of regional organizations and of popular publications for workers to supplement *Iskra,* the enthusiasm for which was extremely difficult to dampen even among *Iskra*'s warmest supporters.

In any event these minor qualifications scarcely tarnished the impression of a phenomenal swing into the *Iskra* camp. The growing revolutionary atmosphere in 1902—the revival of terrorism, the peasant uprisings, the general strike in Rostov—contributed to the further dissolution of local loyalties and persuaded many local *praktiki* to look beyond their own group for the signal to strike the "decisive blow" against tsarism. Correspondingly, *Rabochee Delo* lost out during these months because it ceased to supply practical

aid and the over-simplified slogans and dogmas so ardently desired. The demoralizing frequency of arrests especially rendered
local committees susceptible to the blandishments of the seemingly invulnerable *Iskra* conspirators, who entered and left the committees almost at will.

From this it must not be concluded, however, that the *Iskra* jug-
gernaut met no resistance. The highhanded tactics employed by
Iskra agents generated friction where even a little tact might have
won sympathy. *Iskra* was faced with a series of unexpected "counter-revolutions" which seriously threatened to upset her plans.
First came reports in December of 1902 that the decisions of the
St. Petersburg and Kiev Committees to support *Iskra* had been
reversed and that the oppositionists had won over the workers.
Before long it became apparent that disaffection was rife in nearly
all the major committees (Ekaterinoslav, Odessa, Rostov). Lenin
was thoroughly dismayed, as he had been convinced by his agents'
reports (and by his own preconceptions) that the workers strongly favored *Iskra*. He was even more vexed by the fact that documents on these schisms were being published in the rival Social
Democratic publications abroad while his local agents seemed to
be oblivious to these developments and conveyed misleading information. To the Samara bureau Krupskaia reported:

> We are hurrying with the Congress because now the situation has
> radically changed; the St. Petersburg schism served as a signal for
> a series of scandals. Everywhere the *rabochedeltsy* are raising their
> heads and stirring up the workers against the intelligentsia. They
> send in special representatives and try to make it appear as if the
> workers are rebelling against the leadership of *Iskra* in bringing
> about unity.[46]

It is typical of the mentality of the conspirator to attribute to
enemy intrigue (in this case quite absent) unpleasant developments brought about by intrigues of his own. The actual cause of
the revolts, however, is not very far to seek. *Iskra* agents who in-
filtrated local committees were under instructions to effect the
reorganization of local work to conform to the model outlined in

---

[46] Letter of December 28, 1902, *Leninskii Sbornik*, VIII, 308. For Lenin's strictures against the unhappy St. Petersburg *Iskra*ites, see letters to Stasova of December
27, 1902, and January 15, 16, and 28, 1903. *Sochineniia*, XXVIII, 157-58, 161-62,
165-66, and 171-72.

Lenin's mimeographed pamphlet *Letter to a Comrade* (late 1902), which he distributed in small numbers for their guidance.[47] Lenin was ostensibly criticizing a draft statute for local organizations sent to him by a certain "comrade Erema," who sought to ease some of the current friction with the workers by instituting "discussion" circles and factory district meetings. At these, the more experienced workers could at least vent their grievances and seek redress from the Committee, without the inconvenience of a second "workers'" organization. Lenin dismissed the scheme as highly unconspiratorial and inexpedient. Provocateurs could easily gain access to such circles, spot the committee representatives and obtain other information on party affairs. As in 1897, he favored training workers for revolutionary work and co-opting the more talented ones into the committees, but anything that smacked of consulting subordinate worker groups or of appealing committee decisions he rejected outright. District and factory representatives were to be chosen by the Committee and were to discuss only how they could best carry out the latter's instructions. They should regard themselves as agents of the party and as being bound by its discipline. Their chief current functions were to distribute political proclamations and to inform factory cells of the time and place of demonstrations. This mechanism, Lenin felt, should be capable of "mobilizing the whole working population of St. Petersburg in one night." In other words Lenin simply gave his unqualified support to the structure which had evolved in the era of politics and made any compromise with worker aspirations tantamount to heresy.

Although the majority of the local *praktiki* probably preferred Lenin's mode of operation for the reasons discussed earlier, they were far more sensitive than the *Iskra* conspirators to the rumblings of worker discontent and had often entered into various degrees of compromise to mollify it. Also, in a few committees, such as St. Petersburg and Kiev, there were strong factions which consciously rejected *Iskra* centralism and still adhered to the worker-oriented philosophy.

In all likelihood, the well documented situation in Ekaterinoslav was representative of most of the counter-revolutions of the win-

---

[47] See *Sochineniia*, V, 179–92 for the text.

ter of 1902–1903.[48] The Ekaterinoslav Committee including its worker contingent was avidly pro-*Iskra* in spirit even though it continued to operate on the "elective" principle. Because of arrests, the Committee welcomed the arrival of comrade "Valentin" (Martov's younger brother Levitskii), deputized to them by the O.C. However, when Levitskii demanded in the name of the O.C. the immediate abolition of the elective principle and the reinstatement of the former system (whereby the Committee was to consist of four or five hard-core self-perpetuating "professional revolutionaries" who were to appoint the membership of a separate Workers' Committee), the reaction of the lower instances, the district worker groups, was immediate and violent: they refused to accept any further literature from the official Committee for distribution and demanded that the inspirer of these innovations defend them before a joint meeting of all the district groups.

About one hundred workers showed up at a meeting place out on the steppe to hear the unknown comrade "Komar" present his case. The leader of the disaffected workers, David Braginskii, demanded that "Komar" first identify himself and state what group he represented. "Komar" did not dare to comply (there were certainly provocateurs in such a large gathering), and he left, followed by several intelligentsia members of the Committee. The workers elected Braginskii their chairman and constituted a new "Committee," in essence, reasserting their sovereign rights as they had done the previous year. The O.C. soon dispatched new agents to shore up their rump "Committee" and circulated a special leaflet declaring their Committee to be the official one by virtue of the O.C.'s authority as a "provisional" all-party organization. The workers countered with another leaflet (they had captured the former Committee's press and the official seal) exposing the irresponsible group which had usurped the name of the Ekaterinoslav Committee and had been elected by no one.[49] The O.C.'s next agent "Zemliachka" (R. S. Zalkind) had been followed by the police, and although she escaped herself, she "infected" the other *Iskra* supporters, who were arrested shortly thereafter. Another

---

[48] There are accounts in *Istoriia ekaterinoslavskoi* by Polonskii, Beliavskii, and Nogin in addition to police reports and intercepted correspondence. In addition there is the lengthy account in Levitskii, II, chap. 5.

[49] For the text of the leaflets, see *Istoriia ekaterinoslavskoi*, pp. 393–94.

O.C. member, Aleksandrova, followed her in order to patch things up. She sent word back to the O.C. that "the forces of the rebels are many times greater than those of the Orthodox, who sit without a penny, without technical apparatus, without ties [to the workers]."[50] Nevertheless, two members of the rump Committee, Vilenskii and Makhlin, represented Ekaterinoslav at the Second Congress, whereas the workers' "Ekaterinoslav Committee" was not consulted at all. A new agent, Viktor Nogin (who had fled exile), apparently possessed a little more tact than his predecessors and managed to negotiate a compromise with the dissident Committee on the very eve of the summer general strike. The workers surrendered their rigid insistence on the elective principle and cut up their Committee seal in the presence of their rivals. This solemn act was consummated in the midst of the strike, during which the former enemies cooperated in perfect harmony. It was a far better outcome than the *Iskra*ites deserved, but it indicated that the workers did not actually seek a radical break with the party, but were fighting for their legitimate status within it. Mass arrests and Nogin's departure, however, soon erased the benefits of the reconciliation; until 1905 there was no further trace of an active workers' group in Ekaterinoslav.

The other counter-revolutions also proved to lack durability. By the time of the Second Congress, the *Iskra* organization had restored order in every locality except Voronezh (which was not represented at the Second Congress). In cases where the worker-oriented groups proved intractable, as in Odessa, Ekaterinoslav, and St. Petersburg, the Organizing Committee simply granted recognition to the *Iskra*-dominated group and ignored their opponents. In other cases, as in Rostov, arrests conveniently removed the dissidents. B. I. Gorev, dispatched by Lenin to the O.C. with specific instructions to secure the election of pro-*Iskra* delegates, was able with impunity to nominate the delegates from Moscow (one of whom, N. E. Bauman, had long since escaped prison and fled abroad). For St. Petersburg he chose himself and a worker, A. Shotman, who was known for his boundless devotion to the

---

[50] *Istoriia ekaterinoslavskoi,* p. 392. Four letters from "Zemliachka" and one from Aleksandrova to the O.C. are reprinted in this collection. They were preserved, like most correspondence of this period, because they were intercepted by the police.

author of *Chto delat'?*, but had previously been little involved in committee work.[51]

Rozanov, though a "soft" *Iskra*ite and a critic of the ruthless tactics of the O.C., confessed that even in the South only the Tiflis Committee consulted the workers on the choice of a delegate. He admitted his own complicity in by-passing the Odessa worker-oriented group *Rabochaia Volia* and requesting delegates only from the *Iskra*-dominated Committee. He limply explained that "it just did not seem possible with the conspirative practices of that time to democratize things."[52] The success of *Iskra*'s tactics in securing hand-picked, loyal delegates to the Second Congress was overwhelming.

In notes made just before the Second Congress assembled, Lenin calculated the probable balance of forces: the *Iskra*ites, whom he significantly divided into "firm" and "soft" categories, numbered twenty-six and thirteen, respectively; the "Economists" —only eight, of whom five represented the Bund and two the now-defunct Union of Russian Social Democrats Abroad.[53] Of local organizations only the vote of the dissident St. Petersburg Committee represented the voice of the opposition by virtue of a last minute decision of the Congress' special credentials committee (Gorev had been arrested at the border anyway). Lenin was now able to turn his attention toward his next major struggle—with the infirm elements in the *Iskra* camp itself.

The victory of *Iskra,* or rather of Lenin, had indeed been complete, but it was a victory bought at a price. At the very time when the *Iskra* organization was concentrating on taking over local committees, a golden opportunity was slipping by for Social Democracy to recover its leadership of both the workers' movement and the nation-wide opposition to the autocracy. In mid-1902, as pointed out above, the majority of Social Democratic Committees were in a state of demoralization due to the combined effects of inordinate arrests, the manifest failure of "political" demonstrations, and the signs of renewed vigor on the part of rival

---

[51] See Gorev, p. 62 ff. Gorev notes that it was the intention of the supporters of Lenin, should their efforts fail to secure a majority of *Iskra*ites at the Second Congress, to boycott it and call their own congress of pro-*Iskra* organizations.

[52] *Nasha Zaria,* No. 6, 1913, p. 38.

[53] See *Vtoroi S'ezd,* pp. 458–59.

revolutionary groupings. The former slogans of seizing the leadership and placing the workers at the forefront of the nation-wide struggle for political liberty now took on a very hollow sound. Appearing equally futile were the much touted tactics of mass demonstrations and general strikes which were to climax in a coordinated armed uprising directed by the Social Democratic party.

At this low ebb of fortune (November, 1902) there erupted in Rostov a general strike of phenomenal proportions. This was no mere demonstration which the authorities could easily dispatch by force. The entire normal life of a sizable provincial city came to a standstill, and for days on end political orators were able to harangue large crowds while the Cossacks and police helplessly looked on. Not only were the factories and workshops effectively closed down (10,000 strikers), but also the stores, schools, cabbies, delivery boys, doormen, and even government offices stood idle. The strike had originated in the railroad workshops over minor economic issues, but the railwaymen decided to broaden their demands to a nine-hour day, the abolition of fines, and schools for their children, in support of which they called for sympathy strikes. The Social Democratic Committee had been caught napping, but in short order it was turning out reams of leaflets and supplying orators for the street crowds, which registered their enthusiasm for "political" speeches. The railroad workers had originally wished to keep the intelligentsia and "politics" out of the affair, but they were soon compelled by the logic of their actions (a general strike, demands presupposing a political solution) and the swelling of outside support to surrender to the prevailing mood.[54] The techniques which the Social Democrats had so carefully fashioned for the era of politics proved to be relevant after all.

The Rostov events made an enormous impression on both the Social Democrats and their rivals. The underground press lost no opportunity to broadcast detailed accounts much as they had done with the textile strike of 1896. To be sure the O.C. issued a special leaflet calling upon other centers to organize similar affairs

---

[54] A short account of the Rostov strike may be found in *Obshchestvennoe dvizhenie v Rossii*, I, 210–11. It was described in many underground publications of the time in hopes of inspiring imitation. The best of these accounts appeared in *Krasnoe Znamia*, Nos. 2 and 3 (December, 1902 and January, 1903).

and Lenin penned for *Iskra* readers a carefully reasoned article, underscoring the revolutionary significance of the strike.[55] Nevertheless, as there was no immediate sequel elsewhere and further heavy arrests ensued, the *Iskra* organization soon devoted its full attention to preparations for the Congress and to squelching worker revolts.

Ironically, at precisely the time when the cream of *Iskra's* "professional revolutionaries" were wending their way via secret routes to Brussels for the Second Congress, a new series of general strikes rocked the industrial Southland, this time including the Caucasus. Early in June, 30,000 to 40,000 oil workers and railwaymen struck in Baku for nearly two weeks, halting in the process all major public services (trams, electricity, newspapers, telegraph and telephones). Their example was followed in rapid succession by Tiflis, Batum, Odessa, Kiev, Ekaterinoslav, and Nikolaev. Crowds numbering tens of thousands assembled in the streets to hear political orators, while frequent "flying speeches" kept the workers in the factory districts in a constant state of agitation. Infantry units fired into crowds and Cossacks charged using the flat of their swords, leaving dead and severely wounded. There was no sequel to these strikes the following year (the war with Japan was a temporary distraction), but their unprecedented scope augured the approach of a day of reckoning.[56]

The Social Democrats played a somewhat ambiguous and varied role in these events. The renewed demonstrations of the strength of the proletariat after several years of economic depression should have bolstered their self-esteem vis-à-vis other revolutionary factions. However, their consciences were disturbed by the fact that again they had been overtaken by events, and that they had only very imperfectly been able to keep in step with the capricious moods of the workers. Moreover, their orators had been obliged to share the streets with Social Revolutionaries, anarchists, Zionists,

---

[55] See *Sochineniia*, V, pp. 206–10.

[56] See *Obshchestvennoe dvizhenie v Rossii*, I, 213–14; V. Pravdin (N. Valentinov), *Revoliutsionnye dni v Kieve* (Geneva, 1903); the memoirs of Polonskii and Nogin and a contemporary anonymous account "Ekaterinoslavskii Komitet ob avgustovskykh sobytiiakh 1903 goda," in *Istoriia ekaterinoslavskoi*; and "K stachechnomu dvizheniiu na iuge Rossii v 1903 godu," *Arkhiv Istorii Truda*, No. 6–7 (1923), pp. 183–87.

assorted radicals and free lancers. In Ekaterinoslav, the Social Democrats eventually caught up with the movement and became its acknowledged leaders. In Kiev, they were successful in setting it in motion, but exercised little control or influence once it was under way; in Odessa, the avalanche was actually set loose by the Zubatov unions and was soon beyond the control of any of the organized groups (Social Democrats, the Bund, the S.R.'s). The strikers in Odessa were for the most part illiterate dockers, stokers and tram operators who had previously never been exposed directly to Social Democratic agitation and had little interest in "politics." In Nikolaev, where the local committee carefully mapped out a campaign on the model of the others, it was cut short by the energetic measures of the local military commander.[57]

The ambiguous behavior of the Social Democrats was conditioned by the fact that the new dispensation of "politics" had spoiled their taste for the workers' economic concerns; intimidated by *Iskra*'s polemics they wished above all to avoid any taint of the heresy of "Economism." The Kiev Committee, reviewing developments in Odessa, very nearly decided against declaring a strike for fear that it could not be guided into political channels (in which case it was undesirable). In the end, they approved the strike, rationalizing that even an "economic" strike on such a scale was a "political" event. Their fears proved to be ungrounded, as the response to both economic and political slogans was enormous. However, there was one unwelcome consequence of the revival of "economics": as strike fever began to infect the bakers, the seamstresses, and the tram operators, contributions from "society" rapidly dried up. Persons of social standing welcomed the strike insofar as it was directed against the autocracy, but they soon sensed a threat to themselves in the unfolding "anarchy" and the workers' inordinate economic demands. The very success of the general strikes threatened to drive a wedge between Social Democracy and other oppositional groups whose support was essential for tipping the scales against absolutism. This unwelcome sequence, reflecting a basic inconsistency in the revolutionary

---

[57] An excellent source pinpointing the differing characteristics of each strike is the report of the Director of the Department of Police, Lopukhin. See "Zapiska Direktora departamenta politsii Lopukhina o stachkakh v iuge 1903 g.," *Krasnaia Letopis'*, No. 4 (April, 1922), pp. 382–95.

formula of the Social Democrats, was to be repeated with tragic consequences in the last few months of 1905.

In spite of the monumental scale of these events, they marked the end rather than the beginning of Social Democratic influence within the revolutionary movement. The severe punitive measures taken by tsarist authorities in the wake of the strikes cut heavily into the worker and intelligentsia cadres of local organizations. Most experienced committeemen, if they survived arrests, resorted to the by then standard practice of "departing" to new localities where they were unknown to police (they were usually co-opted without question, if they came with recommendations by trusted comrades). Before local organizations had the opportunity to re-form, the heralds of the respective factions returned from the Second Congress and devoted themselves to "capturing" this or that committee for the Bolshevik or Menshevik viewpoint. The unique opportunity afforded by the summer strikes passed by, as the blight of intra-party strife descended. Social Democracy was now divorced from the workers' movement, which drifted along its own undiscerned paths until Bloody Sunday in 1905.

With the fiasco of the Second Congress, the Russian Social Democratic movement had come full circle. Conceived in a blush of optimism over the revolutionary potentialities of the industrial proletariat, it had inspired the radical intellectuals of the 1890's to seek out the workers and immerse themselves in the working class milieu. The determination to find a means to engage the masses, rather than a mere handful of indoctrinated workers, in revolutionary action had led to the discovery of the technique of strike agitation, which by 1901 had indeed brought into being a mass workers' movement subject to a Social Democratic influence.

There was, however, an ambiguity in the motivation of intellectuals attracted to the movement which was obscured by the temporary ascendancy of the "economic" struggle over the "political." On the one hand, they were heartened by the emergence of a vigorous worker leadership from the ranks which proved itself more and more capable of acting independently. On the other, they could not divest themselves of the assumption that the leadership of the movement in its political phases, particularly the task of constructing a revolutionary party, belonged by right to the intelligentsia. True, the fact that a truly revolutionary situation did not yet exist, whereas a workers' movement was already a palpable reality, persuaded many *praktiki* to subordinate their political aspirations to the current needs of the latter. Still, only the most devout partisans of *Rabochaia Mysl'* forsook revolutionary ambitions entirely, while the majority adhered happily to the ambiguous formulas of *Ob agitatsii*. Insofar as the inner inconsistencies of the movement evoked conflict, it consisted of sporadic episodes in which the real issues at stake scarcely intruded upon the consciousness of the participants.

With the maturing of a nation-wide mood of political protest in 1901, the Social Democratic intellectuals became acutely aware that the historic moment demanding their political leadership had arrived: Russian Social Democracy was appointed to link up the ferment in "society" with the workers' movement to effect the "bourgeois revolution," a goal which in their minds was very closely bound up with efforts to create a strongly centralized party with firm ideological leadership. *Iskra*'s dramatic rise simply registered this new mood among the party's adherents. However, the conversion to "politics" imperceptibly loosened the cords which bound the intellectuals to common actions and perspectives with the worker leadership. *Iskra*ism as it evolved by the end of 1902 came to mean the close fraternity of those revolutionary intellectuals who were fanatically convinced of their historical mission in the forthcoming decisive stage of the revolutionary movement. Careerism, intrigue, condescension toward the uninitiated rank and file now became the hallmark of a movement hitherto noteworthy for its comradely and democratic spirit.

Political agitation among the masses sharply reversed the direction of communications. Whereas economic agitation presupposed the careful assembling of information from the workers and the accurate formulation of their grievances, political agitation tended to overtax the workers' ideological maturity and self-discipline by demanding blind adherence to slogans decided upon by the leadership, slogans designed more to articulate the mood of "society" than of the workers. The worker leaders certainly registered their feelings over this state of affairs often enough, but the new generation of *praktiki* inspired by grand political vistas and re-educated by *Iskra*, showed themselves singularly oblivious to the workers' desire for participation in party affairs.

The full measure of the Marxist intelligentsia's alienation from the class it purported to lead came to light as a result of the summer strikes of 1903. Here was a dramatic reconfirmation of the revolutionary significance of the laboring masses and a unique opportunity for Social Democracy to recover its position of "hegemony" in the battle against the autocracy. A decade of unremitting propaganda and agitation had not passed in vain. Yet, paradoxically, the strikes occurred, not because of Social Democratic leadership, but in spite of it. On the eve of the strikes the bitterness of the workers toward the *Iskra*-dominated committees reached its height and was only temporarily glossed over by the strikes themselves. In actuality the Social Democratic elite was so absorbed in its intramural affairs that it was mentally quite unprepared to capitalize on the opportunity to heal the breach with the workers. After the strikes the "professional revolutionaries" still moved about unimpeded from place to place, penetrating local committees wherever they chose, whereas the workers were systematically excluded. Neither the Bolsheviks nor the Mensheviks maintained significant contacts with the workers except with those handpicked by themselves. The seasoned worker leaders who had acquired status among their peers by hard-earned effort had by now lost all hope of working through the regular Social Democratic organizations and either turned to other revolutionary groups (Anarchists, S.R.'s), to "legal" activities (consumer cooperatives, the newly approved elections of factory elders) or gave up political activity entirely.[58]

---

[58] Although this process is very difficult to trace with exactness, evidence of it recurs constantly in the sources. Novomirskii from Odessa and Moisei Lure became anarchists. One gets the impression that most of Gapon's lieutenants were disaffected Social Democrats. See the account of former Social Democrat A. E. Karelin, "Deviatoe ianvaria i Gapon," *Krasnaia Letopis'*, No. 1 (January, 1922), pp. 106–21. L. Ia. Gurevich explicitly refers to Gapon's workers as having "gone through the party school" ("Narodnoe dvizhenie v Peterburge," *Byloe*, No. 1 (January, 1906), p. 196. Earlier Zubatov had very skillfully played upon the hostility of arrested worker Social Democrats toward the intelligentsia and was able to make use of them to launch his police socialism. He was particularly successful in the Jewish movement with his "Independent Workers' Party," consisting for the most part of former worker Social Democrats. Unfortunately for Zubatov, the involvement of his agent Shaevich in the Odessa general strike led to his undoing; otherwise he would undoubtedly have been able to attract many of the disaffected workers. After all, the Zubatov organization allowed them to do many things the Social Democrats hoped to achieve by revolution—to organize, to discuss their own needs, and, within limits, to strike. See the interesting documents on Zubatov in "Novoe o Zubatovshchine," *Krasnyi*

It was indeed ironic that the political ideology which had conceived of the idea of a mass workers' movement and nurtured it into being found itself totally incapable of coming to terms with that movement once it was a reality. Akselrod was not far from the truth when he characterized the Leninist ideology as in essence an expression of "bourgeois radicalism" of the intelligentsia rather than a consistent ideology of the working classes.[59] He would have been closer to the truth had he acknowledged that the Social Democratic movement was tainted with this flaw from its very inception. The primary commitment of the Social Democratic intellectual, like that of his Populist counterpart, had always been to the mystique of revolution itself, to the vision of a faultless society purged of the anomalies of the existing order in which the "intelligentsia" had no place. The workers' movement had always served him as a vehicle through which the world of values he rejected could be overthrown. During the earlier phase of the movement, when belief in the defeat of the autocracy through a mass workers' movement was still an act of revolutionary faith, the Social Democrats were capable of heroic feats of dedication and self-sacrifice to advance the interests of the workers. But as revolution became ever more a concrete possibility, the inmost springs of their faith impelled them along a path parallel to and influenced by rival groupings of the intelligentsia. Right up until October of 1905 they found it easier to communicate and make common cause with their political rivals than to resolve their differences with the workers.

It is true that Menshevism as it emerged from its ideological debates with the Bolsheviks represented in theory a return to the worker-oriented, democratic philosophy of the early Social Democratic movement. But in practice the Mensheviks ventured little further than the Bolsheviks in restoring friendly relations with the workers. Garvi, working in the Menshevik-dominated Kiev Com-

---

Arkhiv, No. 1 (1922), pp. 289-328. For two excellent contemporary discussions of the problem see the above cited pamphlet "Rabochii," *Rabochie i intelligenty v nashikh organizatsiiakh,* and [M. Panin-Makodziub] *Kustarnichestvo i partiinaia organizatsiia* (Geneva, 1904). These well informed observers support my own conclusions on the exodus of workers from the movement.

[59] See the introduction to his *Bor'ba sotsialisticheskikh i burzhuaznykh tendentsii v russkom revoliutsionnom dvizhenii* (St. Petersburg, 1907), pp. xix-xx.

mittee in late 1904, expressed his dismay at the lack of contacts with the workers and stated that this situation persisted in most of the major committees until the general strikes of October, 1905.[60] The strategy of the Mensheviks on the eve of the 1905 Revolution was based on Akselrod's idea of pushing the zemstvo and liberal circles further to the left by having hand-picked workers make speeches at political banquets: in other words, a strategy which reckoned more on a radicalization of the intelligentsia and liberal circles than on a revival of the mass workers' movement. Bloody Sunday was a rude awakening for both wings of Russian Social Democracy and vividly demonstrated its failure to maintain leadership over the very social force which had been the product of its own vision. Perhaps the worst aspect of this failure was the almost total alienation of the invaluable worker cadres which years of collaborative effort had brought into being. Any hopes for Social Democracy to play a significant role in the forthcoming "bourgeois revolution" depended heavily on the existence of a capable worker leadership to weld the working class into an organized force. The fate of the "worker intelligentsia" is one of the key factors to be considered in assessing the historical significance of Russian Social Democracy. Its odyssey was far from over in 1903 when the researches for the present study end, but many of the patterns of inner conflict had been set and the same inherent dilemmas continued to plague the movement until its tragic denouement in 1917.

---

[60] See Garvi, p. 440.

Bibliography

THE following is designed to be a useful bibliography of printed works relevant to the present investigation, not a complete bibliography of Russian Social Democracy. I have omitted popular works, which are of minor interest to the investigator, and articles, for which adequate guides and indexes exist.

A large part of the original sources employed in this study consists of illegal pamphlets and journals of the various Social Democratic groups, which are too numerous to be listed. A complete bibliography of these publications is given in *Ukazatel' sotsial-demokraticheskoi literatury na russkom iazyke,* while a systematic listing of the holdings in main Western European libraries is conveniently arranged in Zaleski. (See Part A of the bibliography for information on both these works.) The richest collections of such materials are available in the rare book room of the Columbia University Library and at the Bibliothèque de la Documentation Internationale Contemporaine in Paris. The Slavonic collection of the New York Public Library frequently bridges the gaps, and use of its printed catalogue can save unnecessary trips. A complete collection of legally published books and journals before 1917 (and therefore of the legal Marxist and Populist works), is located in Helsinki, Finland, in the library of the state university. One of four depository libraries of the Russian Empire, this collection has remained completely intact. Moreover, the excellent facilities and helpful staff of this library make it a delight to use.

Police reports—at times surprisingly perspicacious, at other times incredibly obtuse—are an indispensable source of information. Even before the opening of the archives in 1917, a defecting officer of the

Okhrana, Leonid Menshchikov, had important materials printed in Paris with the aid of the S.R. historian Vladimir Burtsev. His *Okhrana i Revoliutsiia,* printed after the revolution, gives an over-view of the revolutionary groups based on police surveillance reports. The year by year police surveys, *Obzory vazhneishikh doznanii* (available at the Hoover Institution, Stanford University), are of less use than the reports they are based upon, a number of which have been reprinted in historical journals and collections of sources.

Memoirs on this period are abundant, but, like all memoirs, they must be evaluated with care. Written for the most part some thirty years after the events, they abound in errors of both fact and retrospective evaluation. Those published in the Soviet Union present the added difficulty of both intentional and unintentional distortion through the influence of the official party viewpoint. Furthermore, since chiefly Bolsheviks were in a position to write of their experiences, the available selection is not exactly representative. Nevertheless, up to the late twenties, when Stalin began to impose his own conceptions of party history, there appeared a surprising number of candid and useful memoirs. The 1890's being for many party figures the heroic era of their youth, their reminiscences of this period were more likely to be fresh and unimpaired by party scruples than those of the *Iskra* period. In addition, these memoirs can be weighed against more than a few excellent non-Bolshevik memoirs, such as those of Martov, Garvi, Takhtarev, Tuchapskii, and Levitskii. It should be pointed out that there are, besides the full-length works, an incredible number of fragmentary eyewitness accounts scattered throughout the historical journals and source collections that often contain surprising bits of information and authentic expressions of attitudes. For these, the journal indexes and bibliographical aids must be scoured; it is even worthwhile to go through the journals issue by issue, as articles are sometimes not recorded in any of the guides.

During the early and mid-1920's Soviet scholars published an enormous number of documentary sources, for the most part meeting acceptable standards. In the late 1920's this productivity rapidly fell off quantitatively and qualitatively, until almost nothing appeared that was not heavily edited in a Stalinist spirit. The last refuge of the non-Stalinist Bolsheviks, *Katorga i Ssylka,* was closed down in 1935 (other journals had died out along the way). For over two decades scarcely a single new document or memoir of importance appeared in the Soviet press. The carefully selected and edited reprints merely echoed the stereotyped postulates of Stalin's *Short Course on the His-*

tory of the C.P.S.U., while the secondary works were footnoted almost exclusively with the writings of Marx, Lenin, and Stalin.

In recent years there has been a genuine renaissance of scholarly activity in the Soviet Union on the history of the party. New sources are being published, old ones reprinted, and monographs of real value are appearing that refer to unpublished materials (Kazakevich, Polevoi). An indispensable and fairly complete index to the scholarly output of the 1920's is now available in *Istoriia SSSR: Ukazatel'*, edited by K. P. Simons. (The names of Trotsky, Kamenev, Zinoviev, and Bukharin, as well as others closely connected with various "oppositions" of the 1920's, do not appear, despite the fact that most of them made contributions to party history.) A new multi-volume history of the party based on the new scholarly activity is now being written, the first volume of which has already appeared (Pospelov). While it retains the Stalinist habit of pressing events into the mold of official party canons, it at least takes cognizance of the existing sources and provides an orderly, if selective, catalogue of the facts.

Of the existing general treatments in Russian very few are satisfactory, because so few authors were in a position to benefit from the fruits of the Soviet scholarship of the 1920's before the curtain of Stalinism descended. The one solid work of the early Soviet period is that of V. I. Nevskii, but his labors were interrupted midway and his account only comes up to around 1898. The pre-1917 accounts of Martov and Liadov, while close to the events, are considerably limited by the authors' angle of vision and the selection of facts available to them (both were in exile during most of the period). The short account of the unrepentant Economist Akimov is a refreshing and interesting antidote based on a conscientious effort to assemble the relevant facts and re-interpret them in an anti-*Iskra* spirit. Although there are a number of excellent monographs, there is not as yet a good general treatment in the English language. An excellent standard work does exist in German, that of Dietrich Geyer. It is not only a gold mine of information, but offers stimulating, and from my viewpoint generally sound, interpretations. Its translation into English would make any further effort at synthesis unnecessary for some time to come.

A. *Bibliographical and Reference Works*

Biographical Dictionary of Mensheviks. Assembled by Grigorii Aronson and Ladis K. Kristoff. In preparation under the auspices of the Inter-University Project on the History of the Menshevik Movement.

Deiateli revoliutsionnogo dvizheniia v Rossii. Bio-Bibliographiche-skii slovar'. Ed. V. I. Nevskii, F. Kon, V. Vilenskii-Sibiriakov, *et al.* 5 vols. Moscow: *Vsesoiuznoe Obshchestvo Politicheskikh Kator-zhan,* 1927–31. Vol. V: *Sotsialdemokraty 1880–1904, A-G.*

Further volumes unfortunately did not appear.

Gesamtverzeichnis russischer und sowjetischer Periodica und Se-rienwerke in den Bibliotheken der Bundesrepublik und West-Berlins. Ed. Werner Phillipp. Berlin, 1960–.

A systematic catalogue of periodical holdings in German li-braries. Nine volumes, up to the letter "R," have appeared to date.

Istoriia SSSR. Ukazatel' sovetskoi literatury za 1917–1952 gg. Ed. K. P. Simon. 2 vols. and a supplement. Moscow: *Akademiia Nauk SSSR,* 1958. Vol. II: *Period kapitalizma.*

Detailed bibliography of books and articles on Russian Social Democracy in Soviet publications.

Russkaia periodicheskaia pechat' (*1895–Oktiabr, 1917*). *Spravoch-nik.* Ed. M. C. Cherepakhov and E. M. Fingerit. Moscow, 1957.

Guide to periodicals only, not to articles.

Ukazatel' sotsialdemokraticheskoi literatury na russkom iazyke, 1883–1905 gg. Paris, 1913.

Indispensable for illegal publications of the period.

Ulianov, N. A., and Ulianova, V. A. *Ukazatel' zhurnal'noi litera-turi. Alfavetnyi, predmetnyi, sistematicheskii, 1896–1910.* 2 vols. Moscow, 1911–13.

Guide to articles in the major legal journals.

Zaleski, Eugene. *Mouvements Ouvriers et Socialistes. Chronologie et bibliographie. La Russie.* 2 vols. Paris: L'Institut Français d'His-toire Sociale, 1956. Vol. I: 1725–1907. Vol. II: 1908–1917.

The basic bibliographical reference work for publications of and about the Russian revolutionary movement from the begin-ning to the present.

B. *General Histories and Investigations*

Akimov, V. [V. Makhnovets.] *Materialy dlia kharakteristiki razvitiia rossiiskoi sotsial-demokraticheskoi rabochei partii.* Geneva, 1905.

Short but provocative study of Vilna, St. Petersburg, and Kiev.

Arkomed, S. T. *Rabochee dvizhenie i sotsial-demokratiia na Kav-kaze.* Moscow, 1923.

Baron, Samuel H. *Plekhanov: The Father of Russian Marxism.* Stanford: Stanford University Press, 1963.

Excellent standard biography emphasizing intellectual evolution.

Dan, Fedor. *Proizkhozhdenie bol'shevizma*. New York, 1946.
General Menshevik account of revolutionary movement. Only two chapters on early Social Democracy.

Geyer, Dietrich. *Lenin in der russischen Sozialdemokratie*. Cologne: Böhlau Verlag, 1962.
Best available general history.

Haimson, Leopold. *The Russian Marxists and the Origins of Bolshevism*. Cambridge: Harvard University Press, 1955.

Istoriia VKP(b). Ed. E. Iaroslavskii. 4 vols. Moscow, 1926–30.
Though detailed, little of value. No references to sources. For early period essentially a reworking of Nevskii.

Kazakevich, P. A. *Sotsial-demokraticheskie organizatsii Peterburga kontsa 80-kh–nachala 90-kh godov*. Leningrad, 1960.

Keep, J. L. H. *The Rise of Social Democracy in Russia*. London: Oxford University Press, 1963.
General treatment through the Revolution of 1905. While very informative on 1905, far less balanced and detailed than Geyer on early history of the movement.

Kindersley, R. *The First Russian Revisionists: A Study of "Legal Marxism" in Russia*. Oxford, 1962.

Kulczycki, Ludwik. *Geschichte der russischen Revolution*. 3 vols. Gotha, 1910–14. Vol. III: *Vom Beginn der sozialdemokratischen Bewegung bis zum Ausbruch der Unzufriedenheit in der russischen Gesellschaft (1886–1900)*.
Useful primarily for Polish developments.

Liadov, M. N. *Istoriia rossiiskoi sotsial-demokraticheskoi partii*. 2 vols. St. Petersburg, 1906–7.
Very biased Bolshevik account, but contains useful information on Moscow organization in which author participated from 1893 to 1895.

Martov, Iu. O. *Istoriia rossiiskoi sotsial-demokratii*. 3d ed. Petrograd, 1923
Slightly revised and expanded version of his essay in *Obshchesvennoe dvizhenie v Rossii v nachale XX-ogo veka*. Vol. I. A very brief Menshevik account.

Mendel, A. P. *Dilemmas of Progress in Tsarist Russia*. Cambridge: Harvard University Press, 1961.

Nevskii, V. I. *Ocherki po istorii rossiiskoi sotsial-demokraticheskoi partii*. Moscow, 1925.
The one notable achievement of Soviet historiography. Though

Bolshevik in interpretation, it shows a genuine respect for historical accuracy.

——. *Istoriia RKP(b). Kratkii Ocherk.* Leningrad, 1926.

Another edition of above work.

Obshchestvennoe dvizhenie v Rossii v nachale XX–go veka. L. Martov, A. N. Maslov, and A. N. Potresov. 4 vols. St. Petersburg,
1909–14. Vol. I: *Predvestniki i osnovnye prichini dvizheniia.*

Popov, N. N. *Ocherk istorii VKP(b).* Moscow, 1933.

A useless Stalinist account.

Paialin, N. P. *Zavod imeni Lenina 1857–1918.* Moscow, 1933.

A few useful facts on workers' circles despite heavy Stalinist
editing.

Pipes, Richard. *Social Democracy and the St. Peterburg Labor
Movement, 1885–1897.* Cambridge: Harvard University Press,
1963.

Polevoi, Iu. Z. *Zarozhdenie marksizma v Rossii, 1883–1894 gg.*
Moscow, 1959.

The first general work since the revival of Soviet scholarship.

Pospelev, P. N., *et al. Istoriia KPSS. Tom pervyi. Sozdanie bol'she-
vistskoi partii, 1888–1903.* Moscow and Leningrad, 1964.

New standard Soviet account.

Zavialov, S. *Istoriia izhorskogo zavoda.* Moscow, 1934.

C. *Memoirs and Correspondence*

[Babushkin, V. I.] *Vospominaniia I. V. Babushkina.* Leningrad,
1925.

Chernov, V. N. *Zapiski sotsialista–revoliutsionera.* Berlin, 1922.

Ermanskii, O. A. *Iz perezhitogo (1888–1927 gg.).* Moscow, 1927.

Garvi, P. A. *Vospominaniia sotsial-demokrata.* New York, 1946.

Goldman, L. I. *Organizatsiia i tipografiia "Iskry" v Rossii.* Moscow,
1928.

Gorev, B. I. [B. I. Gol'dman.] *Iz partiinago proshlago.* Leningrad,
1924.

Khinoi, Mark. *V podpolnykh tipografiiakh.* Inter-University Project
on the History of the Menshevik Movement; Paper No. 2. New
York, 1960. (Mimeographed.)

Kizevetter, A. A. *Na rubezhe dvukh stoletii. Vospominaniia 1881–
1914.* Prague, 1929.

Krupskaia, N. D. *Vospominaniia.* Moscow, 1926.

Lalaiants, I. Kh. *U istokov bol'shevizma Zarozhdenie R.S.–D.R.P.*
2d ed. Moscow, 1934.

Lepeshinskii, P. N. *Na povorote* (*ot kontsa 80-kh godov k 1905 g*). Leningrad, 1925.

Levitskii, V. O. *Za chetvert' veka*. 2 vols. Moscow, 1926.

Maklakov, V. A. *Iz vospominanii*. New York: Chekhov Publishing House, 1954.

Martov, Iu. O. *Zapiski sotsial-demokrata*. Berlin, 1923.

Mikhailov, I. K. *Chetvert' veka podpol'shchika*. Moscow, 1928.

Miliukov, P. N. *Vospominaniia 1889–1917*. 2 vols. New York: Chekhov Publishing House, 1955.

Mitskevich, S. I. *Revoliutsionnaia Moskva*. Moscow, 1940.
    Expanded version of earlier memoirs.

Perepiska G. V. Plekhanova i P. B. Akselroda. Ed. B. I. Nicolaevsky, P. A. Berlin, and V. S. Voitinskii. 2 vols. Moscow, 1935.

Petrunkevich, I. I. *Iz zapisok obshchestvennago deiatelia*. Vol. XXI of *Arkhiv Russkoi Revoliutsii*. Berlin, 1934.

Pis'ma P. B. Aksel'roda i Iu. O. Martova. Ed. F. Dan, B. N. Nicolaevsky, and L. O. Tsederbaum-Dan. Berlin, 1924.

Posse, V. *Moi zhiznennyi put'*. Moscow and Leningrad, 1929.

Shotman, A. *Iz partiinago proshlago*. Moscow, 1924.

Silvin, M. A. *Lenin v period zarozhdeniia partii. Vospominaniia*. Moscow and Leningrad, 1958.
    Posthumous memoirs. A major contribution of recent Soviet scholarly activity.

Takhtarev, K. M. *Rabochee dvizhenie v Peterburge, 1893–1901 gg*. Leningrad, 1924.
    An expanded version of the 1902 edition; it contains much exact data and personal recollections omitted in earlier editions to avoid giving helpful information to the police.

[Takhtarev, K. M.] "Peterburzhets" (pseud). *Ocherk peterburgskago rabochego dzizheniia 90-kh godov*. London, 1902.
    Invaluable firsthand account, written very soon after events described. Important documentary materials included.

Tuchapskii, P. L. *Iz perezhitago. Devianostye gody*. Odessa, 1923.

Tyrkova-Viliams, A. *Na putiakh k svobode*. New York: Chekhov Publishing House, 1952.

Valentinov, N. *Vstrechi s Leninym*. New York: Chekhov Publishing House, 1953.

Zakharova-Tsederbaum, K. I., and Tsederbaum, S. O. *Iz epokhi "Iskry" (1900–1905)*. Moscow, 1926.

Zelikson-Bobrovskaia, Ts. *Zapiski riadovogo podpol'shchika*. Moscow, 1922.

D. *Printed Sources and Works*

Akselrod, P. B. *Bor'ba sotsialisticheskikh i burzhuaznykh tendentsii v russkom revoliutsionnom dvizhenii.* St. Petersburg, 1907.
    A collection of Akselrod's most important writings of the period 1895–1905.

Dimanshtein, S. (ed.). *Revoliutsionnoe dvizhenie sredi evreev.* Moscow, 1930.
    Invaluable collection of memoirs relating to the 1890's by participants. Still undisturbed by Stalinist historiography.

Gorbunova, M. I., *et al. Perepiska V. I. Lenina i rukovodimykh partiinykh organov s sotsial-demokraticheskimi organizatsiami Ukrainy (1901–1905).* Kiev, 1964.
    Important new contribution. Includes previously unpublished correspondence of *Iskra* organization.

Istoriia ekaterinoslavskoi sotsial-demokraticheskoi organizatsii (1889–1903). Ed. M. A. Rubach. Ekaterinoslav, 1923.
    Memoirs and documents. Best collection on a local organization.

Istoriia R.K.P.(b) v dokumentakh. Ed. Sh. M. Levin and I. L. Tatarov. Leningrad, 1926.
    Little that is unique.

Istoriko-revoliutsionnyi sbornik. Ed. V. I. Nevskii. 3 vols. Leningrad, 1924.
    An important collection of sources on the revolutionary movement, much of it on Social Democracy.

Itogi revoliutsionnago dvizheniia v Rosii za 40 let. Ed. G. A. Kuklin. London, 1903.
    Program statements of all the various revolutionary factions. Important.

K dvadtsatipiatiletiiu pervago s'ezda partii (1898–1923). Moscow, 1923.
    Invaluable memoirs and documents.

Lenin, V. I. *Sochineniia.* 3d ed. 30 vols. Moscow, 1928–37.
    Best edition; contains valuable notes. (All footnote references are to this edition.)

———. *Sochineniia.* 5th ed. Moscow, 1959–.
    A few relevant works not contained in earlier editions.

Leninskii Sbornik. 33 vols. Moscow, 1924–40.
    Basic collection of documents relating to Lenin.

Listovki peterburgskogo "Soiuza Bor'by," 1895–97 gg. Ed. S. N. Valk. Moscow, 1934.

Listovki revoliutsionnykh s.-d. organizatsii Ukrainy, 1896–1904.
Kiev, 1963.

Literatura Moskovkogo rabochego soiuza. Ed. N. P. Miliutin and
S. I. Mitskevich. Moscow, 1930.

Materialy k istorii evreiskago rabochego dvizheniia. St. Petersburg,
1906.

An official history of the Bund published by the party. Valuable documents.

Menshchikov, L. P. *Okhrana i revoliutsiia.* 4 vols. Moscow, 1925–32.

Author was a former official in the *Okhrana* and wrote from
documents in his possession.

Minuvshee. Russkii politicheskii sysk zagranitsei. Ed. L. Menshchikov. Paris, 1914.

Reports of *Okhrana* agents Rataev and Rachkovskii, 1898–1905.

Na zare rabochego dvizheniia v Moskve. Ed. S. I. Mitskevich. Moscow, 1932.

A collection of short memoirs and documents.

Ot gruppy Blagoeva k Soiuzu Bor'by (1886–1894). Rostov-on-Don,
1921. Memoirs.

Pervyi S'ezd R.S.–D.R.P. Dokumenty i materialy. Moscow, 1958.

A useful, although poorly edited, collection of previously
printed documents.

Pervyi S'ezd R.S.–D.R.P. Sbornik statei i materialov. Ed. V. A. Alga-
sov. Kiev, 1923.

A valuable collection of the most relevant previously printed
memoirs and studies (A. Kremer, B. Eidelman, P. Tuchapskii,
and others).

Rabochee dvizhenie v Rossii v XIX–om veke. 4 vols. Ed. A. M.
Pankratova, L. M. Ivanov, *et al.* Moscow and Leningrad, 1950–
63.

Vol. IV, parts 1 and 2, cover the years 1890–1900. Valuable collection primarily of leaflets and police sources, many printed here
for first time. A major contribution of present day Soviet scholarship.

Revoliutsionnoe dvizhenie v Rossii v dokladakh ministra Murav'eva.
Ed. L. Martov. St. Petersburg, 1907.

Sotsial-demokraticheskoe dvizhenie v Rossii. Ed. A. N. Potresov and
B. I. Nicolaevsky. Moscow, 1928.

Correspondence of Potresov, 1895–1914. Documents.

Vtoroi S'ezd R.S.–D.R.P. Protokoly. Moscow, 1959.

Besides the proceedings, many relevant materials on the Second Congress are included.

E. *Historical Journals*

Byloe. 22 nos. St. Petersburg; January, 1906, to October, 1907.

Byloe. 35 nos. Leningrad, 1917–26.

Golos Minuvshago. Moscow, 1913–23.

Golos Minuvshago na Chuzhoi Storone. 19 nos. Berlin, Prague, and Paris, 1923–28.

Katorga i Ssylka. 116 nos. Moscow, 1921–35. Publication of *Obshchestvo byvshikh politicheskikh katorzhan i ssylno-pocelentsev.*

Krasnaia Letopis'. 64 nos. Leningrad, 1922–36.

Krasnyi Arkhiv. 106 nos. Moscow, 1922–41.

Letopis' Marksizma. 10 nos. Moscow, 1926–29.

Letopis' Revoliutsii. Ed. E. I. Grzhebin. No. 1. Berlin, 1923.
    Only issue to appear.

Letopis' Revoliutsii. 10 nos. Kharkov, 1922–25.
    Rare historical journal on Social Democratic organizations in the South. Subsequently appeared in the Ukrainian language.

Minuvshie Gody. 12 nos. St. Petersburg, 1908.
    Appeared in place of *Byloe* in 1908.

Proletarskaia Revoliutsiia. 113 nos. Moscow, 1921–40.
    The most important historical journal on the history of the Social Democratic movement and of the party.

Zapiski Instituta Lenina. 3 nos. Moscow, 1927–28.

Index

Aizenshtadt, I. L., 44, 110, 155
Akimov, Vl. (Makhnovets), 34 n., 40 n., 41 n., 43 n., 52, 53, 62, 63 n., 68–69, 83 n., 84, 86 n., 120 n., 127 n., 130, 132 n., 158 n., 159 n., 160, 162 n., 164 n., 165 n., 167 n., 168 n., 169, 171, 172, 174, 176 n., 177 n., 183, 185, 188 n., 198 n., 207, 213
Akselrod, P. B.: as Populist, 27; on agitation, 28; rift with young Social Democrats, 80 n.; on tactics (1898), 142–43, 144; editor of *Rabotnik*, 156–57; and *Rabochaia Gazeta*, 164–67; negotiations with Kremer (1897), 160, 172 n.; and Plekhanov, tactics, 184; and Martov, 237 n.; as Menshevik, views, 58, 190, 252–53
Aleksandrov, M. C., 33 n.
Aleksandrova, V. M., 239, 244
Alekseev, N. A., 119
Alexander II (tsar), 1, 216
Alexander III (tsar), 2 n.
Anarchists and anarchism, 194, 205, 247, 251
Andreev, Ia. A., 120–22, 126
Andropov, Sergei, 201–8, 231
Astyrev Circle, 12 n.
Autocracy and tsarism: object of political agitation, 12, 78, 81–84, 86, 135, 150–51, 216–18; as political system, x, xi, 1–2, 4 n., 21, 22, 125–26, 134, 163, 182, 252; revolutionary struggle against, 11, 15, 17, 27, 28, 137, 139, 143, 150–51, 184–85, 190, 196, 197, 208, 209, 215, 224, 240, 245, 248,

251, 252; tsarist government and representatives, 5, 78, 249

Babushkin, I. V., 37 n., 53–54, 56, 61, 94–95, 96, 103–7, 128 n., 174 n., 187–88
Bagaev, M., 50, 108 n., 174 n.
Bakunin and Bakunism, 27, 31, 228
Baron, Samuel, x, xiii, 148 n.
Batyrev, Mikhail, 127 n.
Bauman, N. E., 244
Beltov (*see* Plekhanov, G. V.)
Berdyaev, Nicholas, 25, 147 n.
Berenshtam, N. V., 201
Berlin, P. A., 25, 141 n., 147
Bernstein, Eduard, and Bernsteinism, 26, 128, 131, 140–49, 150, 206, 207, 226
Black Repartition, 27–28
Bloody Sunday (1905), 249, 253
Bogdanov, N. M., 35 n., 125 n.
Bogolepov (Minister of Education), 26, 215
Bogoraz, N. A., 119, 123 n.
Bolsheviks and Bolshevism: roots of, 12, 98 n., 101–2, 181, 190; Lenin and, 99, 229; after Second Congress, 90, 249, 251–53
Braginskii, David, 243
Brizgalov (university inspector), 4
Broida, Eva, 209–10
Brusnev Circle (St. Petersburg, 1889–92), 30 n., 33 n., 36 n., 40 n., 94, 102
Buchholtz, 127, 128
Bulgakov, Sergei, 14, 24, 25, 214
Bund, 60 n., 116 n., 160 n., 173, 174,

Pipes, Richard, x, 28 n., 29 n., 36 n., 59, 62, 73–75, 83, 102 n.

Plekhanov, G. V.: as Populist, 27, 29 n., 32 n.; founder of Russian Marxism, 27, 149; and Liberation of Labor Group, 17; author, 14, 17, 19, 21, 23 n., 25; theoretician, 102, 131, 137–38, 145, 147–48, 153 n., 162, 181–82, 184; and Lenin, 156, 229, 238 n.; and *Rabochaia Mysl'*, 132, 139, 144, 147; and *Rabochee Znamia*, 206–7

Pobedonestsev, Konstantin, 1–2, 22

Poles and Polish S. D. Movement, xiii, 18, 37, 38–41, 51, 60, 72, 81, 87, 175, 185, 193, 196, 203, 224; Union of Polish Workers, 38, 39; "Proletariat," 38; SDKP, 39; P.P.S. 175–76, 181, 193

Polevoi, Iu. Z., 30 n., 36 n., 110 n., 127 n.

Poliakov, Vasilii, 119, 121, 125, 126, 136

Police, tsarist, 13, 67, 68, 76, 78, 90, 120, 189, 199, 203, 209, 218–19, 227, 246, 249; arrests, 13, 15, 49, 51, 55, 57, 77, 79, 93–94, 105, 122, 130, 132, 150, 166, 186, 198, 207, 212, 216, 217, 222, 235, 236, 241, 247; reports, ix, 48, 49 n., 62, 74 n., 75 n., 78, 79, 82, 87–88, 108–9, 193 n., 198 n., 203 n., 204 n., 212 n.; surveillance, 24, 25, 61, 116, 186, 193 n., 198 n., 205 n., 207, 212, 236

Political freedom and civil liberties, 10, 84, 86, 108, 109, 135, 136, 138, 145, 149–50, 163, 182 n., 184–85, 197, 209, 215, 246

"Political" struggle (*see* Economic aims)

Popova, O. N., 24

Populists and Populism: Populist intelligentsia, 2–4, 8–11, 102, 124, 252; and students, 4, 12; conflict with Marxism, 18–26, 182, 202, 209; worker propaganda, 27–34, 72, 90–91, 127; and Moisei Lure, 194, 203; revival of revolutionary Populism (1901–3), 26, 192, 209–10, 212, 217; ex-Populists, 214

Posse, Vladimir, 14, 24, 25, 205, 215

Potresov, A. N., 9 n., 14, 16, 17, 21, 24, 25, 98, 160, 223, 225, 226

Prokofev, 54, 93, 102

Prokopovich, S. N., 14, 15, 25, 143-44

Rabochaia Gazeta, 79, 160–70, 172 n.,

173, 174 n., 175, 176, 177, 180, 181, 182, 183, 186, 223

Rabochaia Mysl', origins, 119–23; St. Petersburg group, 85, 112–13, 127–33, 180 n., 198, 200–202; the journal, 116 n., 188, 191, 195, 197, 220; ideology, 123–26, 137–49; symbol of "Economism," 69 n., 88, 119, 123–24, 143, 191, 206–7, 226, 250; symbol of worker independence, xi, 112, 118–19, 123, 130, 133, 136–39, 144–45, 148, 149, 189, 200; and Revisionism, 128, 140–41, 143; Lenin and, 119, 123–24, 143, 226, 229

Rabochaia Volia (Kiev, 1901), 215

Rabochaia Volia (Odessa, 1903), 245

Rabochee Delo, 80 n., 85, 136 n., 139, 140 n., 143 n., 144, 188, 206, 213, 220, 224, 225, 229, 237, 240

Rabochee Znamia, xii, 114, 127, 130, 169 n., 170, 189, 215, 216, 231

Rabotnik, 48 n., 80 n., 92 n., 96 n., 139, 157

Rachkovskii (chief of secret police abroad), 193 n., 203 n., 204 n.

Radchenko, I. I., 227, 234–35, 237, 238, 239

Radchenko, L. N., 227

Radchenko, Stepan, 50, 52, 56, 98, 99, 109, 127, 128, 130, 160, 174, 176 n., 180 n., 183, 186, 187, 199, 201

Revisionism (*see* Bernstein and Bernsteinism)

Revolution of 1905, xi, 67, 249, 253

Riazanov, D. B., 29 n., 36 n.

Romm, I. M., 195

Rostov/Don, 80, 221; Don Committee, 57, 85, 188, 222, 240, 241, 244; Mine Workers' Union, 222, 240; general strike of 1902, 59, 240, 246–47

Rozanov, V. N., 223, 237, 239, 245

Russian Social-Democratic Workers' Party (R.S.–D.R.P.), 130, 150, 176–77, 187–89, 195, 196, 202; idea of party congress, 152, 156–57, 207, 223, 224; First Congress (Minsk, 1898), xii, 85, 105, 195, 199, 226, 235 n.; Second Congress (Brussels and London, 1903), xii, 58, 117, 176, 181, 190, 213, 214, 224, 233 n., 241, 244, 245, 247, 249; Organizing Committee for Second Congress, 236–40, 243–45, 246; Pskov Conference of Organizing Committee, 238–39; Orel Conference of Organizing Committee, 239; Kievan Conference of S. D.

31; participant in S. D. movement, 123 n., 172 n.; participant in *Rabochaia Mysl'*, 128–32, 229; conflict with Lenin on "Economism" and worker independence, 98–101; ideologist of *Rabochaia Mysl'*, 137–38, 140, 143–44

Tatarov, Nikolai, 203, 204, 211, 212

Tesler, 164, 165 n.

Tochiiskii Circle, 30 n., 152

Tolstoy, Count Leo, 3, 6–7, 196

Tolstoyans and Tolstoyanism, 6, 8, 9, 196, 202, 203

Trade unions and unionism, 69 n., 78, 79, 83, 123, 126, 138, 141, 144, 163, 220

Trotsky, 56, 116 n., 169

Trutovskaia, 109

Tsederbaum, Sergei (Ezhov), 201, 207–8, 227, 231, 232, 233 n., 235

Tsoglin, V. (David Kats), 44 n., 171 n., 172, 174, 175, 176 n., 185, 186

Tsyperovich, G., 110

Tuchapskii, P. L., 158, 162 n., 164, 166, 168 n., 174, 176 n., 182, 183

Tugan-Baranovskii, M. I., 14, 24, 25, 205, 210, 214, 228

Tyshko (Iogikhes), L., 39

Ulianov, Alexander, 3

Union of Polish Workers (*see* Poles and Polish S. D. Movement)

Union of Social Democrats Abroad, 80 n., 144, 172 n., 181, 188, 226, 245

University Statute of 1884, 1, 4, 11

Vannovskii, Viktor, 174–75, 176 n., 235 n.

Venturi, Franco, 29 n., 102 n., 128

Vestnik Evropy, 8, 9, 10 n., 16

Vetrovskaia demonstration (*see* Street demonstrations)

Vigdorchik, N. A., 155, 162, 168, 176 n., 186

Vilenskii, I. I., 44, 103 n., 174 n., 223

Vilna and Vilna S. D. organization, 39, 40–45, 51, 54, 61, 103, 105, 152, 153, 156, 159, 160, 170–73, 224, 231

Vinokurov, 39, 101

Vorontsov, V. ("V.V."), 8, 10, 19 n., 22, 124

Vpered (Kiev, 1897–1902), 85, 161, 232

Vyshnegradskii, Ivan (Minister of Finance), 5, 8, 21 n.

Witte, Sergei (Minister of Finance), 21, 24, 26, 66, 76, 77

Workers: workers' funds (*kassy*), 43, 60, 94–98, 103, 113–14, 218, 221, 242; worker intelligentsia, 31–33, 34–35, 37, 41–42, 46–47, 51–54, 89, 115–17; workers' opposition, xi–xiii, 90, 130–31, 191, 219–21, 241–44, 245, 250–52; workers' organizations, 92, 94–95, 124, 137–38, 144, 146, 194–95, 218, 219–21, 243–44

Zakharova, K. I., 227, 231 n.

Zalkind, R. S. ("Zemliachka"), 243

Zasulich, Vera, 25, 172 n.

Zavialov, S., 120 n., 122 n., 123 n., 126 n.

Zelikman, M., 104

"Zemliachka" (*see* Zalkind, R. S.)

Zemstvos, 2, 3, 6, 8, 10, 16, 22, 26, 142, 214, 234, 253

Zhizn', 25, 205

Zubatov, xiii, 90, 186, 222, 237, 248, 251 n.

Zvezdochetova, Olga, 201–3